THE MOST ACCURATE PRICE GUIDE FOR GB STAMPS

In this book you'll find...

USEFUL ADVICE & TIPS

- **06** Why stamps are worth money • **08** Where to buy stamps
- **11** The A-Z of philatelic terms • **22** Market trends
- **26** The story of presentation packs, booklets & miniature sheets
- **32** How to look after your stamps • **34** Where to see stamps
- **37** How this price guide works • **227** Key philatelic contacts

ACCURATE PRICES YOU CAN TRUST

BRITISH STAMP MARKET VALUES 2006 is the only British stamp price guide compiled by totally independent experts – thus giving you the exact worth of your GB collection, NOT shop prices that British stamps are sold to customers at

- **39** Queen Victoria issues (1840-1901)
- **48** King Edward VII issues (1901-1911)
- **51** King George V issues (1911-1936)
- **57** King Edward VIII issues (1936)
- **59** King George VI issues (1937-51)
- **64** Queen Elizanbeth II pre-decimal issues (1952-1970)
- **82** Machin definitives (1967-2005)
- **108** Queen Elizabeth II special stamps (1971-2005)
- **188** GB Officials
- **191** Regional issues (including Guernsey, Jersey & Isle of Man)
- **202** Postage Dues
- **206** Prestige Stamp Books
- **213** Presentation Packs, Year Packs & Year Books

BRITISH STAMP MARKET VALUES 2006

Editorial team
Editor • Steve Fairclough
Consultant Editor • Richard West
Art Director • Sheradon Dublin
Production Editor • Roger White
Senior Listings Editor • J.P. Hill
Listings Editors • Helen Rainbow, Liz Briggs, Chantelle Rainbow
Special thanks • James Miller, James Skinner, Allan Grant, Paul Dauwalder, Arthur Ryan, Packs & Cards.

Editorial address
IPC Media, Leon House, 233 High Street, Croydon, Surrey CR9 1HZ.
Tel: 020 8726 8000.

Advertisement team
Advertisement Manager • Jay Jones
Advertisement Executives •
Rachel Hearn, Uty Rohrs
Ad Production • Charlotte Blunden

Distributed by
MarketForce, King's Reach Tower, Stamford Street, London SE1 9LS.
Tel: 020 7633 3300.

Pre-press by CTT; printed by Broglia Press Ltd.

BRITISH STAMP MARKET VALUES 2006 has been produced by the team behind STAMP MAGAZINE. STAMP MAGAZINE is an IPC Media Ltd. publication that's in good newsagents on the second Thursday of every month. For more details about where to buy it just go to www.stampmagazine.co.uk and click on the 'nearest newsagent' link or take a look at the subscription offers that are available on the site!

Why

stamps are worth money

At first it isn't clear why some stamps are worth more than others. We explain the key factors that make British stamps worth money

It's fair to say that working out how stamps become valuable isn't rocket science. Clearly, rarity has something to do with value, as does condition and the length of availability but stamps are somewhat different to other collectables in that mistakes can be priceless. In addition to this there have been a few occasions when stamps have been issued by mistake (a factor that makes them highly desirable).

Errors on stamps can be missing colours, missing or irregular perforations, inverted watermarks, inverted printings, double printings or missing elements of artwork. Although errors did occur prior to the QEII reign, it was in the 1960s that an explosion of errors came about. This was because more multicoloured stamps were issued and, consequently, there was more

This Prussian Blue error of colour from 1935 means this Silver Jubilee 2½d is £8,500 mint

chance that missing colour examples would appear.

Some of the early Victorian era stamps are worth money because they had very high original face values and only a few people could afford them originally. Examples include the 10/- and £1 values from the 1867-83 series (when the average pay was under £1 a week).

Other Victorian stamps that are worth money are the so-called 'Abnormals' that were printed from plates which were never out into regular use and the famous Penny Red from plate 77. This plate produced stamps that were regarded as sub-standard but a few of them got to the public and any existing examples are now worth over £100,000 each.

Missing colours, and values, on this 1966 British Birds issue block make its value rocket upwards

This Queen Victoria 1½d from 1870 without plate number in the design increases its value

BEING COMPLETE

Although not all of us can afford to buy great rarities most GB collectors will go for completeness. In other words if you are a QEII collector of GB material you will probably try to buy all items (this can be done by standing order from the Philatelic Bureau in Edinburgh). The multicolour-printing era saw immediate results in value as the 1961 Savings Bank centenary set saw examples with missing colours turning up.

The most valuable modern GB rarity is the missing 'p' from the Roses 13p stamp of 1976. In 2003 a missing '£' sign on the high value £2 slate blue Machin definitive turned out to be the biggest flaw found on a GB definitive for many years. Clearly something went awry during the printing process but it has never been officially revealed exactly what happened.

MARKET DEMANDS

Another factor that makes stamps worth money is market demands. Over the past two years the British stamp market has begun to go through a boom period due to a mixture of high prices paid at philatelic auctions, new GB rarities

L-R: Early high value GB stamps can be rare; as are missing items from printings (PO Tower)

emerging, and a scramble among collectors to get hold of the best possible material. One of the more modern influences on this has been the online trading of stamps, both through dealers and auction websites such as eBay. Internet bidders are forcing up the prices being paid for the much sought-after material such as the Welsh language Princess Diana pack from 1998 with online auctions now requiring successful bidders to bid over £100 to secure one of the packs.

Whatever factors determine the price of British stamps, the truth is that, at the moment, the market is vibrant and there has arguably never been a better time to buy British stamps! ∎

Where to buy
GBSTAMPS

If you've decided to start a GB collection you'll need to know where to look for stamps. We give you a few handy hints

The great majority of GB definitives and special issues can be purchased from your local post office on the day of their issue. For more unusual material such as some booklets that are normally issued only in a certain area, regional or country stamps, pictorial aerogrammes, coils, postage due labels (now obsolescent) and PHQ cards, you will have to pay a visit to a philatelic counter. These are located only in the largest post offices. These are now categorised as Post Shops, Post Shops Plus and Collections.

You can save yourself a lot of hassle by signing up to one or other of the services provided by the Royal Mail's Philatelic Bureau in Edinburgh. You can subscribe to a standing order, which means you will automatically receive all commemoratives and special issues, as singles or cylinder blocks, or you can order specific items from the monthly stock list. Once you are on the mailing list, your requested philatelic material will come to you automatically.

STARTING OFF

Many beginners get a tremendous boost to their collection by acquiring a bumper mixed packet of stamps, usually as a present. At one time most stationers and newsagents carried extensive lines in packets of mixed stamps, from 50 to 1,000 all different, but sadly that method of retailing seems to have all but vanished. Some dealers specialise in the packet trade and can offer packets with up to 100,000 different stamps, which is guaranteed to put most collectors right off the hobby!

Some traditional stamp shops still exist, like **Gustamps** in Brighton

Once you become rather more advanced in the hobby you might try a bag of kiloware. Originally this term denoted officially sealed parcels, weighing a kilogram; the stamps in these kilo bags consisted mainly of high values clipped off parcel cards and commemoratives cut off unsold first day covers. The term is now used for any mixtures of stamps on paper, sold by weight.

SHOPS AND AUCTIONS

There was a time when every British town had at least one stamp shop, but today many shops have closed and many dealers concentrate on mail order or the fairs circuits (details are published in STAMP MAGAZINE each month). In London, traditionally stamp shops were in and around the Covent Garden area and a few still survive including Stanley Gibbons, The Stamp Centre and Vera Trinder.

Usually there's a monthly fair in most towns, and these gatherings offer you the chance to shop around and find a dealer who specialises in your interests. Purchases by mail order or direct from a dealer satisfy most collectors, but stamp auctions offer the opportunity to acquire everything, from whole collections to individual rarities. Auctions range from the club auction where members dispose of surplus material, to the great international sales.

While you can get the sale catalogue and put in bids by post (indicating the maximum you are prepared to pay for each lot), it is often preferable to attend the sale and see who you are bidding against. It's best if you can attend a few sales in person and observe how they are conducted. You can pick up terrific bargains this way, but you can also get carried away and end up paying far more than a stamp is worth.

Don't overlook general auctions and house sales which sometimes yield some surprising material that should have been consigned to a

Rushstamps is a long established GB dealer that now sells a lot of stamps via its website

philatelic auctioneer; not good for the vendor but lucky bidders have been known to hit the jackpot.

Once again a glance at the advertisement pages in STAMP MAGAZINE every month will help to guide you to auctions, your nearest stamp shop or give details on fair and exhibitions. There are normally around five or six major exhibitions in the UK every year. Most, like Stampex and Philatex, tend to take place in London. At all of these shows dealers, auction houses, postal bureaux and societies will be present to sell, swap or simply give advice on what stamps to look out for.

WEBSITES FOR STAMPS

A wealth of philatelic material is available for purchase online. This makes it easy to buy anything from around the world, but the snag with this is that you don't get the chance to view the items at close quarters. If you go into the Internet with a generic term such as 'stamps' you'll be bombarded with thousands of sites, so look for 'GB stamps' as a search. What websites do allow you to do is to browse through stamp lists and types at your leisure, and you'll probably also pick up a few more buying tips along the way.

■ For a list of recommended buying contacts turn to page 227 of this book. ■

Many collectors will go to major shows such as Stampex to buy new material for their collections

OF PHILATELIC TERMINOLGY

To help you to understand all of the key philatelic terminology contained in BRITISH STAMP MARKET VALUES 2006, here's an easy-to-understand guide to the descriptions that have been used

ADHESIVE
A stamp issued with gum on the back for sticking to mail, as opposed to one printed directly on to an envelope or card.

ADVERTISING
At different times commercial advertising has been presented alongside GB stamps in stamp booklets and on labels attached to stamps in booklets. Advertising has also appeared on the back of stamps (most notably the advertisements for Pears' Soap on the back of some GB Queen Victoria stamps that were produced on an experimental basis).

AEROGRAMME/AIR MAIL
Any item of post that's been sent to its destination by air is said to have gone 'by Air Mail'. Most post offices sell ready stamped, specially printed air letter sheets on lightweight paper – these are known as aerogrammes, air letters or air mail forms.

ALBINO
A colourless impression which is usually produced in embossing.

ALPHABET LETTERS
The different styles of lettering printed in the corners of British (Queen Victoria) stamps from 1840-1887. Each stamp in a sheet had its own letters – the stamps in the top row were lettered

AA, AB, AC and so on; those in the second row, BA, BB, BC and so on. This pattern continued throughout the sheet. Originally GB stamps had the letters in the lower corners only, with stars in the top corners. Later the letters also appeared in the top corners but in the reverse order.

ARROWS
The margins of many sheets of stamps feature arrows that are designed to help post office clerks to divide the sheets into sections.

BACKSTAMP
Postmark on the back of an envelope, usually applied in transit or arrival.

BANTAMS
Stamps printed in a reduced format.

A first day cover that commemorated England's win in the 1966 World Cup Final

L-R: An Inland Revenue official stamp overprinted 'I. R./OFFICIAL'; a regional stamp for Scotland

BI-SECT
Stamp cut in half (normally diagonally) for use as a stamp of half the usual value, in times of shortage. For example, 2d stamps may be bisected to meet a 1d postal rate.

BLEUTE
French term denoting paper blued by chemicals in the printing ink or in the ingredients used in its manufacture.

BLIND PERFORATION
Perforation in which the stamp paper is merely dented owing to blunt teeth incorporated in the perforating machine.

BLOCK
Four or more stamps joined together; also used in Europe as a synonym for a miniature sheet.

BOOKLET
A small book containing one or more pages (known as panes) of stamps within a card cover. Today GB booklets fall into key main types – the everyday definitive booklet of stamps that usually contains standard GB 1st class definitives

and prestige stamp booklets that are issued roughly twice a year for special stamps and offer a combination of pages (panes) featuring historic background and mixed stamps (definitives and commemoratives). Since the first ever GB stamp book (in 1904) the covers of booklets have come in various guises – pictorial; with advertising; or plain merely stating what's inside.

CACHET
A mark applied to cards and covers, other than the postmark; it is often private or unofficial in nature.

CANCELLATION
Postmark applied to stamps to prevent re-use.

CANCELLED TO ORDER (CTO)
Stamps postmarked in bulk, usually for sale to collectors on 'first day covers' but often ordered even after stamps have been issued and manufactured retrospectively. It is usually advisable to try to obtain stamps that have been cancelled as a result of performing their intended postal duty.

CHALK-SURFACED PAPER
Paper with a security coating to prevent re-use by cleaning off the cancellation. When rubbed with silver a black mark will appear.

CHANGELING
A stamp whose colour has altered through immersion in water or exposure to sunlight.

CHARITY STAMPS
Stamps issued to support a charity. Usually such issues will be sold at a price above their postal face value with the additional monies donated to the charity.

COILS
Stamps issued in reels (usually used in vending machines) and often collected in strips. May be identified by being imperforate on two opposite sides or by having sideways watermarks.

COLOUR TRIALS
Proofs produced in various colours prior to issue to determine the most suitable colour.

COMB PERFORATION
Perforation applied to three sides of a stamp at a single stroke. This is aimed at providing stamps where perforations meet perfectly at the corners.

COMMEMORATIVES
Stamps issued to mark an occasion or anniversary and on sale for not more than 12 months.

COMPOUND PERFORATION
Perforation of different gauges on different sides of a stamp.

CONDITION
The condition of stamps is very important. The preference for collectors tends to be for unused stamps with their gum intact (known as 'mint' or 'unmounted mint') as issued by Royal Mail, but finding stamps in such condition prior to the reign of King George VI can be quite difficult. Used stamps are best collected with clear, clean, circular cancellations. Unused stamps that have the gum disturbed, and used stamps that show a poor cancellation, command lower prices than perfect examples.

CONTROL (NUMBERS)
Letters and numerals printed in the sheet margins of British stamps (from 1881-1947) for accounting purposes. For example the letter 'Y' would indicate which half of the year the stamps were printed and '36' would indicate 1936.

CORNER BLOCK
Stamps from the corner of the sheet with margins showing controls, cylinder or plate numbers and/or printer's imprint.

COVER
Envelope or wrapper with stamps affixed or pre-printed.

CYLINDER NUMBERS
Tiny numeral printed in the sheet margin denoting the cylinder from which it was printed. This is done for security reasons and there is usually one number for each colour in which the stamp is printed, the number appearing in the respective colours. Cylinder numbers are collected – this is usually done in a block of four, six or eight stamps with the sheet margin containing the cylinder numbers still attached. Most collectors refer to the cylinder numbers of recess (intaglio) printed stamps as 'Plate Numbers'. With many Queen Victoria period GB stamps the plate number was incorporated into the design of the stamp. Because of the relative ease with which the plate number can be

L-R: An example of a Maltese Cross cancellation; Pears' Soap advert on the back of a GB stamp

Millennium 1999/22
Right to learn/A Drummond

44

An example of what are now known as 'stamp cards' reproducing a 1999 GB Millennium issue

identified there is an interest in collecting stamps from each of the plates used during the printing.

DEFINITIVES
Stamps in general use over a period of years as opposed to the GB Special Stamps and commemoratives, which have a limited lifetime.

DIE
For recess (intaglio) printed stamps the design has to be engraved on to a piece of soft steel called the die.

DIE PROOF
A proof impression taken pulled from the die to check that it is satisfactory.

DOCTOR BLADE
With photogravure printing a blade is used to wipe off excess ink from the printing cylinder.

Sometimes a build-up of dust will occur that forces the blade away from the cylinder for a moment. This results in a streak of ink appearing across the printed sheet of stamps – this type of streak is known as a 'doctor blade variety'.

DUMB CANCELLATION
Postmark with no inscription or identifying mark, often applied to naval mail in wartime for security reasons.

DUTY PLATE
Plate used to print the 'duty' (i.e. the value) in conjunction with the key plate, a different duty plate being used for each denomination.

EMBOSSED
A stamp or a portion of stamp, in which the design is raised up.

ERROR
Stamp deviating from the normal in some respect with missing, shifted or inverted colours,

perforations, surcharges or overprints or mistakes in the design. Errors are usually only collectable if they have affected just a few sheets, otherwise a widespread error might be destroyed or simply issued in bulk (making it much less collectable). Despite widespread checking at printing stage errors do slip though the net and some are sold at post offices. The value of an error depends on the numbers known and the visual effect of the error.

ESSAY
Preliminary stamp design, often not subsequently used. However, essays can be produced using the eventual design but with experiments in colour.

EXHIBITION CARDS
Cards produced specifically for sale at major stamp exhibitions. They bear suitable stamps, cancellations and cachets.

FAKE
A genuine stamp that has been tampered with in some way to make it more valuable. This is usually by forging an overprint or removing a fiscal cancellation.

FISCAL
Stamp intended for fiscal or revenue purposes – such stamps are often authorised for postal use.

FIRST DAY COVER (FDC)
Souvenir envelope bearing stamps postmarked on the first day of issue. Many early GB first day covers comprised blank envelopes but later envelopes were designed to match the stamps. The British Post Office (now referred to as 'Royal Mail') started producing envelopes for first day covers with the Shakespeare Festival set of stamps in 1964. In May 1963, for the Paris Postal Conference stamp, the Post Office made a postmark (it was applied by machine) available for the first time which read 'FIRST DAY OF ISSUE'. Today handstamps bearing the same inscription are available on the day of issue of each new stamp release from many British post offices. In addition, Royal Mail usually produces two special pictorial handstamps for each new stamp issue with a direct relevance to the stamp issue. A

number of private companies usually sponsor additional special handstamps to coincide with the day of issue of new British stamps. These are then used on first day covers produced by the companies who sponsored the handstamps.

FLAW
Defect in printing, resulting in a constant blemish on the same stamp in every sheet.

FRANK
A mark or label that indicates that mail is transmitted free of postage. This is widely used by government departments and armed forces.

GRANITE PAPER
Paper containing tiny coloured fibres as a security device.

GRAPHITE LINES
Black lines found on the back of some British stamps (between 1957 and 1959) in connection with electronic sorting experiments. The first such trials were conducted in the Southampton area.

GUM
The adhesive on the back of stamps. For many years the natural product, gum arabic (this has a shiny appearance), was used. Later a synthetic

A mixture of early GB stamp booklets including the first ever one from 1904 (with red cover)

gum, called polyvinyl alcohol (PVA) gum, was developed – this is colourless but it's usually given a yellow tinge by printers. Later dextrin was added to this gum (this was known as PVAD gum) and this produced a bluish tinge.

GUTTERS

When the British printing firm Harrisons and Sons (now amalgamated into the De La Rue print group) installed a printing machine called Jumelle, it was capable of printing in several colours and perforating in one operation, it became necessary to change the layout of sheets of stamps. Because the circumference of the printing and perforating cylinders differed it was necessary to arrange sheets of special issues in the form of two blocks of stamps separated by a white central margin. This margin has become known as 'the gutter'.

GUTTER PAIRS

Stamps from adjoining panes with the gutter in the middle are known as gutter pairs.

IMPERFORATE

Stamps without any means of separating them and requiring to be cut apart with scissors. Early Victorian-era GB stamps were imperforate before the concept of perforating stamps became a practical reality. Stamps imperforate on one or more adjoining sides may be from booklets; those with no perforations on opposite sides come from coils.

IMPRIMATUR

The name given to the first sheet of stamps off the printing press that's marked to indicate that it has been approved. All imprimatur sheets should have been retained by Royal Mail but some of these have 'escaped' and come to market.

IMPRINT

Marginal inscription giving the printer's name or logo, the date of printing or other details.

INVERT

A stamp with part of the design upside down in relation to the rest.

IVORY HEAD

An outline of the portrait of Queen Victoria that can be seen on the backs of certain GB stamps printed on blued paper.

JUBILEE LINES

Lines of printer's rule reinforcing the edges of the printing plate, first used on the British 'Jubilee'

From 1998 the famous Diana memorial presentation pack in Welsh. GB packs officially began in 1964

L-R: An example of a control number and Jubilee line; error from 1965, missing Post Office Tower

series of 1887. Appear as bars of colour at the foot of the sheet.

KEY PLATE
A plate that provides the main part of a stamp design (usually the sovereign's head and border design) for a design that requires two separate printings (usually for two colour issues). The key plate is used in conjunction with the duty plate so the same basic design can be reproduced with different values (using different duty plates).

KILLER
Cancellation designed to obliterate the stamp very heavily.

KILOWARE
Originally sealed kilo bags of stamps on paper, but now applied to any mixtures of stamps sold by weight.

LINE PERFORATION
A form of perforation where both the horizontal perforations and vertical perforations are applied by separate processes. This frequently results in ragged edges at the corners of stamps.

LOCALS
Stamps whose validity is restricted to a single town or district and which cannot be used on national or international mail. Many collectors refer to them as 'labels'. A good example is stamps attached to items carried from offshore islands to the mainland where they are then placed into the main postal system. The labels cover only the charge to get the mail item to the mainland and the additional mainland postage must also be covered by additional mainland stamps to a certain value.

MACHINS
British definitive stamp designs that feature a profile of the Queen's head and have been issued since 1967. The 'Machins' name is after the designer of the profile head artwork – Arnold Machin.

MALTESE CROSS
The name given to the cancellation used for the first British stamps (from 1840 to 1844). It's named after its shape.

METER MARKS
Marks applied by meter to indicate pre-payment of postage. They usually consist of an indicium (country name and value), a dater die and a slogan advertising a firm or organisation.

MINIATURE SHEET
A small sheet containing a single stamp or a small group of stamps, often with broad decorative margins. Sometimes a stamp may only be issued within a miniature sheet and in no other format.

MINT
Unused stamp with full, original gum.

OBLITERATION
Postmarking of stamps to prevent re-use.

OFFICIAL STAMPS
Stamps produced solely for the use of government departments.

OVERPRINTS
Printing applied to a stamp after the original printing to convert it to some other purpose or mark some other event.

PANE

Originally a portion of a sheet divided by gutters, but now it's also a term applied to the blocks issued in booklets.

PEN CANCELLATION

Stamp cancelled in manuscript by pen and ink, usually applied to fiscal stamps but sometimes used postally. Modern stamps that miss machine postmarking are sometimes cancelled with a ballpoint pen, but these have no value.

PERFINS

Stamps perforated with the initials of firms or government departments as a security measure to prevent pilferage or improper use.

PERFORATION

Form of separation using machines which punch out tiny circles of paper. Different stamp printings and varieties can sometimes be identified by a difference in their perforations.

PHOSPHOR BANDS

Almost invisible lines applied to the face of stamps to facilitate electronic sorting.

PLATE

Flat or curved piece of metal from which stamps are printed.

PLATE NUMBERS

See 'Cylinder Numbers'

POSTAGE DUES ('TO PAY') LABELS

Labels denoting the amount of postage to be recovered from the addressee, on unpaid or underpaid mail.

POSTAGE PAID IMPRESSION (PPI)

Mark printed or handstruck on bulk postings denoting prepayment of postage.

POSTAL STATIONERY

Stationery sold by Royal Mail that has already been stamped (usually within its design) to the required basic postal rate. Occasionally postal stationery is issued bearing Special Stamp designs – this tends only to be on sale for a limited period.

PRE-CANCELS

Stamps used in bulk postings, with printed or handstruck marks to prevent re-use. Widely used in Belgium, France, Canada and USA but now largely superseded by meter marks or PPIs.

PRESENTATION PACKS

British presentation packs date back to 1964, when the Post Office issued the five stamps from the Shakespeare Festival set mounted within a black card and contained in a folder which gave additional details of the issue. This constitutes a presentation pack and the basic constituents remain the same to this day. In 1960 the Post Office repackaged certain definitive items and theses are regarded as presentation packs by collectors and as such are listed in this publication.

PRINTING

British stamp printing is put out to tender among printing firms with each individual issue or type of issue (e.g. booklets, self-adhesives or definitives) being awarded to a particular specialist printer. Stamp printing is carried out by a variety of different processes, described as follows.

Intaglio (aka recess)

This process requires the design to be engraved into the printing cylinder. When the ink is applied it fills the engraved recesses and any excess ink is wiped away. On contact with the paper the design is transferred as the ink leaves the recesses. Such a stamp can be identified because the ink parts of the design feel raised when run over by your fingers.

Typography (aka surface printing, letterpress)

These three names refer to the same process – the design to be printed stands up away from the surface of the printing cylinder. The ink is just applied to the raised parts and only the design is printed on contact with the paper.

GB miniature sheet from 2000 – these stamps were only available on this sheet, not singly

Photogravure (aka gravure)

For this process the cylinder consists of a large number of very small cells (each containing ink) with the depth of the cells determining how dark the colour will finally be reproduced. The printed stamp appears as a series of minute dots, each dot representing one cell and each being of equal size.

Lithography

The design of a lithography printed stamp will likewise appear as a number of dots, but here the dots will differ in size – the larger the dot the deeper the colour. A way of spotting a lithographed stamp against a photogravure printed stamp is to look at any lettering. On a photogravure stamp the lettering will be made up of dots but it will appear solid on a lithographed stamp.

PROVISIONALS

Stamps temporarily overprinted or surcharged to meet a shortage of regular issues.

RE-ENTRY

Part of an intaglio plate which is re-engraved or re-entered by the transfer roller, usually detected by slight doubling of the lines.

REPRINTS

Stamps from the original plates, printed long after the issue has ceased and usually distinguishable from the originals by slight differences on colour, paper or watermark.

RETOUCH

Repair to letterpress plates or photogravure cylinders to touch out a flaw.

ROULETTE

Form of separation using serrated instruments to produce cuts in the paper.

SELF-ADHESIVE(S)

Stamps that are attached to a backing paper and when peeled off have existing sticky adhesive on the back that is sufficient to stick them to envelopes and cards (no wetting agent is required). British self-adhesives are a fairly recent addition with the first such stamps being self-adhesive Machins issued in October 1993.

SE-TENANT

Two or more stamps of different designs, values or colours, printed side by side on sheet or as pair.

SHEET

Stamps are usually printed in sheets, which are then put into books and sold through post offices.

SMARTSTAMPS

In early 2004 Royal Mail introduced a service whereby small businesses could order their own special postal barcodes online for a monthly, or annual, fee to save them from having to continuously go to post offices to buy stamps. The service allows businesses to include their own logos within the 'stamps' but it's still in its infancy and widespread collecting of SmartStamps isn't yet known.

SPECIAL STAMPS

About 10 or 11 months out of every 12 Royal Mail issues a new set of 'Special Stamps'. These are in addition to the standard GB definitives. For example, in October 2005 six GB Special Stamps will be issued to commemorate the 200th anniversary of the Battle of Trafalgar.

SPECIMEN

Stamp perforated or overprinted thus, or its equivalent in other languages, for record or publicity purposes and having no postal validity.

STAMP CARDS (AKA PHQ CARDS)

Postcards issued by Royal Mail that reproduce enlarged versions of new British stamp issues on the front. The first such stamp card came in July 1973 when a 3p County Cricket stamp was 'blown up' on a postcard (two months after the actual stamp went on sale). At first stamp cards were issued randomly but today every new GB stamp issued tends to be accompanied by a stamp card reproducing it.

SURCHARGE

An overprint that alters the face value of a stamp.

TESTING LABELS

Labels used for testing stamp vending machines. Their design has earned them the name of 'poached eggs' among stamp collectors.

TÊTE-BÊCHE

French term denoting two adjoining stamps, upside down in relation to each other.

TRAFFIC LIGHTS

The name given by collectors to the solid circles of colour which appear in the margins of many sheets of stamps. These are intended to act as a check to prove that all colours have been printed.

TRAINING LABELS

Stamps found with thick black bars on the front have probably been used at the Post Office Training Schools – the bars render the stamps invalid for postage. When decimal currency was introduced Post Office staff were trained in its use with special labels bearing just the denomination (value of the stamps) but printed in the same colours as the respective definitives.

THEMATICS

A form of stamp collecting in which collectors pick a theme – e.g. transport – and then collect all relevant philatelic material surrounding their chosen theme.

UNDERPRINT

A term used to describe the motif found on a number of modern GB stamps – it's generally used to indicate that such stamps have been sold at a discount off face value. Such 'underprints' appear on the gummed side, usually printed on top of the gum. They have taken such forms as the letter 'D' or a star pattern. They tend to appear on stamps that were issued in booklets at a special discount price. A 12p Machin definitive from the 1980s exists with an underprint on stamps sold at full face value in sheets – this was to use up paper that had been intended for printing a discount booklet that, in the end, didn't materialise.

USED

A stamp that has performed its postal function and has had a cancellation applied. Collectors prefer the cancellations on stamps to be neat and clear so that they can be easily read but don't obscure too much of the stamp design.

VARIETY

Any variation from the norm, in shade, perforation, watermark etc. A variety differs from an error in that it usually occurs when small corrections are made to the printing cylinder by hand (usually on only one position on a sheet) and thus it will be noted on every sheet printed.

VENDING MACHINE LABELS

In the mid-1980s machines were developed that 'printed' a range of denominations on labels on insertion of the appropriate amount in coins. Such machines are known by the name of 'Frama' and the labels thus produced as called 'Frama labels' by collectors. From May 1, 1984 until April 30, 1985 the British Post Office installed four such machines on an experimental basis. The labels so produced are listed at the end of the special issues' section.

VIGNETTE

The central pictorial portion of a stamp design.

WATERMARK

A translucent impression used as a security device in the paper that's usually only visible when held up to the light. ∎

PROTECTIVE SHIELD

In a market filled with many pitfalls, it's good to know who you can rely on.

Members of the Philatelic Traders' Society agree to abide by a strict code of ethics, which ensures that you can deal with them in total confidence.

Established over 60 years, the PTS is the premier British dealer organisation with over 500 members respected throughout the philatelic community.

For more information on the society and its members, which also organises the world famous, twice yearly Stampex national stamp exhibitions held in London, go to
www.philatelic-traders-society.co.uk

The Philatelic Traders' Society Limited,
P.O. Box 371, Fleet, Hampshire GU52 6ZX.
Tel: 01252 628006 Fax: 01252 684674

Market forces

From high auction prices to rising stamp price indices and a spate of modern GB rarities, all the indicators are that British stamps are currently going through a 'golden age'. We explain why

Sceptics might think that a book like this will simply suggest that GB stamps are worth buying because the market is 'doing well'. But it's now true to say that, after some lean years, the past 18 months have seen a resurgence in auction prices obtained by British stamps from all reigns, plus the emergence of a number of modern rarities that will have significant financial benefit for even the most casual collector.

In the past year a number of significant philatelic collections have come under the hammers of various British auction houses. Among these was the previously unknown collection compiled in secret by Sir Gawaine Baillie, an amateur racing driver, with the emphasis on mint items and great rarities. The first part of Baillie's sale was at Sotheby's London in September 2004 when over £3,500,000 was raised.

This sale heralded the beginning of a renaissance in classic GB items such as the 'Seahorses' designs, the 1935 Prussian Blue error of colour 2½d Silver Jubilee stamp, and a wide variety of classic GB errors such as the black missing from the 2½d Post Office Savings Bank pre-decimal QEII issue of 1961.

The values of the famous 'Seahorses' designs have gone up due to recent auction realisations

Rare classic such as the £5 orange from 1882-3 and modern errors (Machin misperf) are rising

In fact, if you examined auction trends over the past 12 months they are very much on the up, with bidders fighting strongly over items. This has been helped by the strength of material, coming to market but clear trends are modern GB errors (mainly missing colours) such as the 6d from the 1966 British Technology issues with blue missing, and fine and rare classic material (mainly from the Queen Victoria reign) like the £5 orange of 1882-3.

Although philatelic auctions are more likely to throw up the more rare items, the general upward trend in the GB stamp market is perhaps better illustrated by the fact that even issues which were produced in comparatively large numbers still retain relatively high market prices. Key examples

ABOVE: Multiple printing and, right, missing colours affect worth

of such stamps are the £5 orange of 1882 (over 250,000 produced), the 1858 1d red plate 225 and the 1870 ½d rose plate 9 (about 2,500,000 issued).

It may seem strange that such items are worth money but many have fallen by the wayside as they pre-date the more active period of collecting GB stamps (that principally began from King George V's reign onwards). The best advice for any collector is to talk to one of the key established GB dealers such as Rushstamps, Dauwalders, Arthur Ryan and B. Alan. All are capable of helping you to build a GB collection that will significantly grow in value over a number of years.

The oldest GB dealer – Stanley Gibbons – has recently published figures of its price index that lists the 30 most rare GB stamps and follows their price progress (much liked a share index). The upshot of this is that, over the past seven years (since 1998),

the value of the most rare GB stamps has risen by over 100%. In other words if you had bought the 30 rare items back in 1998 they would have had a market price of around £423,500 but today you would have to pay out around £861,000 for the same stamps. It's little wonder that many investors are now turning to stamps as a 'safe bet' compared to share markets.

Another factor that may also impact upon the value of GB stamps in the future is the fact that from April 2006 stamp collections can be added into Self-Invested Pensions (SIPs). This odd piece of legislation effectively allows you to sell your collection to yourself and have a cheque written out in your favour (provided you have enough funds in your pension to do so).

Followers of month-by-month market trends through the pages of STAMP MAGAZINE will already know that the key trend

Modern rarities include the Rowland Hill miniature sheet (below) and presentation packs such as the Classic Locos and Entente Cordiale

in the past 12 months has been the emergence of modern 'rarities'. These rarities aren't errors or but are simply the result of comparatively low printings of items which have been high in demand. Among these are the GB and French language versions of the Entente Cordiale presentation packs of 2004; the Classic Locomotives miniature sheets and presentation packs of 2004; and the Ocean Liners and Royal Horticultural miniature sheets (from 2004).

Despite the fact that Royal Mail doesn't reveal the extent of its print runs on philatelic items it seems that it struck gold last year in issuing a number of philatelic issues that struck a chord way beyond then usual regular philatelic customers.

For example, Classic Locomotives would have been collected by thematic collectors of train stamps and by rail enthusiasts – presentation packs

are already fetching over £30 less than 18 months after such packs sold for under £4.

What is also happening is that excess amounts of even comparatively 'straightforward' GB issues are being snapped up so that less material is on the market. Among such tips is the £10 Britannia stamp from 1993, and the very short-lived Castles set of four that was printed by Dutch printing house Enschedé in 1997.

In the definitive arena (Machins) a couple of modern errors have emerged, most notably the '£' sign missing error from the £2 value of July 2003. This is given added value by the fact that the high value Machin range of mid-2003 survived for under nine months before being swept aside for the use of the incredibly dull printed Post Office labels that now cover so much of our parcel postage costs.

If the collecting bug does bite you hard and this book has merely whetted your appetite, take a look at STAMP MAGAZINE every month. Its price tipster, 'Phil Attlee', will be able to guide you regularly towards making the most astute purchases of GB material possible! ■

GBBOOKLETS, packs and sheets

Stamps are just one aspect of collecting British issues. Many collectors now choose to collect presentation packs, sheets and booklets. We look at the history of these philatelic items

Amazingly enough British stamp booklets date back to 1904 when the British Post Office issued its first booklet – it contained 24 of the then current King Edward VII 1d stamps arranged in four panes of six. Since then the British stamp book has gone through a variety of key changes including allowing advertising to appear within booklets, the introduction of selling them by vending machines (in 1937), the era of the 'prestige stamp booklet' (the PSB first came out in 1969

with the famous Stamps for Cooks book), and the tradition of selling self-adhesive stamps in booklets (from 1993).

Initially booklets were issued as a functional way to buy stamps in bulk but the British public still preferred to buy its stamps as required over post office counters across the land. The big shift in habits came as late as 1987 when Royal Mail allowed stamps to be sold in non-Post Office outlets. Suddenly British people could buy in newsagents, garages and the like and the new 'retail books' incorporated barcodes on the back to make it easy for non-postal shops to sell them.

Later developments in books have included the use of 'non-value indicator (NVI) stamps simply inscribed '1st' or '2nd' in books. This meant that less reprints of stamps were required if any changes in postal rates happened. But what books should the collector look out for?

AGE CONSIDERATIONS

Several types of GB stamp books are worth looking for if you wish to make money. Early booklets were stapled together but a metal shortage during World War I meant that the method of binding was changed to stitching (a practice that remained in place for almost 60 years). Age

ABOVE: Travellers' Tale presentation pack from the Royal Mail's Millennium series of stamps, February 1999

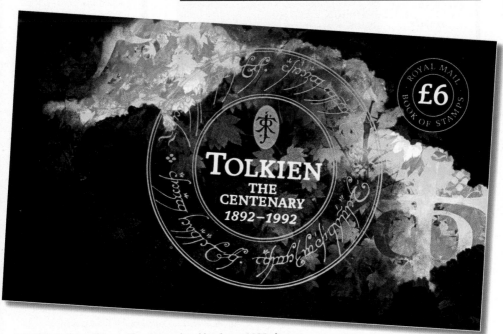

BELOW: Tolkien £6 prestige stamp booklet from 1992 that marked the author's J.R.R. Tolkien's birth centenary

does not necessarily mean value with booklets but often it's the rarity of a stamp contained within that makes a book worth more money. For example, the £1 Story of Wedgwood booklet from 1972 is valuable, as its is the only place in which Machin collectors can get hold of the GB ½p Machin side band (the book is worth around £40 today).

A similar story has emerged within the past two years from the A Perfect Coronation PSB of 2003 which include a £1 version of the Edmund Dulac designed 1/3 Coronation stamp if 1953.

ABOVE: One of the 3/8 packs from 1960 that contained definitives. Many regard this as being the first GB presentation pack

The stamp doesn't exist anywhere else and, as about half of the print run of the A Perfect Coronation PSB was sold to a book company, the chances of collectors getting it were immediately halved. BRITISH STAMP MARKET VALUES recommends that you try and get hold of the PSB as it could be worth hundreds of pounds in the not-too-distant future.

PRESENTATION PACKS

Presentation packs are a much more modern phenomena than British booklets, with the first one emerging in April 1964 as a part of the stamp set to commemorate the Shakespeare Festival. However, some collectors argue that

the low-value Wildings, Castle high values, 'phosphor-graphite' definitives, and the regional stamps that were issued in packs for London's first ever international stamp exhibition in 1960 are actually Britain's first ever packs.

SUBJECT BACKGROUND

For any collector, packs are fascinating as they usually contain extra information about a particular stamp issue as well as the background to the stamp designs or the subject matter depicted on the stamps.

Whatever argument you subscribe to which pack was officially first in the mid-1960s, pack releases were sporadic and it wasn't until the World Cup set of 1966 that demand really picked up. Soon packs would accompany every special issue of British stamps and after the debut of the famous Machin definitives in 1967 packs started to include low and high value British definitive stamps and country stamps (from England, Scotland, Wales and Northern Ireland).

The basic format of GB packs changed in 1982 with the issue to commemorate Charles Darwin so that stamps now appeared below rather than to the right of, the descriptive panel. Foreign language versions of GB presentation packs began in 1968 with the Paintings pack that had a German version.

In addition, for a period standard GB packs were also provided with insert cards, with the text in Dutch or Japanese. In fact, the Royal Silver Wedding pack of 1972 was additionally printed in Japanese. Also, Welsh language packs were produced for the Investiture pack for the Prince of Wales (in 1969) and for a commemorative pack for Diana, Princess of Wales (issued in February 1998).

Some GB packs contain errors – for example, the Anniversaries stamp packs of 1970 misspelt the name of one of the designers, Marjorie Saynor (it said 'Majorie') and also the word descendants (it appeared as 'decendants').

SHORT PRINT RUN

As far as value is concerned a number of British packs stand out. The aforementioned Welsh language Princess Diana pack from 1998 is rare because only around 6,500 were printed and it was exclusively sold in post offices in Wales. It regularly fetches over £100 on the Internet auction site eBay. Other noteworthy packs to look out for (due to their comparative rarity) are the 1964 Opening of Forth Road Bridge pack, which is worth closer to £300 today

In addition the 2002 Wilding I pack (celebrating 50 years of the first ever QEII definitives) is worth three figures – only 8,500 of this pack were sold and the rest of the print run is believed to have been destroyed (due to the fact that they contained errors).

Another modern pack that's worth keeping an eye on is the 2004 Classic Locomotives pack that is said to exist in two main forms – with stamps from the set and with a miniature sheet version. Although Royal Mail has been at pains to deny that it mistakenly let out a few versions of this pack containing miniature sheets by mistake these do exist and are already changing hands at £30 plus (that's in comparison to an original pack price of under £4).

MINIATURE SHEETS

Britain didn't begin to produce miniature sheets until as recently as 1978 when a Historic Buildings sheet was printed with a 10p surcharge above the value of the stamps contained on it in order

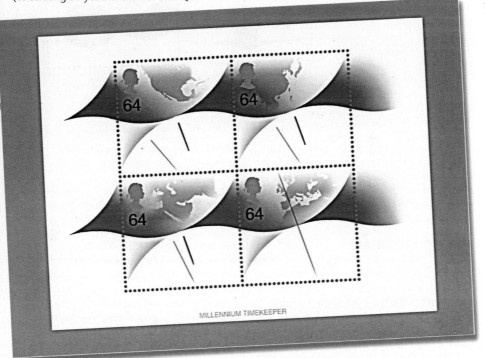

MILLENNIUM TIMEKEEPER

ABOVE: Millennium Timekeeper sheet from December 1999 shown here on a stamp card

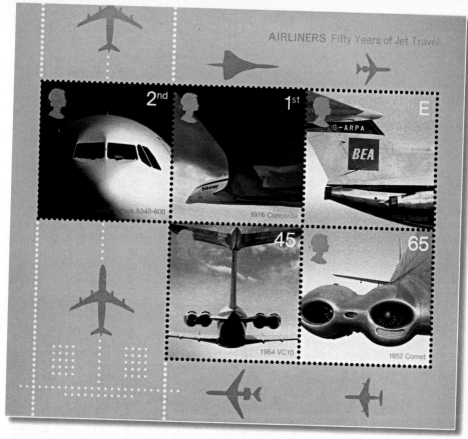

to fund the London 1980 International Stamp Exhibition. It seems almost bizarre nowadays but the first GB sheet issued that wasn't linked to an international exhibition was as recently as 1999, when Royal Mail produced a special sheet for the Solar Eclipse of August 11, 1999.

TRANSPORT THEME

Since that milestone British miniature sheets have become more commonplace with an established series on a transport theme (that began with the Buses sheet in 2001) and although not every British special issue is accompanied by a miniature, around half of them are so there are now about six new GB sheets every year.

A notable royal sheet from 2000 for the 100th birthday of the Queen Mother featured four

ABOVE: Airliners sheet from May 2002 featuring the five designs from the set

generations of the British Royal Family: the Queen Mother, Her Majesty Queen Elizabeth II, Prince Charles and HRH Prince William.

The current popularity of miniature sheets is perhaps best illustrated by the fact that in March 2005 the Ocean Liners and Royal Horticultural Society sheets from 2004 became the first ever British sheets to sell out before their scheduled on sale period came to an end. If you've managed to tuck away some of these and/or the Classic Locomotives sheet (also from 2004) then you've probably got a nice investment if you can hold onto them for a few years. ■

Caring for your stamps

Once you've bought your stamps it's vitally important to look after them. We give you some top tips on how to care for your collection

Most collectors are justifiably proud of their stamp collections, as they will often have spent much time and money on compiling it. However, many people can be a tad careless about protecting it. So here are a few basic rules that should ensure that your stamps are well kept.

Always handle stamps, indeed any philatelic material, with tweezers. It's vital to use proper stamp tweezers, not those intended for other purposes (eyebrows etc.).

Keep your stamps safe, probably in a stockbook (a sort of 'holding album' before you decide to place stamps on exhibition sheets or mount them on album pages). Do not overfill the stockbook and be careful as you insert or remove items. It is surprisingly easy to fold over the corner perforations of a stamp as you slip it within the strips of a stockbook.

INTERLEAVES FOR PROTECTION

Keep your stockbooks in an upright position, turning over the pages from time to time. Look for quality when you buy a stockbook. Interleaving between the pages will protect the stamps.

Remember that the holding strips in stockbooks might cause damage to your stamps. The top edge of the strips could leave a mark on your stamps, so check the strips carefully.

Take care of covers, miniature sheets and blocks. Many collectors store such items in boxes (shoe boxes are popular), but whatever methods you choose ensure your items are kept safe from any damage.

STORAGE CONDITIONS

Much the same applies if you use stamp albums. It's best to opt for the highest quality that you can afford. Not all paper is suitable for housing a stamp collection, and nothing looks worse than a bulging album caused by the leaves not being strong enough to hold the material. Again, avoid over-filling, and keep the albums upright, turning over the leaves from time to time.

Always store your albums and stockbooks in the right conditions. Avoid extremes of heat, light and humidity. Be very wary, and take immediate action if you have any suspicions of dampness, or signs of discolouring.

If removing stamps from paper, do so carefully, and do not be in too much of a hurry. Wait until the stamps slide easily off the piece of envelope. Also, dry the stamps with care.

When mounting, if using stamp hinges, again use the best, and remember to apply as little moisture as possible to the part of the hinge that affixes to the stamp. Don't forget that the hinge is placed just below the perforations. You should never place a hinge over perforations.

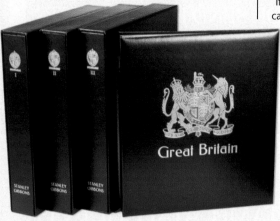

A selection of dedicated GB albums is available to hold your collection

If using protective mounts, again opt for the best quality. Do be careful as you cut the mount to fit the stamp. Also remember that the stamp should be removed from its mount from time to time.

Seek the best possible condition for your stamps, and other material. Naturally condition is relative: a modern stamp should be perfect, whereas such condition may be more difficult to achieve with an older stamp.

THOSE LITTLE PERFORATIONS

Perforations are all important. Are all the perforation teeth present? Avoid perforation teeth that have been 'pulled' (i.e. missing) and especially check the corners of your stamps (remember that stamps with line perforations will have uneven corners).

Is the stamp well centred within the

You should always use proper philatelic tweezers – not those for eyebrows – when 'handling' stamps

perforations? Some stamps are only found badly centred; nevertheless, always try to achieve the best possible.

Remember that your stamps should never be torn or thinned in any way. Do check the backs of stamps very carefully. Avoid any which have a wad of old hinges stuck to them.

Cancellations should be neat and clean. Of course, it does depend on the purpose of your collection. If you need to read the postmark, its clarity might be more important than seeing the stamp beneath. But if the stamp is the important aspect, then a thick, heavy postmark shouldn't obscure its design. Your stamps are important to you – always seek the best, and keep them that way. ■

Where to see
GBSTAMPS

If you want to whet your appetite for British stamps there are several key places that showcase the best of GB issues from 1840 to the present day

U nless you've just won the lottery or have been successful in business it's fair to say that you will be building up your collection on a budget. However, that doesn't mean that you can't get the chance at least to see some of the most rare British stamps known. Arguably, the best known collection of stamps held in Britain is that of the British Library at Euston in London. The collection has millions of rare pieces from all over the world and it can show only a fraction if its collections at one time. The overall library collection has its roots in the collection formed by H.T. Tapling in the 19th century which was donated to the British Museum after Tapling's death at the age of just 39.

Since Tapling's historic bequeathal many other famous philatelists from around the world have chosen the British Library as the place to put their collections. In the large foyer of the British Library there is always a huge display of frames that can be pulled out from the walls to allow you to view some of Britain's (and the world's) most rare stamps. In addition to this if you become a dedicated philatelist who wants to research, further appointments can be made via the library's philatelic staff.

BRITISH POSTAL MUSEUM

In a similar vein to the British Library, what is now known as the British Postal Museum & Archive (BPMA) was inspired by the donation of a single collection – that of Reginald Phillips, which was donated in the mid-1960s. Unfortunately, at the end of 1998 the old British

ABOVE: Stamp albums as they are stored in the Royal Philatelic Collection's safe room

Postal Museum closed its doors, but recent announcements have revealed that a revamped BPMA is set to open at Royal Woolwich Arsenal in London in 2008.

All of this doesn't mean that stamps from the BPMA can't be seen by the public. At its current premises at Freeling House, Farringdon, London, there are exhibitions of parts of the collection that can be freely viewed. Like the policy adopted by the British Library, the BPMA also allows scheduled visits for more detailed research on specific GB issues.

The bi-annual national British stamp exhibition, Stampex, will often have great displays of GB

ABOVE: Collectors browing at Stampex in London
RIGHT: The new British Library at Euston

material – either by individual philatelists who have entered their collections into competition or by invited displays by the BPMA, or even by philatelic societies which collect GB philately.

ROYAL PHILATELIC COLLECTION

Until the late 1990s the Royal Philatelic Collection (kept at a royal palace in London) was something of a 'mythical beast' that wasn't seen in public too often. Since then the policy of the last two keepers of the collection – Charles Goodwyn and Michael Sefi – has been to make more of the collection available for exhibitionaround the world.

During 2002 it went on a Golden Jubilee tour of Royal residences across Britain and some of the best parts of it were seen at the last London international shown – The Stamp Show 2000. You will need to keep an eye on the philatelic press (such as STAMP MAGAZINE, out monthly) to see where and when parts of the Royal Philatelic Collection will be displayed.

As mentioned, another route to seeing British stamps is through your local philatelic society. During the season (usually September to June) societies meet about twice a month and often are visited by guest exhibitors talking about British stamps. The best one for truly dedicated GB collectors is the Great Britain Philatelic Society, which celebrated its 50th anniversary in 2005. ■

LEFT: The Kirkcudbright Penny Black cover

How this guide works

An explanation of the prices given and the abbreviations used

BRITISH STAMP MARKET VALUES 2006 is unique in that it offers independent and accurate price information about all GB stamps issued between 1840 and 2005. We don't quote inflated prices that dealers might hope to achieve but merely state the accurate market price for each stamp issued over the past 165 years. We are not affiliated to any dealer and we give you accurate pricings that allow you to pinpoint the exact worth of your collection. Throughout this extensive listing the prices are shown as follows.

• **Queen Victoria**: prices are given in two columns – mounted unused (the left-hand column) and fine used (right-hand column). The exception is for the imperforate issues, where fine used are priced for both three and four margins.

• **King Edward VII and King George V**: prices are given in three columns – unmounted mint (left-hand column), mounted unused (middle column), and fine used (right-hand column).

• **King Edward VIII, King George VI and Queen Elizabeth II**: prices are given in two columns – unmounted mint (left-hand column) and fine used (right-hand column).

• **In the prestige stamp booklet and presentation pack listings** the prices quoted are simply for mint condition items. When a dash (–) appears in a price column it means that the stamp doesn't exist in the particular states (i.e. used or unused) or simply that it is impracticable to price the stamps (i.e. used stamps where only a gum difference exists).

Because of the proliferation of modern GB special stamps, often a price for a 'set' of basic stamps will be given. The basic stamps are listed first and when any variation occurs they are given a prefix such as (a) or (b). Unused set prices include any se-tenant combinations where applicable; used set prices are for the stamps as singles.

While the question of a stamp's condition can be a personal one, the used prices here are for fine used copies – stamps with a clear, circular datestamp (steel) after 1880 or with a light Duplex cancellation prior to 1880. Prices quoted are for clean stamps with full perforations (or with reasonable margins for imperforate stamps). Modern, mounted unused material should be available at lower prices.

The philatelic dealers who have kindly helped with the pricings of this book are:
• Arthur Ryan (Queen Victoria, King Edward VII and King George V).
• Rushstamps (QEII special stamps).
• B. Alan (Machins).
• Dauwalders (King Edward VIII and King George VI).
• Packs & Cards (presentation packs and stamp cards).

The following abbreviations are used:
Des – designer; Perf – perforation; Wmk – watermark
Names of stamp printers:
Harrison – Harrison and Sons (High Wycombe) Ltd
Waterlow – Waterlow and Sons Ltd
De La Rue – Thomas De La Rue and Co Ltd
Bradbury Wilkinson – Bradbury Wilkinson and Co Ltd
Questa – The House of Questa
Courvoisier – Helio Courvoisier SA, Switzerland
Enschede – Joh. Eschedé en Zohen, Holland
Format – Format International Security Printers Ltd
Waddington – John Waddington and Co Ltd
Delrieu – Imprimerie Delrieu

QUEEN VICTORIA

Prices in this section are for lightly mounted unused and fine used only: care should be excercised when buying unmounted mint because of cases in regumming are known. In view of the wide variation in pricing, for the 1840-1841 imperforate stamps, fine used are priced for copies with either four margins or three margins.

Id black

1840
Engraved by Charles and Frederick Heath. Printed in recess by Perkins, Bacon, Wmk: Small crowns, Imperforate. Letters in lower corners only.

	Unused	Fine used Four margins	Three margins
Id black (May 6)	£4,500	£180	70.00

(*- This stamp was distributed to Post masters on May 1, but could not be officially used until May 6: covers dated prior to May 6 do however exist.)

2d blue (May 8)	£10,000	£450	£125

2d blue, 1841

1841
Details as above, but white lines added to design of 2d

Id red brown (February 10)	200.00	9.00	3.00
2d blue (March 13)	£2,100	50.00	12.00

1854
As above but perf: 16

Id red-brown February 1854)	£175	10.00
2d blue (March 1, 1854)	£1,900	60.00

NB - trials leading up to the perforating of stamps were conducted between 1848 and 1853 by Henry Archer and by the Government.

1855
As above but perf: 14.

Id red-brown (January 1855)	£400	40.00
2d blue (March 4, 1855)	£3,500	£140

1855
As above but wmk. Large crown and perf: 16

Id red-brown (May 15, 1855)	700.00	65.00
2d blue (July 20, 1855)	£5,000	£220

1855
As above but perf: 14

Id red-brown (August 18, 1855)	£150	8.00
2d blue (July 20, 1855)	£1600	30.00

1858-1870.
As above with wmk: 'half penny' extending over three stamps (½d) or Large Crowns (1d, 1½d, 2d). Perf: 14 but letters in all four corners. These plates have the number included in the design of the stamps and as such stamps from the individual plates are collected.

½d rose-red

½d rose-red (October 1, 1870)	75.00	10.00

Plates

1	£180	50.00
3	£120	25.00
4	£100	18.00
5	75.00	10.00
6	80.00	10.00
8	£200	60.00
9	£3000	£550
10	85.00	10.00
11	80.00	10.00
12	80.00	10.00
13	80.00	10.00
14	80.00	10.00
15	£115	24.00
19	£140	28.00
20	£170	50.00

Id rose-red

Id rose-red (April 1, 1864)	12.00	1.50

Plates

71	22.00	2.00
72	27.00	2.50
73	24.00	2.00
74	25.00	1.50
76	25.00	1.50
77	£160,000	£100,000

78	45.00	1.50		139	40.00	12.50
79	22.00	1.50		140	14.00	1.50
80	30.00	1.50		141	£100	7.00
81	35.00	1.50		142	50.00	22.00
82	85.00	2.75		143	40.00	12.00
83	£110	6.00		144	75.00	16.00
84	40.00	1.60		145	23.00	1.75
85	27.00	1.60		146	25.00	4.50
86	35.00	2.75		147	30.00	2.00
87	22.00	1.50		148	25.00	2.00
88	£150	7.00		149	25.00	4.50
89	25.00	1.50		150	12.00	1.50
90	25.00	1.50		151	40.00	7.50
91	35.00	4.50		152	40.00	4.00
92	21.00	1.50		153	90.00	7.00
93	30.00	1.50		154	30.00	1.50
94	28.00	4.00		155	30.00	1.75
95	25.00	1.50		156	35.00	1.50
96	28.00	1.50		157	30.00	1.50
97	25.00	2.50		158	23.00	1.50
98	30.00	4.50		159	23.00	1.50
99	35.00	4.00		160	23.00	1.50
100	40.00	1.50		161	40.00	5.00
101	40.00	7.50		162	30.00	5.00
102	28.00	1.50		163	30.00	2.00
103	30.00	2.75		164	30.00	2.00
104	60.00	4.00		165	35.00	1.50
105	55.00	5.50		166	35.00	4.50
106	35.00	1.50		167	35.00	1.50
107	40.00	5.00		168	30.00	6.00
108	60.00	1.75		169	30.00	6.00
109	65.00	2.50		170	21.00	1.50
110	40.00	7.50		171	12.00	1.50
111	36.00	1.75		172	23.00	1.50
112	50.00	1.70		173	48.00	6.50
113	30.00	9.00		174	23.00	1.50
114	£240	9.00		175	40.00	2.50
115	85.00	1.75		176	40.00	1.75
116	60.00	7.50		177	32.00	1.50
117	28.00	1.50		178	40.00	2.50
118	30.00	1.50		179	30.00	1.75
119	28.00	1.50		180	40.00	4.00
120	12.00	1.50		181	36.00	1.50
121	25.00	8.00		182	75.00	4.00
122	12.00	1.50		183	35.00	2.00
123	25.00	1.50		184	23.00	1.75
124	22.00	1.50		185	30.00	2.00
125	25.00	1.50		186	35.00	1.75
127	35.00	1.75		187	30.00	1.50
129	25.00	6.50		188	50.00	7.50
130	35.00	1.75		189	50.00	5.50
131	45.00	12.00		190	30.00	4.50
132	£125	18.00		191	23.00	5.50
133	£105	7.50		192	30.00	1.50
134	12.00	1.50		193	23.00	1.50
135	70.00	22.00		194	30.00	6.50
136	65.00	17.00		195	30.00	6.50
137	22.00	1.75		196	30.00	4.00
138	14.00	1.50		197	35.00	7.00

198	32.00	4.50
199	35.00	4.50
200	40.00	2.00
201	23.00	4.00
202	40.00	6.50
203	23.00	13.00
204	35.00	1.75
205	35.00	2.25
206	35.00	7.00
207	40.00	7.00
208	35.00	12.50
209	30.00	8.00
210	45.00	10.00
211	50.00	18.00
212	40.00	10.00
213	40.00	10.00
214	45.00	15.00
215	45.00	15.00
216	50.00	15.00
217	50.00	6.00
218	45.00	7.00
219	80.00	58.00
220	32.00	6.00
221	50.00	15.00
222	60.00	30.00
223	75.00	50.00
224	90.00	45.00
225	£1,800	£500

1½d red-rose

1½d red-rose (October 1, 1870)	£250	25.00

Plates
1*	£400	45.00
3	£250	25.00

(* plate number 1 does not in fact appear in the stamp design)

2d blue (July 1858)	£250	15.00

Plates
7	£875	40.00
8	£800	25.00
9	£250	8.00
12	£1350	£100
13	£260	15.00
14	£340	16.00
15	£320	16.00

10d embossed

1847-1845, Embossed issue.
Die engraved at the Royal Mint by William Wyon. Printed using the embossed process at Somerset House. Wmk: VR (6d), unwatermarked (10d, 1/-).
Imperforate.

6d lilac (March 1, 1854)	£4,500	£500
10d brown (November 6, 1848)	£3,600	£750
1/- green (September 11, 1847)	£5,000	£500

NB – the above are priced cut square; examples cut to shape are worth considerably less.

The following issues are printed by the surface printed process by De La Rue. Perf: 14 (except where stated).

4d carmine

1855-1857
4d carmine (Wmk: Small Garter) (July 31, 1855)	£3,600	£250
4d carmine (Wmk: Medium Garter) (February 25, 1856)	£4,000	£300
4d carmine (Wmk: Large Garter) (January 1857)	£950	50.00

6d lilac

1856
Wmk: Emblems.
6d lilac (October 21, 1856)	£700	60.00
1/- green (November 1, 1856)	£880	£150

9d bistre

1862-1864
Wmk: Large Garter (**4d**), Emblems (**3d, 6d, 9d, 1/-**).

3d carmine (May 1, 1862)	£1,100	£200
4d red (January 15, 1862)	£800	50.00
6d lilac (December 1, 1862)	£950	45.00
9d bistre (January 15, 1862)	£2,500	£250
1/- green (December 1, 1862)	£1,700	£180

NB: the 1/- exists with either a number 1 in the border or with a number 2.

10d brown

Designs as above, but with large corner letters (all values). The designs of the 3d and 4d values are as 1862 issue.

1865-1867.
Wmk: Larger Garter (**4d**), Emblems (**3d, 6d, 9d, 10d, 1/-**).

3d carmine (March 1, 1865)		
(plate 4)	£900	£100
4d vermilion (July 4, 1865)	£375	35.00
6d lilac (April 1, 1865)	£600	50.00
9d bistre (December 1, 1865)		
(plate 4*)	£1,800	£325
10d brown (November 11, 1867)		
(plate 1)	-	£22,000
1/- green (February 1, 1865)		
(plate 4)	£1,000	£110

(*- copies from an 'Imprimatur sheet' of plate 5 are known to exist.)

Plates:
4d

7	£425	60.00
8	£375	38.00
9	£375	38.00
10	£450	80.00
11	£375	35.00
12	£375	35.00
13	£375	35.00
14	£425	55.00

6d

5	£600	£500
6	£1750	90.00

2/- blue

(Other designs as previous issue).

1867-1880.
Wmk: Flowering rose.

3d red (July 12, 1867)		£350	30.00
6d lilac (June 21, 1867)	260	£360	50.00
9d bistre (October 3, 1867)			
(plate 4)		£1,200	£180
10d brown (July 1, 1867)		£1,700	£200
1/- green (July 13, 1867)		£480	25.00
2/- blue (July 1, 1867)			
(plate 1)		£1,700	£110
2/- brown (February 27, 1880)			
(plate 1)		£11,000	£2,000

Plates:
3d

4	£600	£100
5	£350	30.00
6	£375	30.00
7	£450	32.00
8	£380	30.00
9	£380	32.00
10	£500	65.00

6d

8	£360	50.00
9	£360	50.00
10	-	£16,000

10d

1	£1700	£200
2	£17,000	£6,000

1/-

4	£600	40.00
5	£480	25.00
6	£600	25.00
7	£700	45.00

6d grey, 1973

1872-1873.
Wmk: Flowering Rose.

6d brown (April 12, 1872) £400   30.00

Plates:

11	£400	30.00
12	£1500	£150

6d grey (April 24, 1873)
(plate 12)   £950   £125

£1 brown

1867-1868
Wmk: Maltese Cross. Perf: 15 x 15.

5/- red (July 1, 1867)	£3,500	£400
10/- grey-green (September 26, 1878) (plate 1)	£30,000	£1,750
£1 brown (September 26, 1878) (plate 1)	£35,000	£2,500

5/- plates

1	£3,500	£400
2	£5,000	£550

1882-1883
Wmk: Large Anchor. Perf: 14.

5/- red (November 25, 1882) **(plate 4)**	£12000	£1750
10/- grey-green (February 1883) **(plate 1)**	£46000	£2500
£1 brown (December 1882) **(plate 1)**	£60000	£5000
£5 orange (March 21, 1882) (plate 1)	£7500	£3000

1873-1880
A) Wmk: Small Anchor

2½d mauve (July 1, 1875) £35000   50.00

Plates:

1	£350	50.00
2	£350	50.00
3	£550	75.00

B) Wmk: Orb

2½d mauve (May 16, 1876)	£300	30.00
2½d blue (February 5, 1880)	£300	20.00

2½d (mauve)

3	£675	65.00
4	£300	30.00
5	£300	30.00
6	£300	30.00
7	£300	30.00
8	£300	30.00
9	£300	30.00
10	£325	35.00
11	£300	30.00
12	£300	30.00
13	£300	30.00
14	£300	30.00
15	£300	30.00
16	£300	30.00
17	£950	£170

2½d (blue)

17	£300	35.00
18	£325	20.00
19	£300	20.00
20	£325	20.00

C) Wmk: Flowering Rose.

3d red (July 5, 1873)	£275	28.00
6d buff (March 15, 1873) (plate 13)	-	£12,000
6d grey (March 31, 1874)	£280	55.00
1/- green (September 1, 1873)	£450	45.00
1/- brown (October 14, 1880) **(plate 13)**	£2,400	£400

Plates:
3d (red)

11	£275	28.00
12	£300	28.00
14	£350	28.00
15	£275	28.00
16	£275	28.00
17	£300	28.00
18	£300	28.00
19	£275	28.00
20	£375	50.00

6d (grey)

13	£280	30.00
14	£280	30.00
15	£280	30.00
16	£280	30.00
17	£450	75.00

1/- (green)

8	£450	55.00
9	£450	55.00
10	£450	75.00

11	£450	25.00
12	£425	45.00
13	£425	45.00
14	-	£17000

D) Wmk: Large Garter.
4d vermilion (March 1, 1867)

	£1,250	£200
4d green (March 12, 1877)	£700	£150
4d brown (August 15, 1880)		
(plate 17)	£1,100	£250
8d orange (September 11, 1876)		
(plate 1)	£850	90.00

NB – an **8d** red-brown was prepared for use but not issued.

Plates:
4d (vermilion)

15	£1250	£150
16	-	£18000
4d green		
15	£750	£150
16	£700	£150
17	-	£11,000

(3d on 3d)

1880-1883
Wmk: Imperial Crown.

2½d blue (March 23, 1881)	£300	12.00
3d red (February 1881)	£350	45.00
3d (in red) on 3d lilac		
(January 1, 1883)		
(plate 21)	£375	75.00
4d brown (December 9, 1880)	£275	35.00
6d grey (January 1, 1881)	£280	40.00
6d (in red) on 6d lilac		
(January 1, 1883) (plate 18)	£400	75.00
1/- brown (May 29, 1881)	£375	75.00

Plates:
2½d (blue)

21	£325	15.00
22	£300	15.00
23	£300	12.00

3d (red)

20	£450	80.00
21	£350	45.00

4d (brown)

17	£275	35.00
18	£275	35.00

6d (grey)

17	£320	40.00
18	£280	40.00

1/- (brown)

13	£450	75.00
14	£375	75.00

5d indigo

1880-1881.
Wmk: Imperial Crown.

½d green (October 14, 1880)	30.00	6.00
1d brown (January 1, 1880)	15.00	2.00
1½d red-brown (October 14, 1880)	£120	25.00
2d red (December 8, 1880)	£160	50.00
5d indigo (March 15, 1881)	£500	55.00

1d lilac

(varieties – 14 dots in corner and 16 dots in corner).

1881
Wmk: Imperial Crown.
14 white dots in each corner

1d lilac (July 12, 1881)	£130	12.00

ii) 16 white dots in each corner

1d lilac (December 12, 1881)	1.75	0.75

5/- red, 1884

1883-1884
Wmk: Large Anchor.

2/6 lilac (July 2, 1883)	£300	60.00
5/- red (April 1, 1884)	£600	85.00

Great Britain 1839–1951

The Graeme Webster collection of Seahorses

1913 Waterlow £1 deep green, a
magnificent corner copy

1915–18 De La Rue 10s., the 'true' Cambridge
or 'Powder' blue, the only example presently in
private hands. Ex Dodd and Shaida.

A full colour brochure of selected items from this superb collection is available on request

Andrew G Lajer
The Old Post Office, Davis Way, Hurst
Berkshire RG10 0TR, United Kingdom
T: +44 (0)1189 344151 F: +44 (0)1189 344947
E: andrew.lajer@btinternet.com

Andrew Claridge
PO Box 1999, Witham
Essex CM8 1RZ, United Kingdom
T: +44 (0)1376 584412 F: +44 (0)1376 585388
E: andrew.claridge@btinternet.com

10/- blue (April 1, 1884)   £1300   £275

£1 green, 1891

1884-1891
A) Wmk: Imperial Crowns.
£1 brown (April 1, 1884)	£18,000	£1,750
£1 green (January 27, 1891)	£2,000	£450

B) Wmk: Orbs.
£1 brown (February 1, 1888)	£40,000	£2,500

(2d, 6d green - same design)
(Design of ½d as 1880 issue)

1884, April 1 (except 9d)
Wmk: Imperial Crown (sideways on **2d, 2½d, 6d, 9d**)
½d blue	12.00	3.00
1½d lilac	75.00	20.00
2d lilac	£125	35.00
2½d lilac	55.00	5.00
3d lilac	£120	35.00
4d green	£275	95.00
5d green	£250	90.00
6d green	£250	95.00
9d green (August 1, 1883)	£650	£300
1/- green	£675	£150

9d violet, blue

1887, January 1. Jubilee issue (*).
Wmk: Imperial Crown.
i) Wmk upright.

½d orange	1.25	0.50
½d green (April 17, 1900)	1.30	0.60
½d purple, green	10.00	2.00
2d green, red	18.00	8.00
2½d purple (blue paper)	14.00	0.75
3d purple (yellow paper)	18.00	1.50
4d green, brown	22.00	7.00
4½d green, red	7.00	25.00
5d purple, blue	26.00	5.00
6d purple (red paper)	20.00	5.00
9d violet, blue	45.00	25.00
10d purple, red	40.00	24.00
1/- green	£150	40.00
1/- green, red (July 11, 1900)	45.00	70.00
Set	£400	£200

Wmk inverted		
½d orange	25.00	20.00
½d green	25.00	25.00
1½d purple, green	£650	£225
2d purple, red	£650	£300
2½d purple (blue)	£900	£350
4d green, brown	£650	£250
5d purple	-	£400
6d purple (red)	£1,500	£500
9d violet, blue	£1,800	£550
10d purple, red	£2,200	£600
1/- green	£650	£350
1/- green, red	£1,000	£500

(*- so called by collectors because 1887 marked Queen Victoria's Golden Jubilee, but the issue wasn't specifically issued to commemorate the Golden Jubilee)

KING EDWARD VII

For this reign the stamps are priced in three columns: unmounted mint, mounted unused and fine used, except for booklet panes which are only priced at mounted unused.

To help distinguish the work in three printers in the series it is worth noting that the De La Rue printings are generally cleaner, with good centering and clean perforations. By comparison the Harrison and Somerset House printings are coarser, the centerings are poor and the perforations are ragged.

½d yellow-green	5/- red

King Edward VII (within differing border designs) (all values – designs similar to Queen Victoria 'Jubilee' issuses and 1883-84 high values.)

1902, January 1, 1911.
A) Surface printed by De La Rue. Wmk. Imperial Crown (½d to 1/-), Large Anchor **(2/6, 5/-, 10/-)**, three Imperial Crowns (£1). Perf:14.

½d blue-green	2.00	1.00	0.70
a) yellow-green	2.00	1.00	0.70
1d scarlet	1.75	1.00	0.50
1½d purple, green	60.00	30.00	10.00
a) chalky paper	60.00	30.00	10.00
2d green, red (March 25, 1902)			
	70.00	30.00	10.00
a) chalky paper	60.00	28.00	12.00
2½d blue	25.00	12.00	3.00
3d purple (yellow paper)	70.00	30.00	7.00
a) chalky paper	60.00	30.00	10.00
4d green, brown	95.00	40.00	18.00
a) chalky paper	65.00	30.00	15.00
4d orange (November 1, 1909)	32.00	15.00	10.00
5d purple blue (May 14, 1902)	90.00	40.00	15.00
a) chalky paper	85.00	45.00	15.00
6d purple	60.00	28.00	14.00
a) chalky paper	60.00	30.00	14.00
7d grey	10.00	7.00	16.00
9d purple, blue	£170	70.00	40.00
a) chalky paper	£155	60.00	40.00

10d purple, red
(July 3, 1902)	£210	60.00	40.00
a) chalky paper	£175	55.00	40.00

1/- green, red
(March 24, 1902)	£165	60.00	20.00
a) chalky paper	£165	60.00	24.00
2/6 lilac (April 5, 1902)	£450	£200	75.00
a) chalky paper	£450	£300	90.00
5/- red (April 5, 1902)	£600	£280	£120
10/- blue (April 5, 1902)	£1100	£500	£350
£1 green (June 16, 1902)	£2000	£1100	£600

Wmk inverted
½d yellow-green	20.00	12.00	12.00
1d scarlet	7.00	5.00	6.00
5d purple, blue	£4000	£2800	£2000
2/6 lilac	£3000	£2000	£1000

NB – a vast range of shades exists on all printings of this series: full details of these are beyond the scope of this publication.

Booklet panes

Wmk upright or inverted

	Upright	Inverted
Pane of five se-tenant with one label showing St. Andrew's Cross	£400	£400
Pane of six ½d	55.00	90.00
Pane of six 1d	40.00	70.00

B) As above but printed by Harrison.

Wmk upright

½d yellow-green
(May 3, 1911)	3.50	2.00	1.30
1d red (May 3, 1911)	10.00	6.00	8.00
2½d blue (July 10, 1911)	70.00	45.00	18.00

3d purple (yellow paper)
(September 12, 1911)	£140	80.00	£140
4d orange (July 13, 1911)	£130	60.00	46.00

Watermarked inverted

½d yellow-green	25.00	15.00	12.00
1d red	28.00	15.00	10.00
2½d blue	£850	£750	£450

Booklet panes

Wmk upright or inverted.

	Upright	Inverted
Pane of five ½d se-tenant with one label showing the St. Andrew's Cross	£700	£700
Pane of six ½d	80.00	£110
Pane of six 1d	70.00	90.00

C) As above but printed at Somerset House
i) Wmk upright.

1½d purple, green
(July 13, 1911)	50.00	25.00	12.00

2d green, red
(March 11, 1912)	46.00	24.00	11.00

5d purple, blue
(August 7, 1911)	50.00	28.00	11.00

6d purple
(October 31, 1911)	50.00	26.00	14.00
a) chalky paper	50.00	28.00	60.00
7d grey (August 1, 1912)	15.00	11.00	15.00

9d purple, blue
(July 24, 1911)	£105	65.00	40.00

10d purple, red
(October 9, 1911)	£125	75.00	45.00

1/- green, red
(July 17, 1911)	£115	58.00	25.00

2/6 purple
(September 27, 1911)	£425	£180	£585

5/- red
(February 29, 1912)	£600	£280	£120
10/- (January 14, 1912)	£1200	£600	£400

£1 green
(September 3, 1911)	£2000	£1150	£700

Wmk inverted
1/- green, red	£275	£175	-

D) As above, but printed by Harrison with perf: 15x14

½d green
(October 30, 1911)	50.00	30.00	30.00

1d red
(October 5, 1911)	32.00	16.00	8.50

2½d blue
(October 14, 1911)	45.00	21.00	7.00

3d purple (yellow paper)
(September 22, 1911)	55.00	30.00	13.00

4d orange
(November 22, 1911)	48.00	26.00	10.00

Stamp booklets

2/- booklets (Stamps by De La Rue)
a) 24 at 1d (sold at 2½d)	£350
b) 12 at 1d, 23 at ½d	£900
c) 18 at 1d, 11 at ½d	£1000
d) as above but the stamps by Harrison	£1400

2d Tyrian Plum

NB – A 2d value in new design printed in Tyrian plum was prepared for use with the intention that it be issued in May 1910. The death of King Edward VII prevented its release, although copies are known unused and one example used.

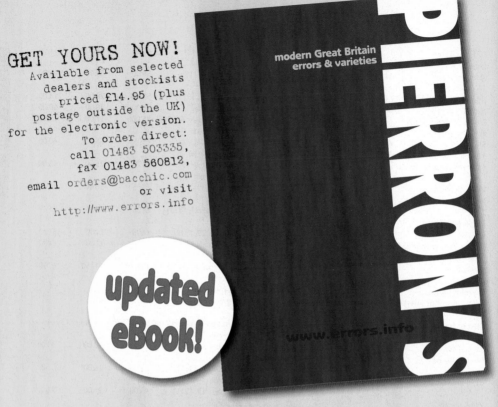

KING GEORGE V

In this section the stamps are priced in three columns: unmounted mint, mounted unused, fine used.

½d green 1912

1911-1912
Des: Bertram Mackennal and G. W. Eve. Portrait based on photograph by Downey. Die engraved by J. A. C. Harrison. Printed in typography by Harrison. Perf: 15 x 14.
A) Wmk: Imperial Crown
i) Wmk upright

½ d green (June 22, 1911)	7.50	3.50	2.00
1d red (June 22, 1911)	6.50	3.00	1.50

(NB-once again, many of the stamps of this reign can be found in large numbers of shades. The above two stamps exist either with waterm arks sideways, being scarce thus, or printed in error with perf: 14.)

ii) Wmk inverted

½d green	15.00	7.50	3.50
1d red	12.50	7.00	3.00

Booklet panes
Wmk upright or inverted

	Wmk upright	Wmk inverted
Six ½d	80.00	£120
Six 1d	75.00	£110

B) Wmk: Crown with script GVR (Royal Cypher)
Issued August 1912 in booklets
i) Watermark upright or inverted (prices same way either way)

½d green	70.00	30.00	28.00
1d green	35.00	16.00	18.00

Booklet panes
Watermark upright or inverted

	Wmk upright	Wmk inverted
Six ½d	£500	£500
Six 1d	£250	£240

The following differ in design from the above in that the King's hair is lighter on the ½d and the lion is shaded on the 1d

1912
A) Wmk: Imperial Crown
i) Wmk upright

½d green (January 1, 1912)	8.50	4.50	1.00
1d red (January 1, 1912)	5.00	2.00	0.80

ii) Wmk inverted

½d green	£750	£500	£300
1d red	£450	£350	£175

B) Wmk. Crown with script GVR (Royal Cypher)
i) Wmk upright

½d green (August 1912)	8.00	4.00	1.25
1d red (August 1912)	7.00	3.50	1.00

ii) Wmk inverted

½d green	225.00	140.00	60.00
1d red	22.00	14.00	12.00

C) Wmk: Multiple Royal Cypher (Crown and script GVR)
i) Wmk upright

½d green (October 1912)	12.00	7.00	9.00
1d red (October 1912)	15.00	9.00	4.50

ii) Wmk inverted

½d green	15.00	12.00	12.50
1d red	20.00	15.00	16.00

iii) Watermark sideways

½d green	-	-	£2,750
1d	£220	150.00	£160

1d red, 1911-13

1911-1913
Designed and engraved as before. Printed in typography by Harrison (all values except 6d) and at Somerset House (½d, 1d, 1½d, 2, 2½d, 3d, 4d, 5d, 6d, 7d, 8d, 9d, 10d, 1/-)
A) Wmk: Crown and script GVR (Royal Cypher)
i) Wmk upright

½d green (January 1913)	1.00	0.40	0.40
1d red (October 1919)	1.00	0.40	0.40
1½d brown (Oct 1912)	3.50	2.00	0.80
2d orange (August 1912)	3.50	1.75	0.60
2½d blue (October 1912)	16.00	8.00	2.25
3d violet (October 1912)	7.00	3.75	1.00
4d green (January 1913)	16.00	7.00	1.50
5d brown (June 1913)	18.00	8.00	4.00
6d purple (August 1913) (chalky paper)			
	18.00	8.00	2.00
7d green (August 1913)	28.00	11.00	7.50
8d black (*yellow paper*) (August 1913)			
	42.00	20.00	11.00
9d black (June 1913)	20.00	10.00	3.75
9d green (Sept 1922)	£180	75.00	24.00

10d blue (August 1913)	32.00	15.00	18.00
1/- brown (August 1913)	28.00	13.00	1.80

ii) Wmk inverted

½d green	3,00	2.25	1.10
1d red	3.00	2.25	0.90
1½d brown	8.00	4.00	1.60
2d orange	16.00	10.00	8.50
2½d blue	70.00	45.00	45.00
3d violet	90.00	65.00	65.00
4d green	40.00	25.00	25.00
5d brown	£600	£400	£400
6d purple	65.00	35.00	35.00
7d green	65.00	40.00	40.00
8d black (*yellow paper*)	130.00	85.00	85.00
9d black	125.00	80.00	85.00
9d green	£1,000	£700	£625
10d blue	£3,500	£2,000	£1,400
1/- brown	£200	£140	£110

Booklet panes
Wmk upright or inverted

Six ½d	35.00	45.00
Six 1d	35.00	45.00
Six 1½d	60.00	75.00
Four 1½d se-tenant with two advertising labels		
	£750	£750
Six 2d	80.00	£130

B) Wmk: Multiple Royal Cypher (Crown and Script GVR)
i) Wmk upright

½d green (August 1913)	£160	£100	95.00
1d red (August 1913)	£350	£225	£180

ii) Wmk inverted

½d green	£500	£350	£350
1d red	£800	£600	£600

1924-1926
As before, but printed typography by Waterlow (all values except 6d), Harrison (all values) or at Somerset House (1½d, 6d)
Wmk: Multiple Crown and block GVR
i) Wmk upright

½d green (February 1924)	0.60	0.30	0.20
1d red (February 1924)	0.85	0.35	0.20
1½d brown (Feb 1924)	0.90	0.40	0.20
2d orange (Sept 1924)	2.00	0.85	0.70
2½d blue (October 1924)	7.50	4.00	1.10
3d violet (October 1924)	11.00	5.00	1.00
4d green (Nov 1924)	18.00	7.00	1.40
5d brown (Nov 1924)	28.00	12.00	2.00
6d purple (*chalky paper*, September 1924)			
	14.00	9.00	1.75
(a) *ordinary paper*	3.80	1.50	0.50
9d green (Dec 1924)	20.00	7.00	2.50
10d blue (Nov 1923)	65.00	28.00	22.00

1/- brown (October 1924)	35.00	16.00	1.40
ii) Wmk inverted			
½d green	4.00	2.00	1.00
1d red	4.00	2.00	1.25
1½d brown	2.50	1.25	1.00
2d orange	30.00	20.0	16.00
2½d blue	35.00	35.00	24.00
3d violet	50.00	35.00	24.00
4d green	100.00	65.00	48.00
5d brown	70.00	50.00	40.00
6d purple (*chalky paper*)	50.00	40.00	28.00
a) *ordinary paper*	48.00	38.00	24.00
9d green	70.00	55.00	48.00
10d blue	£2,500	£1,950	£800
1/- brown	£550	£400	£240

Watermark sideways

½d green	10.00	5.00	4.00
1d red	24.00	14.00	16.00
1½d brown	12.50	5.00	4.00
2d orange	£125	50.00	60.00

Booklet panes
Wmk upright or inverted

	Upright	Inverted
Six ½d	35.00	45.00
Six 1d	35.00	45.00
Six 1½d	60.00	75.00
Four 1½d se-tenant with two advertising labels (a wide range of labels exists)	£125	£125

4d green, 1934-36

1934-1936
As above but printed in photogravure by Harrison. Wmk: Multiple Crown and block GVR, Perf: 15 x 14.
Designs differ in the shading behind the portrait.
Wmk upright

½d green (Nov 19, 1934)	0.25	0.10	0.15
1d red (Sept 24, 1934)	0.25	0.20	0.15
1½d brown (Aug 20, 1934)	0.20	0.15	0.10
2d orange (Jan 21, 1935)	0.50	0.30	0.40
2½d blue (Mar 18, 1935)	1.20	0.75	0.70
3d violet (Mar 18, 1935)	1.50	0.95	0.60
4d green (Dec 2, 1935)	2.00	1.25	0.65
5d brown (Feb 17, 1936)	7.50	3.50	1.75
9d deep green (December 2, 1935)			
	12.00	5.00	2.00
10d blue (Feb 24, 1936)	19.00	10.00	9.00

1/- brown (Feb 24, 1936) 255.00   11.00   75.00

ii) Wmk inverted

½d green	12.50	6.00	3.00
1d red	12.50	6.00	2.50
1½d brown 2.50	1.25	0.60	

Wmk sideways

½d green	8.00	5.50	2.50
1d red	17.50	8.50	12.00
1½d brown 8.00	8.00	5.00	2.00
2d orange	£150	55.00	50.00

Booklet panes
Wmk upright or inverted

	Upright	inverted
Six ½d	60.00	70.00
Six 1d	60.00	70.00
Six 1½d	20.00	25.00
Four 1½d se-tenant with two advertising labels		
	75.00	75.00

2/6 Seahorse, 1913-34 – all values

1913-1934. High values
Des: Bertram Mackennal. Dies engraved by J.A.C. Harrison.
Wmk: single crown with script GVR
(Royal Cypher) Perf: 11 x 12
A) Printed in recess by Waterlow. Released in July 1913

2/6 brown	£300	£125	70.00
5/- red	£500	£225	£140
10/- blue	£900	£450	£225
£1 green	£3500	£1750	£850

B) Printed in recess by De La Rue
Released in December 1915.

2/6 brown	£300	£120	80.00
5/- red	£600	£225	£140
10/- blue	£2550	£850	£350

C) Printed in recess by Bradbury, Wilkinson
Released December 1918

2/6 brown	£200	50.00	25.00
5/- red	£250	85.00	30.00
10/- blue	£450	£200	70.00

(NB: to distinguish the above printings, note that the De La Rue printings have a yellow gum, while the Waterlow design is

about 22mm high, that of Bradbury, Wilkinson is 23mm high. Postmark dates can help separate used copies)

D) Printed in recess by Waterlow by die re-engraved so that the background to portrait consists of horizontal and diagonal lines. Released October 1934

2/6 brown	85.00	40.00	6.00
5/- red	£225	90.00	45.00
10/- blue	£450	£200	35.00

1d, 1½d Lion, Inscribed '1924' and then '1925'

1924-1925. British Empire Exhibition
Des: H. Nelson. Printed in recess by Waterlow
Wmk: Multiple Crown and block GVR. Perf: 14.

1d Red	5.00	5.00	4.00
1½d brown	15.00	6.00	6.00
Set	18.00	8.00	8.00
First Day Cover	-	-	£350

Inscribed '1925' (released May 9, 1925)

1d red	10.00	7.00	12.00
1½d brown	45.00	28.00	25.00
Set	45.00	30.00	30.00
First Day Cover	-	-	£1,500

£1 St. George and the Dragon, 1929

1929, May 10. Postal Union Congress, London 1929.
Des: J. Farleigh (**½d, 2½d**), E. Linzell (**1d, 1½d**) H. Nelson (**£1**). Printed in typography by Waterlow (**½d to 2½d**) or in recess by Bradbury, Wilkinson (**£1**)
Wmk: Multiple Crown and block GRV (**½d to 2½d**) or large

crown and script GVR (**£1**). Perf: 15x14 (**½d to 2½d**), 12 (**£1**).

i) Wmk upright

½d green	1.50	0.50	0.45
1d red	2.50	1.50	1.00
1½d brown	2.00	1.25	0.80
2½d blue	16.00	7.00	5.00
Set	20.00	9.00	6.75
First Day Cover	-	-	£450
£1 black	£750	£450	£450
First Day Cover	-	-	£6,500

ii) Wmk inverted

½d green	20.00	11.00	8.00
1d red	25.00	13.00	14.00
1½d brown	12.00	6.00	4.50
2½d blue	£2,400	£1,750	£750

iii) Wmk sideways

½d green	70.00	25.00	25.00
1d red	90.00	60.00	60.00
1½d brown	65.00	20.00	20.00

Booklet panes
Wmk upright or inverted

	Upright	Inverted
Six ½d	40.00	£120
Six 1d	45.00	£200
Six 1½d	30.00	90.00
Four 1½d se-tenant with two advertising labels		
	£250	£280

2½d (same design – all values)

1935, May 7. Silver Jubilee
Des: B. Freedman. Printed in photogravure by Harrison
Wmk: Multiple Crown and block GVR. Perf: 15x14
i) Wmk upright

½d green	0.80	0.40	0.30
1d red	1.40	0.70	0.70
1½d brown	1.25	0.50	0.40
2½d blue	3.00	2.00	4.00
a) Prussian blue	£8,500	£6,500	£6,500
Set (less Prussian blue)	6.00	3.25	4.75
First Day Cover			
(pictoral cover)	-	-	£800
(plain cover)	-	-	80.00

ii) Wmk inverted

½d green	11.00	6.00	6.00
1d red	11.00	6.00	6.00
1½d brown	2.00	1.00	0.90

Booklet panes
Wmk upright or inverted

	Upright	inverted
Four ½d	30.00	60.00
Four 1d	30.00	60.00
Four 1½d	15.00	20.00

2/- booklet (Silver Jubilee)

Stamp Booklets
2/- booklets

a) 18 at 1d, 12 at ½d (Wmk: Imperial Crown)	£600
b) as above but wmk: Crown with script GRV	£900
c) as above but stamps of 1911-1913 issue	£700
d) 10 x 1½d, 6 x 1d, 6 x ½d	
(Wmk: Crown with script GV)	£1,150
e) as above but wmk: Block GVR, printed by Waterlow	£400
f) as above but Postal Union Congress isuue	£475
g) as above but wmk: Block GVR, printed by Harrison	£450
h) as above but printed in photogravure	£1,000
i) 12 at 1½d, 4 at ½d (Silver Jubilee issue)	80.00

3/- booklets

a) 12 at 1½d, 12 at 1d, 12 at ½d (Wmk: Script Cypher)	£650
b) 18 at 1½d, 6 at 1d, 6 at ½d (Wmk: Script Cypher)	£650
c) 18 at 2d	£700
d) 24 at 1½d	£750
e) 18 at 1½d, 6 at 1d, 6 at ½d	
(Wmk: Block Cypher) stamps printed by Waterlow	£300
f) as above but Postal Union Congress issue	£400
g) as (e) but printed by Harrison	£375
h) as above but printed by photogravure	£340
i) 20 at 1½d, 4 at 1d, 4 at ½d (Silver Jubilee issue)	90.00

3/6 booklets

a) 18 at 2d, 6 at 1d	£850
b) 12 at 2d, 6 at 1½d, 6 at 1d, 6 at ½d	£850

5/- booklets (Wmk: Block Cypher)

a) 34 at 1½d, 6 at 1d, 6 at ½d	
stamps printed by Waterlow	£3,500
b) as above but buff covered	£2,000
c) as above but printed by Harrison	£950
d) as above but printed by photogravure	£2,200

From this point pricing is given in two columns: unmounted mint on the left (mounted unused can normally be obtained for about 50% of the quoted prices), and fine used on the right (except for booklets and booklet panes which are only priced unmounted mint with good perforations).

KING EDWARD VIII

½d green, King Edward VIII (all values)

1936
Printed by Photograuve by Harrison.
Wmk: Multiple Crown and E8R. Perf: 15x14.
i) Wmk upright

½d green (September, 1, 1936)	0.15	0.10
1d red (September 14, 1936)	0.20	0.20
1½d brown (September 1, 1936)	0.25	0.10
2½d blue (September 1, 1936)	0.20	0.30
Set	0.60	0.50

ii) Wmk inverted

½d green	6.00	2.50
1d red	6.00	2.25
1½d brown	0.75	0.80

Booklet panes
Wmk upright or inverted

	Upright	Inverted
Pane of Six ½d	15.00	42.00
Pane osf Six 1d	15.00	42.00
Pane of Two 1½d	10.00	10.00
Pane of six comprising four 1½d se-tenant with two advertising labels	55.00	55.00
Pane of Six 1½d	8.00	14.00

Stamp Booklets

6d – 4 at 1½d	50.00
2/- – 10 at 1½d, 6 at 1d, 6 at ½d	70.00
3/- – 18 at 1½d, 6 at 1d, 6 at ½d	70.00
5/- – 34 at 1½d, 6 at 1d, 6 at ½d	£160

KING GEORGE VI

Unless otherwise stated, all stamps of this reign are printed in photogravure by Harrison
Wmk: Multiple Crown and GVIR. Perf: 15x14

King George VI and Queen Elizabeth (1½d)

1937, May 13. Coronation
Des: E. Dulac.

1½d red-brown	0.25	0.15
First Day Cover (pictorial cover)		20.00
(plain cover)		3.00

(½d, 1d, 1½d, 2d, 2½d, 3d)

(4d, 5d, 6d)   (7d, 8d, 9d, 10d, 11d, 1/-)

1937-47 King George VI Definitive Series
Des: E. Dulac and E. Gill (½d to 6d), E. Dulac (7d to 1/-)
A) Original colours
i) Wmk upright

½d green (May 10, 1937)	0.12	0.10
1d red (May 10, 1937)	0.12	0.10
1½d red-brown (July 30, 1937)	0.15	0.15
2d orange (January 31, 1938)	0.70	0.35
2½d blue (May 10, 1937)	0.25	0.15
3d violet (January 31, 1938)	2.00	0.60
4d green (November 21, 1938)	0.40	0.20
5d brown (November 21, 1938)	2.25	0.30
6d purple (January 30, 1939)	1.00	0.15
7d emerald (February 27, 1939)	3.50	0.50
8d carmine (February 27, 1939)	5.00	0.50
9d deep green (May 1, 1939)	4.00	0.50
10d blue (May 1, 1939)	3.00	0.50
11d brown-purple (December 29, 1947)	2.75	1.00
1/- brown (May 1, 1939)	4.00	0.15
Set	24.00	4.00

ii) Wmk inverted

½d green	7.00	0.50
1d red	20.00	2.50
1½d red-brown	9.00	1.50
2d orange	32.00	2.50
2½d blue	32.00	3.00

iii) Wmk sideways

½d green	0.25	0.30
1d red	15.00	5.00
1½d red-brown	1.00	0.50
2d orange	32.00	25.00
2½d blue	50.00	12.50

Booklet panes
i) Watermark upright or inverted

	Upright	Inverted
Two ½d	10.00	10.00
Six ½d	15.00	25.00
Two 1d	10.00	50.00
Six 1d	15.00	£150
Two 1½d	5.00	10.00
Four 1½d se-tenant with two advertising labels (*)		
	£110	£110

(*- 15 different combinations of labels exist and prices may vary depending on the labels: prices quoted above are for the cheapest types – scarcer panes can be up to twice these prices)

Six 1½d	20.00	25.00
Six 2d	50.00	£200
Six 2½d	50.00	£195

ii) Wmk sideways.

Four ½d	45.00	
Four 1d	70.00	

B) As above but paler colours
i) Wmk upright

½d pale green (September 1, 1941)	0.15	0.10
1d pale red (August 11, 1941)	0.20	0.10
1½d pale red-brown (September 28, 1942)		
	0.60	0.35
2d pale orange (October 6, 1941)	0.50	0.15
2½d pale blue (July 21, 1941)	0.15	0.10
3d pale violet (November 3, 1941)	1.50	0.25
Set	2.25	0.70

ii) Wmk inverted

½d pale green	3.00	0.50
2d pale orange	3.00	0.50
2½d pale blue	1.00	0.40

iii) Wmk sideways

1d pale red	3.00	3.00
2d pale orange	10.00	8.00
2½d pale blue	7.00	6.00

Booklet panes
Wmk upright or inverted

	Upright	Inverted

Two ½d	9.00	-
Six ½d	10.00	25.00
Two Id	9.00	-
Two 1½d	9.00	-
Six 2d	7.50	30.00
Six 2½d pale blue	4.00	15.00

C) As above, but colours changed
i) Wmk upright

½d orange (May 3, 1951) 0.10	0.10	
Id blue (May 3, 1951)	0.10	0.10
1½d green (May 3, 1951) 0.25	0.25	
2d red-brown (May 3, 1951)	0.25	0.25
2½d red (May 3, 1951)	0.10	0.10
4d blue (October 2, 1950)	1.00	0.60
Set	1.50	1.10

ii) Wmk inverted

½d orange	0.20	0.30
Id blue	2.00	1.00
1½d green	2.50	2.00
2d red-brown	4.00	3.50
2½d red	0.75	0.50

iii) Wmk sideways

Id blue	0.20	0.40
1½d green	1.75	2.00
2d red-brown	0.75	0.75
2½d red	1.00	0.85

Booklet panes
Wmk upright or inverted

	Upright	Inverted
Two ½d	9.00	-
Four ½d	7.00	9.00
Six ½d	5.00	6.00
Two Id	9.00	-

Three Id se-tenant with three labels reading
'MINIMUM INLAND PRINTED PAPER RATE 1½d'

	25.00	25.00

Three Id se-tenant with three labels reading
'SHORTHAND IN ONE WEEK'

	35.00	35.00
Four Id	6.00	7.00
Six Id	5.00	20.00

Two 1½d	5.00	-
Four 1½d	6.00	14.00
Six 1½d	8.50	22.00
Six 2d	17.00	60.00
Six 2½d	3.50	6.50

King George VI and   King George VI (10/-,£1)
Coat of Arms (2/6, 5/-)

1939-1948. High Values
Des: E. Dulac (2/6, 5/-), G. R. Bellew (10/-, £1). Printed in
recess by Waterlow
Wmk: Single Crown and GVIR. Perf: 14

2/6 brown (September 4, 1939)	35.00	18.00
2/6 green (March 9, 1942)	7.00	0.50
5/- red (August 21, 1939)	14.00	1.25
10/- dark blue (October 30, 1939)	£180	17.00
10/- ultramarine (November 30, 1942)	22.00	3.50
£1 brown (October 1, 1948)	8.00	12.00
Set	£220	40.00

Queen Victoria and King George VI (all values)

1940, May 6. Centenary of First Adhesive Postage Stamp
Des: H. L. Palmer. Perf: 14½ x 14

½d green	0.20	0.10
Id red	0.30	0.30
1½d brown	0.50	0.75
2d orange	0.90	0.85
2½d blue	1.50	0.30
3d violet	3.00	2.50
Set	4.00	3.50
First Day Cover (pictorial cover)		35.00
(plain cover)		7.50

Signs of industry (2½d)
Signs of peace (3d)

1946, June 11. Victory
Des: H. L. Palmer (2½d), Reynolds Stone (3d)

2½d blue	0.10	0.10

3d violet	0.10	0.15
Set	0.20	0.25
First Day Cover (pictorial cover)		45.00
(plain cover)		9.00

King George VI with Queen Elizabeth
(horizontal design – 2½d; vertical design - £1)

1948, April 26. Royal Silver Wedding

Des: G.T. Knipe and Joan Hassall (photographs by Dorothy
Wilding Studios). Perf: 14 x 15 **(£1)**.

2½d blue	0.10	0.10
£1 blue	27.00	25.00
Set	27.00	25.00
First Day Cover (pictorial cover)		£400
(plain cover)	50.00	

1948, May 10. Liberation of the Channel Islands

Although this set was placed on sale at eight post offices in
Great Britain, it is listed under Regional Issues

Globe surrounded by a Laurel Wreath (2½d)
Globe with Olympic Rings (3d)
Olympic Rings (6d)
Victory and Olympic Rings (1/-)

1948, July 29. Olympic Games

Des: P. Metcalfe, A. Games, S. Scott and E. Dulac

2½d blue	0.15	0.15
3d violet	0.40	0.30
6d purple	0.50	0.75
1/- brown	0.75	0.75
Set	1.25	1.20
First Day Cover (pictorial cover)		35.00
(plain cover)		8.00

Two Hemispheres (2½d)
UPU Monument (3d)
Globe and Compass (6d)

Globe and Posthorn (1/-)

1949, October 10.
75th Anniversary of the Universal Postal Union

Des: Mary Adshed **(2½d)**, P. Metcalfe **(3d)**. H. Fleury **(6d)**,
G. R. Bellew **(1/-)**.

2½d blue	0.15	0.15
3d violet	0.35	0.50
6d purple	0.75	0.65
1/- brown	1.00	0.85
Set	1.50	1.25
First Day Cover (pictorial cover)		47.00
(plain cover)	9.50	

H.M.S. Victory (2/6)

White Cliffs of Dover (5/-)

St. George and the Dragon **(10/-)**

Royal Coat of Arms **(£1)**

Prices: see the notes on page 37

1951, May 3. High Values

Des: Mary Adshead **(2/6, 5/-)**, P. Metcalfe **(10/-, £1)**.
Printed in recess by Waterlow. Wmk: Single Crown and GVIR.
Perf: 11 x 12

2/6 green	9.00	0.50
5/- red	20.00	2.00
10/- blue	15.00	5.00
£1 brown	30.00	12.00
Set	55.00	14.00

(2½d)
Festival of Britain symbol (4d)

1951, May 3. Festival of Britain
Des: E. Dulac (2½d). A. Games (**4d**)

2½d red	0.12	0.15
4d blue	0.30	0.30
Set	0.35	0.35
First Day Cover (pictorial cover)		15.00
(plain cover)	3.00	

Stamp Booklets
6d booklets (stamps in original colours)

a) 4 at 1½d	50.00
b) 2 at 1½d, 2 at 1d, 2 at ½d	£225
c) 4 at 1d, 4 at ½d	£100

1/- booklets

a) 4 at 1½d, 4 at 1d, 4 at ½d	
(pale colours) in panes of two	20.00
b) as above but panes at four	£4500
c) as a) but with changed colours	25.00
d) as b) but with changed colours	20.00

2/- booklets

a) 10 at 1½d, 6 at 1d, 6 at ½d	
(Royal Cypher on cover)	£325
b) as above but with GPO	
cypher on cover	£325

2/6 booklets

a) 6 at 2½d, 6 at 2d, 6 at ½d	
(original colours) – red cover	£750
b) as above but blue colour	£750
c) as above but green colour	£350
d) as above but stamps with pale colours	£350
e) as above but no commercial advertising included	50.00
f) as above but changed colours	30.00
g) 6 at 2½d, 6 at 1½d, 3 at 1d, 6 at ½d	30.00

3/- booklets

18 at 1½d, 6 at 1d, 6 at ½d	£600

5/- booklets

a) 18 at 2½d, 6 at 2d, 6 at ½d (original colours)	£700
b) as above but pale colours	£700
c) as above, but no commercial advertising included	85.00
d) as above but changed colours	45.00
e) 18 at 2½d, 6 at 1½d, 3 at 1d, 6 at ½d	35.00
f) 12 at 2½d, 6 at 2d, 6 at 1½d, 6 at 1d, 6 at ½d	45.00

QUEEN ELIZABETH II
PRE-DECIMALS

In this section all the stamps have the same technical details except where stated:
Printed in photogravure by Harrison. Perf: 15 x 14 for all definitives. Perf: 15 x 14 for all special issues with a horizontal design (or 14 x 15 for all vertical designs indicated by (**V**) after the design description).

(½d, 1d, 1½d, 2d)

(2½d, 3d)

(4d, 4½d)

(5d, 6d, 7d)

(8d, 9d, 10d, 11d)

(1/-, 1/6)

(1/3)

On the 2½d value the top line of the diadem was initially broken (Type I), later corrected (Type II).

1952-1968. The Wilding Definitives
Des: Miss E. Mark (½d, 1d, 1½d, 2d). M.C. Farrar-Bell (2½d, 3d, 4d, 4½d), G. Knipe (5d, 6d, 7d), Miss M. Adshead (8d, 9d, 10d, 11d), E. Dulac (1/-, 1/3, 1/6): portrait by Dorothy Wilding Studios

A) Wmk: Multiple Tudor crown E2R (normally known as the Tudor Crown watermark).
i) Wmk upright.

½d orange (August 31, 1953)	0.10	0.10
1d blue (August 31, 1953)	0.15	0.10

1½d green (December 5, 1952)	0.10	0.10
2d deep brown (August 31, 1953)	0.20	0.15
2½d carmine (type 1) (December 5, 1952)	0.15	0.10
3d violet (January 18, 1954)	1.00	0.20
4d blue (November 2, 1953)	2.75	0.70
5d brown (July 6, 1953)	1.00	2.50
6d purple (January 18, 1954)	2.50	0.75
7d pale green (January 18, 1954)	7.00	3.75
8d magenta (July 6, 1953)	1.00	0.75
9d myrtle-green (February 8, 1954)	18.00	2.00
10d blue (February 8, 1954)	12.00	2.00
11d brown-red (February 8, 1954)	20.00	12.00
1/- bistre (July 6, 1953)	1.00	0.50
1/3 deep-green (November 2, 1953)	6.00	1.50
1/6 grey-blue (November 2, 1953)	12.00	1.25
Set	50.00	20.00
First Day Covers (pictorial covers)		£600
(plain covers)		£140

ii) Wmk inverted.

½d orange	0.30	0.40
1d blue	4.50	2.50
1½d green	0.35	0.30
2d deep brown	16.00	12.00
2½d carmine (type 2)	0.40	0.30
Set	18.00	14.00

iii) Wmk sideways.

1½d green	0.35	0.30
2d deep brown	0.75	0.50
2½d carmine (type 1)	3.50	4.00
Set	4.50	4.50

Booklet panes

	Wmk upright	Wmk inverted
Two ½d	2.00	-
Four ½d	4.00	4.00
Six ½d	2.00	4.00
Two 1d	2.00	-
Four 1d	3.00	25.00

Three 1d se-tenant with three labels reading:

MINIMUM INLAND PRINTED PAPER RATE 1½d	£300	£300
PLEASE POST EARLY IN THE DAY	40.00	40.00
PACK YOUR PARCELS SECURELY/ADDRESS YOUR LETTERS CORRECTLY/AND POST EARLY IN THE DAY	40.00	40.00

Six 1d	8.00	30.00
Two 1½d	2.00	-
Four 1½d	4.00	4.00
Six 1½d	2.00	4.00
Six 2d	27.00	£160
Six 2½d	3.50	3.50

B) Wmk: Multiple St. Edward's Crown E2R (normally known as the Edward's Crown watermark).

i) Wmk upright. Colours as before.

½d (August 1955)	0.15	0.10
1d (September 19, 1955)	0.20	0.10
1½d (August 1955)	0.15	0.10
2d deep brown (September 6, 1955)	0.25	0.30
2d brown (October 17, 1956)	0.25	0.10
2½d (type 1) (September 28, 1955)	0.25	0.15
2½d (type 2) (September 1955)	0.30	0.60
3d (July 17, 1956)	0.25	0.20
4d (November 14, 1955)	1.50	2.00
5d (September 21, 1955)	5.00	2.00
6d purple (December 20, 1955)	3.50	1.00
6d deep purple (May 8, 1958)	3.00	1.00
7d (April 23, 1956)	30.00	6.00
8d (December 21, 1955)	4.00	1.25
9d (December 15, 1955)	12.00	2.00
10d (September 22, 1955)	10.00	2.00
11d (October 28, 1955)	0.50	1.25
1/- (November 3, 1955)	6.50	0.50
1/3 (March 27, 1956)	14.00	1.00
1/6 (March 27, 1956)	20.00	0.75
Set	90.00	25.00

ii) Wmk inverted.

½d	0.20	0.20
1d	0.50	0.50
1½d	0.20	0.20
2d deep brown	7.00	6.00
2d brown	3.00	2.00
2½d (type 2)	0.30	0.30
3d	1.75	1.50
Set	8.00	7.00

iii) Wmk sideways.

1½d	0.20	0.25
2d deep brown	0.50	0.50
2d brown	5.00	4.00
2½d (type 1)	0.75	1.00
3d	5.00	6.00
Set	10.00	9.00

Booklet panes

	Wmk upright	Wmk inverted
Two ½d	3.00	-
Four ½d	4.00	4.00
Six ½d	2.00	3.50
Two 1d	3.50	-

Three 1d se-tenant with three labels reading:

PACK YOUR PARCELS SECURELY/ADDRESS YOUR LETTERS CORRECTLY/AND POST EARLY IN THE DAY

	30.00	35.00
Four 1d	4.00	4.00
Six 1d	2.50	3.00
Two 1½d	3.50	-
Four 1½d	4.00	4.00
Six 1½d	2.00	2.00
Six 2d deep brown	13.00	65.00
Six 2d brown	8.00	22.50
Six 2½d	3.00	3.00
Four 3d	10.00	15.00
Six 3d	6.00	20.00

C) Wmk: Multiple St. Edward's Crown (normally known as Multiple Crowns Watermark).

i) Wmk upright. Colours as before.

½d (November 25, 1958)	0.10	0.10
a) chalky paper (July 15, 1963)	2.00	2.50
1d (November 1958)	0.10	0.10
1½d (December 1958)	0.15	0.15
2d brown (December 4, 1958)	0.10	0.10
2½d (type 1) (October 4, 1961)	0.10	0.40
2½d (type 2) (November 1958)	0.35	0.20
a) chalky paper (July 15, 1963)	0.30	0.25
3d (November 1958)	0.15	0.10
4d blue (October 29, 1958)	0.50	0.25
4d deep blue (April 28, 1965)	0.20	0.12
4½d red-brown (February 9, 1959)	0.12	0.12
5d (November 10, 1958)	0.20	0.10
6d deep purple (December 23, 1958)	0.25	0.10
7d (November 26, 1958)	0.50	0.20
8d (February 24, 1960)	0.35	0.10
9d (March 24, 1959)	0.35	0.20
10d (November 18, 1958)	0.75	0.25
1/- (October 30, 1958	0.35	0.25
1/3 (June 17, 1959)	0.35	0.15
1/6 (December 16, 1958)	3.00	0.15
Set	5.00	1.50

ii) Wmk inverted.

½d	0.30	0.10
a) chalky paper	1.50	2.00
1d	0.20	0.20
1½d	1.00	0.40
2d brown	60.00	40.00
2½d (type 2)	2.00	0.90
a) chalky paper	0.30	0.25
3d	0.25	0.20
4d deep blue	0.35	0.20
Set	65.00	42.00

iii) Wmk sideways.

1½d	0.25	0.15
1d	0.60	0.35
1½d	4.50	3.00
2d	0.50	0.40

2½d (type 1)	0.20	0.25
2½d (type 2)	0.40	0.50
3d	0.25	0.15
4d deep blue	0.35	0.15
Set	5.00	4.00

Booklet Panes

i) Wmk upright or inverted.

	Wmk upright	Wmk inverted
Three ½d (chalky paper)		
se-tenant with one 2½d(chalky paper)	8.00	8.00
Four ½d	2.50	2.50
Six ½d	1.25	2.00
Four 1d	2.50	2.50
Six 1d	1.50	2.50
Four 1½d	2.50	2.50
Six ½d	5.00	6.00
Six 2d	40.00	£500
Four 2½d (chalky paper)	1.00	1.00
Six 2½d	3.00	15.00
Four 3d	2.00	2.00
Six 3d	1.50	1.50
Six 4d deep blue	1.50	1.50

ii) Wmk sideways

two ½d se-tenant with two 2½d (type 2)	1.00
four ½d	2.00
two 1d se-tenant with two 3d	
a) 3d to left of 1d	5.00
b) 3d to right of 1d	5.00
four 1d	3.00
four 1½d	25.00
four 3d	2.00
four 4d	2.00

Graphite Lined Issues

Each stamp has two black lines on the back except for the 2d which has just one line on the right as viewed from the back of the stamp

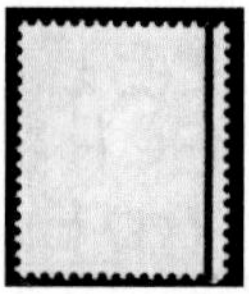

A) Wmk: Multiple St. Edward's Crown E2R upright. Colours as before. Released on November 19, 1957.

½d	20	20
1d	20	20
1½d	40	50
2d brown	3.00	1.25
2½d (type 2)	4.50	5.50
3d	75	50
Set	6.75	7.00
First Day Cover		75.00

B) Wmk: Multiple St. Edward's Crown. Colours as before
i) Wmk upright

½d (June 15, 1959)	3.00	3.00
1d (December 18, 1958)	1.00	1.00
1½d (August 4, 1959)	60.00	50.00
2d (December 4, 1958)	4.75	2.50
2½d (type 2) (June 9, 1959)	6.00	6.00
3d (November 24, 1958)	0.60	0.45
4d (April 29, 1959)	3.25	3.25
4½d (June 3, 1959)	3.50	2.25
Set	70.00	55.00

ii) Wmk inverted

½d	1.00	1.25
1d	1.00	0.75
1½d	20.00	20.00
2½d (type 2)	35.00	30.00
3d	0.55	0.40
Set	60.00	50.00

Booklet Panes

	Wmk upright	Wmk inverted
Six ½d	20.00	12.00
Six 1d	7.50	7.00
Six 1½d	£500	£125
Six 2½d	30.00	£300
Six 3d	4.00	4.00

Phosphor Graphite Issue

Each stamp has two bands of phosphor on the front of the stamp (the **2d** has just one band to the left of the stamp) in addition to the graphite lines on the back.
i) Wmk: Multiple St. Edward's Crown E2R upright. Colours as before. Released on November 18, 1959.

½d	3.00	3.00
1d	9.00	9.00
1½d	2.50	3.00
2d brown	95.00	90.00

ii) Wmk: Multiple St. Edwards Crown upright. Colours as before.

2d brown	4.00	3.00
2½d (type2)	10.00	10.00
3d	14.00	7.50
4d blue	8.00	5.00
4½d	25.00	20.00
Set	45.00	40.00
First Day Cover		75.00

Phosphor Issue

Each stamp has two bands of phosphor on the front except where stated. Colours as before. Released on June 22, 1960 except where stated. Wmk: Multiple St. Edward's Crown.
i) Wmk upright

½d	0.15	0.15
1d	0.10	0.10
1½d	0.12	0.20

2d brown (one band)	14.00	12.00
2d brown (October 4, 1961)	0.20	0.10
2½d (type 2)	0.20	0.20
2½d (type 2 – one band)	1.50	0.50
2½d (type 1 – one band)	30.00	30.00
3d	0.50	0.35
3d (April 29, 1965 – one band at right)	0.30	0.40
3d (as above but band at right)	0.30	0.40
Se-tenant pair	0.60	1.50
3d (December 8, 1966 – one centre band)	0.25	0.25
4d blue	2.75	3.25
4d deep blue (April 28, 1965)	0.15	0.25
4½d (September 13, 1961)	0.15	0.25
5d (June 9, 1967)	0.20	0.25
6d deep purple (June 27, 1960)	0.20	
7d (February 15, 1967)	0.20	0.25
8d (June 28, 1967)	0.20	0.25
9d (December 29, 1966)	0.50	0.25
10d (December 30, 1966)	0.50	0.40
1/- (June 28, 1967)	0.40	0.20
1/3	1.00	1.00
1/6 (December 12, 1966)	2.00	2.00
Set (one of each value)	4.50	5.00

ii) Wmk inverted. Colours as above.

½d	1.00	1.00
1d	0.35	0.30
1½d	5.00	5.00
2½d (type 2)	£135	£120
2½d (type 2 – one band)	19.00	17.00
3d	0.80	0.50
3d (one band at left)	40.00	42.00
3d (one band at right)	6.00	6.50
Se-tenant pair	47.00	49.00
3d (one centre band)	3.00	3.50
4d deep blue	0.25	0.20
Set	£180	£170

iii) Wmk sideways. Colours as before.

½d	5.00	7.50
1d	0.40	0.50
1½d	5.00	7.50
2d	0.30	0.25
3d	1.25	0.55
3d (one band at left)	4.00	4.00
3d (one band at right)	4.00	4.00
Se-tenant pair	8.00	10.00
3d (one centre band)	0.40	0.50
4d deep blue	0.35	0.25
Set	15.00	18.00

Booklet Panes

i) Wmk upright or inverted

	Wmk upright	Wmk inverted
Six **½d**	3.00	4.00
Six **1d**	2.00	2.00
Six **1½d**	8.00	30.00
Six **2½d** (type 2 – two bands)	80.00	£1,100
Six **2½d** (type 2 – one band)	22.00	£140
Six **3d** (two bands)	5.00	5.00
Six **3d** (one band at left or right)	20.00	90.00
Six **3d** (one centre band)	4.00	15.00
Six **4d**	2.00	3.00

ii) Wmk sideways.

Four **½d**	35.00
Two **1d** se-tenant with two **3d** (two bands)	3.00
Two **1d** se-tenant with two **3d** (one band)	
a) **3d** with left band	11.00
b) **3d** with right band	11.00
Four **1d**	5.00
Four **1½d**	35.00
Four **3d** (two bands)	5.00
Four **4d**	1.00

Stamp Booklets

1/- booklets

a) 4 at **1½d**, 4 at **1d**, 4 at **½d** (wmk: Tudor Crown) – panes of two	5.00
b) as above but panes of four	5.00
c) as a) but wmk: St. Edward's Crown	15.00
d) as above but panes of four	5.00
e) as above but wmk: Multiple Crowns	5.00

2/- booklets

a) 4 at **3d**, 4 at **1½d**, 4 at **1d**, 4 at **½d** (wmk: St. Edward's Crown – pink cover)	4.00
b) as above wmk: Multiple Crowns (upright)	6.00
c) as above but yellow cover	6.00
d) as above but wmk: sideways	25.00
e) as above but stamps with phosphor bands	60.00
f) 4 at **4d**, 2 at **1d** se-tenant with 2 at **3d**	3.00
g) as above but stamps with phosphor bands (**3d** with one band at left or right)	8.00
h) as above but 3d has two phosphor bands	4.00
i) 8 at **2½d**, 3 at **½d** se-tenant with 1 at **2½d**	6.00
j) 8 at **½d**, 8 at **2½d** in panes of two **½d** se-tenant with two **2½d**	2.00
k) 8 at **3d**	1.00

2/6 Booklets

a) 6 at **2½d**, 6 at **1½d**, 3 at **1d**, 6 at **½d** - **½d** and **1d** stamps of KGVI, **1½d** and **2½d** of QEII	20.00
b) as above but **1d** stamp of KGVI and rest QEII	20.00
c) as above but QEII stamps only (wmk: Tudor Crown)	30.00
d) as above but wmk: St Edward's Crown	20.00
(NB – Booklets with mixed watermarks exist)	
e) 6 at **2½d**, 6 at **2d**, 6 at **½d** (Wmk: St Edward's Crown)	18.00

3/- booklets

a) 6 at **3d**, 6 at **1½d**, 6 at **1d**, 6 at **½d**

(wmk: St Edward's Crown)	14.00
b) as above but wmk: Multiple Crown s	18.00
c) as above but graphite lined stamps	£150
d) as above phosphor lined stamps	45.00

3/9 booklets

| a) 18 at 2½d (wmk: Tudor Crown) | 22.00 |
| b) as above but wmk: St Edward's Crown | 15.00 |

4/6 booklets

a) 18 at 3d (wmk: St Edward's Crown)	15.00
b) as above but wmk: Multiple Crowns	15.00
c) as above but graphite lined stamps	20.00
d) as above but phosphor lined stamps	22.00
e) 12 at 4d, 6 at 1d (wmk: Multiple Crowns)	14.00
f) as above but phosphor lined stamps	7.00

5/- booklets

a) 12 at 2½d, 6 at 2d, 6 at 1½d, 6 at 1d,	
6 at ½d - ½d, 1d and 2d stamps of KGVI,	
rest of QEII	26.00
b) as above but 1d and 2d stamps of KGVI,	
rest QEII	£175
c) as above but 2d stamps of KGVI, rest QEII	£110
d) as above but QEII stamps only	
(wmk: Tudor Crown)	30.00
e) as above but wmk: St Edward's Crown and	
2d deep brown	20.00
f) as above but 2d brown	22.00
g) 12 at 3d, 6 at 2½d, 6 at 1½d, 6 at ½d	
(wmk: St Edward's Crown)	18.00
h) as above but wmk: Multiple Crowns	20.00
i) as above but with graphite lined stamps	£100
J) as above but with phosphor lined stamps	
– 2½d with two bands	£100
k) as above but 2½d with one band	90.00

6/- booklets

| a) 18 at 4d (wmk: Multiple Crowns) | 18.00 |
| b) as above but with phosphor lined stamps | 22.00 |

10/-

a) 30 at 3d, 6 at 2d, 6 at 1½d, 6 at 1d, 6 at ½d	80.00
b) 30 at 3d, 6 at 2½d, 6 at 1½d, 6 at 1d	80.00
c) 24 at 4d, 6 at 3d, 6 at 1d	18.00
d) as above but phosphor lined stamps – 3d with one side	
phosphor band	8.00
e) as above but 3d with one centre band	5.00

Carrickfergus Castle (2/6)
Caernarvon Castle (5/-)
Edinburgh Castle (10/-)

Windsor Castle (£1)

1955-1968 The Castle High Values.
Printed in recess. Perf: 11 x 12
A) Wmk: Multiple St. Edward's Crown E2R upright.
i) Printed by Waterlow.

2/6 brown (September 23, 1955)	10.00	2.00
5/- carmine (September 23, 1955)	30.00	4.75
10/- blue (September 1, 1955)	60.00	10.00
£1 black (September 1, 1955)	85.00	18.00
Set	£160	30.00
First Day Covers		
(pictorial covers)		£850
(plain covers)		£300

i) Printed by De La Rue. Colours as before.

2/6 (July 17, 1958)	25.00	3.50
5/- (April 30, 1958)	40.00	8.00
10/- (April 25, 1958)	£130	14.00
£1 (April 28, 1958)	£200	30.00
Set	£375	47.00

NB: the top perforation tooth of each side of the stamps from the De La Rue printing is narrower than that found on the Waterlow printing.

B) Wmk: St. Edward's Crown upright.
i) Printed by De LLa Rie. Colours as before.

2/6 (July 22, 1958)	12.00	0.50
5/- (June 15, 1959)	50.00	1.00
10/- (July 21, 1959)	40.00	2.75
£1 (June 23, 1959)	80.00	12.00
Set	£150	15.00

ii) Printed by Bradbury, Wilkinson. Colours as before.

2/6 (July 1, 1963)	0.50	0.15
5/- (September 3, 1963)	2.00	0.40
10/- (October 16, 1963)	3.50	2.50
£1 (November 14, 1963)	9.50	3.00
Set	13.50	7.00

iii) Printed by Bradbury, Wilkinson on chalky paper.

| 2/6 (May 30, 1968) | 0.50 | 0.75 |

NB – the Queen's diadem is more detailed on the Bradbury, Wilkinson printings compared with the De La Rue printing.

C) No wmk. Printed by Bradbury, Wilkinson.

2/6 (July 1, 1968)	30	30
5/- (April 10, 1968)	1.50	75
10/- (April 10, 1968)	8.00	7.00
£1 (December 4, 1967)	3.50	4.00

Set	10.50	10.50

(2½d)
(4d)
(1/3)
(1/6)

1953, June 3. Coronation.
Des: E.G. Fuller (2½d), M. Goaman (4d), E. Dulac (1/3), M.C. Farrar-Bell (1/6). Wmk: Multiple Tudor Crown E2R.
2½d, 4d, 1/3, 1/6

Set	7.50	4.00
First Day Cover		27.00

1955. Castle High Values – see page 68

1955. Wilding definitives with multiple St. Edward's Crown E2R watermark – see page 64

Scout Badge (2½d)
Flying Birds (4d)
Globe within compass (1/3)

1957, August 1. World Scout Jubilee Jamboree.
Des: Mary Adshead (2½d), Pat Keely (4d), W. H. Brown (1/3). Wmk: Multiple St Edward's Crown E2R.
2½d, 4d, 1/3

Set	2.50	2.25
First Day Cover		15.00

NB – these stamps were issued in coils as well as normal sheets.

(4d)

1957, September 12. Inter-Parliamentary Union Conference.
Wmk: Multiple St. Edward's Crown E2R.

4d	0.50	0.50
First Day Cover		70.00

1957, November 19. Wilding definitives; Graphite lined issue – see page 65

Welsh Dragon (3d)
Games emblem (6d)
Welsh Dragon (1/3)

1958, July 18. British Empire and Commonwealth Games.
Des: Reynolds Stone (3d), W.H. Brown (6d), Pat Keely (1/3). Wmk: Multiple St Edward's Crown E2R.
3d, 6d, 1/3

Set	1.25	1.00
First Day Dover		60.00

1958. Wilding definitives with multiple St. Edward's Crown watermark – see page 64

1958. Wilding: Graphite lined issue with multiple St. Edward's Crown watermark – see page 65

1958. Castle High Values with above watermark – see page 68

1959. Wilding: Phosphor Graphite issue – see page 66

1960. Phosphor lined issue – see page 67

Unless otherwise stated, all the following issues have the Multiple St. Edward's Crown wmk (sideways on vertical designs).

1660 Postboy (3d)
1660 Posthorn (1/3)

1960, July 7. Anniversary of General Letter Office.
Des: Reynolds Stone (3d), Faith Jacques (1/3).
3d, 1/3

Set	1.75	1.75
First Day Cover		30.00

Europa emblem (6d, 1/6)

1960, September 19. Europa (First Anniversary).
Des: P. Rahikainen and Reynolds Stone.
6d, 1/6

Set	6.50	3.00
First Day Cover		22.00

Thrift plant (2½d)
Squirrel and stylised tree (3d)
Thrift plant (1/6)

1961, August 28. Post Office Savings Bank Centenary.
Des: P. Gauld (2½d), M. Goaman (3d, 1/6).
i) Printed on a Timson machine.
2½d, 3d, 1/6

Set	1.00	1.00
First Day Cover		30.00

ii)Printed on a Thrissell machine.
2½d, 3d

Pair	1.50	1.50

NB – the portrait of the **2½d** is greyer from the Thrissell machine, while on the **3d** the portrait is much clearer on the Timson printing.

CEPT emblem (2d)
Doves and emblem (4d)
Doves and emblem (10d)

1961, September 18. CEPT (Conference held at Torquay).
Des: M. Goaman and T. Kurperschoek
2d, 4d, 10d

Set	0.25	0.25
First Day Cover		2.50

Roof of Westminster Hall (6d)
Palace of Westminster (1/3)

1961, September 23. Commonwealth Parliamentary Conference.
Des: Faith Jacques
6d, 1/3

Set	1.00	1.00
First Day Cover		17.00

Boxes bearing arrows (2½d)
Arrows over the British Isles (3d)
Joining arrows (1/3)

1962, November 14. National Productivity Year.
Des: D. Gentleman. Wmk: inverted on 2½d and 3d values.
i) Non-phosphor issue.
2½d, 3d, 1/3

Set	1.00	1.00
First Day Cover		20.00

ii) Phosphor issue: **2½d** – one band; **3d, 1/3** – three bands.
2½d, 3d, 1/3

Set	14.00	10.00
First Day Cover		90.00

Ears of Wheat (2½d)
Three Children (1/3)

1963, March 21. Freedom from Hunger.
Des: M. Goaman. Wmk inverted on both values.
i) Non-phosphor issue.
2½d, 1/3

Set	1.25	1.25
First Day Cover		15.00

ii) Phosphor issue: **2½d** – one band; **1/3** – three bands.
2½d, 1/3

Set	12.50	10.00
First Day Cover		22.00

'1863 Paris Postal Conference Centenary' (6d)

1963, May 7. Paris Postal Conference Centenary.
Des: Reynolds Stone. Wmk inverted.
i) Non-phosphor issue.

6d	20	25
First Day Cover		8.00

ii) Phosphor issue – three bands.

6d	3.50	3.00
First Day Cover		18.00

Bee on flowers **(3d)**
Selection of wildlife **(4½d)**

1963, May 16. National Nature Week.
Des: S. Scott **(3d)**, M. Goaman **(4½d).**
i) Non-phosphor issue.
3d, 4½d

Set	0.15	0.20
First Day Cover		12.00

ii)Phosphor issue – three bands.
3d, 4½d

Set	1.75	1.75
First Day Cover		20.00

Helicopter over boat **(2½d)**
Lifeboat **(4d)**
Lifeboatmen **(1/6)**

1963, May 31. International Lifeboat Conference.
Des: D. Gentlemen
i) Non-phosphor issue.

2½d, 4d, 1/6	1.50	1.50
Set		
First Day Cover		17.00

ii) Phosphor issue: **2½d** – one band; **4d, 1/6** – three bands.
2½d, 4d, 1/6

Set	25.00	15.00
First Day Cover		27.00

Red Cross within different borders **(3d, 1/3, 1/6)**

1963, August 15. Red Cross Centenary Congress.

Des: H. Bartram.
i) Non-phosphor issue.
3d, 1/3, 1/6

Set	3.00	3.00
First Day Cover		19.00

ii) Phosphor issue – three bands.
3d, 1/3. 1/6

Set	35.00	25.00
First Day Cover		40.00

Cable over globe **(1/6)**

1963, December 3. Opening of COMPAC Cable.
Des: P. Gauld
i) Non-phosphor issue.

1/6	1.25	1.25
First Day Cover		14.00

ii) Phosphor issue – three bands.

1/6	7.50	7.50
First Day Cover		20.00

Puck and Bottom **(3d)**
Feste **(6d)**
Romeo and Juliet **(1/3)**
Henry V **(1/6)**
Hamlet **(2/6)**

1964, April 23. Shakespeare Festival.
Des: D. Gentleman **(3d to 1/6)**; C. and R. Ironside **(2/6)**. Printed in recess by Bradbury, Wilkinson **(2/6)**. Perf: 11 x 12 **(2/6)**.
i) Non-phosphor issue.
3d, 6d, 1/3. 1/6, 2/6

Set	2.50	2.50
First Day Cover		5.00

ii) Phosphor issue – three bands.
3d, 6d, 1/3. 1/6

Set	6.00	6.00
First Day Cover		8.00

Flats, Richmond Park (2½d)
Shipbuilding, Belfast (4d)
Forest Park, Snowdonia (8d)
Nuclear Reactor, Dounreay (1/6)

1964, July 1. International Geographical Congress.
Des: D. Bailey.
i) Non-phosphor issue.
2½d, 4d, 8d, 1/6

Set	2.00	2.00
First Day Cover		10.00

ii) Phosphor issue: **2½d** – one band, **4d, 8d, 1/6** – three bands.
2½d, 4d, 8d, 1/6

Set	15.00	11.00
First Day Cover		19.00

Spring Gentian (3d)
Dog Rose (6d)
Honeysuckle (9d)
Fringed Water Lily (1/3)

1964, August 5. International Botanical Congress.
Des: Michael and Sylvia Goaman.
i) Non-phosphor issue.
3d, 6d, 9d, 1/3

Set	2.00	2.00
First Day Cover		10.00

ii) Phosphor issue – three bands.
3d, 6d, 9d, 1/3

Set	15.00	11.00
First Day Cover		19.00

Forth Road Bridge (3d)
Forth Road and Railway Bridges (6d)

1964, September 4. Opening of the Forth Road Bridge.
Des: A. Restall.
i) Non-phosphor issue.
3d, 6d

Set	0.25	0.30
First Day Cover		3.50

ii) Phosphor issue – three bands.
3d, 6d

Set	2.50	2.75
First Day Cover		8.00

Sir Winston Churchill (4d, 1/3 – slightly different designs)

1965, July 8. Sir Winston Churchill.
Des: D. Gentleman and Rosaline Dease.
i) Non-phosphor issue.
4d, 1/3

Set	0.30	0.30
First Day Cover		2.00

ii) Phosphor issue – three bands.
4d, 1/3

Set	1.50	1.50
First Day Cover		3.00

iii) Printed on a Timson machine.
4d

	0.10	0.10

NB – this printing shows far more details on the portraits of
Churchill.

Seal of Simon de Montfort (6d)
Parliament Buildings (2/6)
(NB – the 2/6 design measures 59mm by 22mm.)

**1965, July 19. 700th Anniversary of Simon de Montfort's
Parliament.**
Des: S.R. Black (6d), Professor R. Guyatt (2/6).
i) Non-phosphor issue.

6d, 2/6

Set	0.75	0.75
First Day Cover		8.00

ii)Phosphor issue – three bands.

6d	50	60
First Day Cover		15.00

Salvation Army Band (**3d**)
Three Salvation Army members (**1/6**)

1965, August 9. Centenary of Salvation Army.
Des: M.C. Farrar-Bell (**3d**), G. Trenaman (**1/6**).
i) Phosphor issue.

3d, 1/6

Set	0.50	0.60
First Day Cover		11.00

ii) Phosphor issue: **3d** – one band; **1/6** – three bands.
3d, 1/6

Set	1.25	1.35
First Day Cover		14.00

Carbolic Spray (**4d**)
Joseph Lister (**1/-**)

1965, September 1. Centenary of Joseph Lister's Discovery of Antiseptic Surgery.
Des: P. Gauld (**4d**), F. Ariss (**1/-**).
i) Non-phosphor issue.
4d, 1/-

Set	0.50	0.60
First Day Cover		6.00

ii) Phosphor issue – three bands.
4d, 1/-

Set	1.50	1.50
First Day Cover		8.00.

Trinidad Carnival Dancers (**6d**)
Canadian Folk Dancers (**1/6**)

1965, September 1. Commonwealth Arts Festival.
Des: D. Gentleman and Rosalind Dease.
Non-phosphor issue.
6d, 1/6

Set	0.50	0.60
First Day Cover		8.00

i) Phosphor issue – three bands.
6d, 1/6

Set	1.60	1.75
First Day Cover		10.00

Spitfires (**4d**)
Pilot in hurricane (**4d**)
Overlapping wings (**4d**)
Spitfires attacking Heinkel bomber (**4d**)
Spitfire attacking Stuka bomber (**4d**)
Tail wing of Dornier bomber (**4d**)
Anti-aircraft Artillery (**9d**)
St Paul's Cathedral (**1/3**)

1965, September 13. 25th Anniversary of the Battle of Britain.
Des: D. Gentleman and Rosalind Dease (**4d, 1/3**), A. Restall (**9d**).
i) Non-phosphor issue.
4d, 4d, 4d, 4d, 4d, 4d (se-tenant), **9d, 1/3**

Set	4.50	5.00
First Day Cover		12.00

ii) Phosphor issue – three bands.
4d, 4d, 4d, 4d, 4d, 4d (se-tenant), **9d, 1/3**

Set	6.50	6.50
First Day Cover		13.00

Post Office Tower (3d)
Post Office Tower and Nash Terrace (1/3)

1965, October 8. Opening of the Post Office Tower.
Des: C. Abbott.
i) Non-phosphor issue
3d, 1/3

Set	0.25	0.30
First Day Cover		3.00

ii) Phosphor issue: 3d one band; 1/3 – three bands.
3d, 1/3

Set	0.40	0.50
First Day Cover		5.00

UN emblem (**3d**)
ICY emblem (**1/6**)

1965, October 25. 20th Anniversary of United Nations and International Co-operation Year.
Des: J. Matthews.
i) Non-phosphor issue.
3d, 1/6

Set	0.50	0.60
First Day Cover		6.00

ii) Phosphor issue: **3d** – one band; **1/6** three bands.
3d, 1/6

Set	1.50	1.50
First Day Cover		7.00

Telecommunications (**9d**)
Radio Waves (**1/6**)

1965, November 15. International Telecommunication Union Centenary.
Des: A. Restall.
i) Non-phosphor issue.
9d, 1/6

Set	0.50	0.60
First Day Cover		7.00

ii) Phosphor issue – three bands.
9d, 1/6

Set	2.50	2.75
First Day Cover		9.00

Robert Burns (**4d**)
Robert Burns (portrait by Nasmyth) (**1/3**)

1966, January 25. Robert Burns.
Des: G.F. Huntly.
i) Non-phosphor issue.
4d, 1/3

Set	0.30	0.40
First Day Cover		1.50

ii) Phosphor issue – three bands.
4d, 1/3

Set	1.00	1.00
First Day Cover		2.75

Westminster Abbey (**3d**)
Roof of Westminster Abbey (**2/6**)

1966, February 28. 900th Anniversary of Westminster Abbey.
Des: Sheila Robinson (**3d**), Bradbury Wilkinson (**2/6**). Printed in recess by Bradbury Wilkinson (**2/6**). Perf: 11 x 12 (**2/6**)
i) Non-phosphor issue.
3d, 2/6

Set	0.40	0.50
First Day Cover		2.75

ii) Phosphor issue – one band.
3d

Set	0.15	0.20
First Day Cover		8.00

Sussex Downs (**4d**)
Antrim, Northern Ireland (**6d**)
Harlech Castle (**1/3**)
The Cairngorms (**1/6**)

1966, May 2. Landscapes.
Des: L. Rosoman.
i) Non-phosphor issue.
4d, 6d, 1/3, 1/6

Set	0.50	0.60
First Day Cover		3.50

ii) Phosphor issue – three bands.
4d, 6d, 1/3, 1/6
Set   0.50   0.70
First Day Cover   4.00

Two footballers (**4d**)
Four footballers (**6d**)
Saving the ball (**1/3**)

1966, June 1. World Cup (Football Championships).
Des: D. Gentleman (**4d**), W. Kempster (**6d**), D. Caplan (**1/3**)
i) Non-phosphor issue.
4d, 6d, 1/3 ~~2 stamp comes block~~
Set   0.40   0.40
First Day Cover   9.00

ii) Phosphor issue: **4d** – two bands; **6d, 1/3** – three bands.
4d, 6d, 1/3
Set   0.30   0.40
First Day Cover   10.00

Black-headed Gull (**4d**)
Blue Tit (**4d**)
Robin (**4d**)
Blackbird (**4d**)

1966, August 8. British Birds.
Des: J. Norris Wood.
i) Non-phosphor issue.
4d, 4d, 4d, 4d se-tenant
Se-tenant block of four   0.40   2.00
First Day Cover   4.00

ii) Phosphor issue – three bands.
4d, 4d, 4d, 4d se-tenant
Se-tenant block of four   0.40   2.00
First Day Cover   4.00

Two footballers and legend 'ENGLAND WINNERS' (**4d**)

1966, August 18. England's World Cup Victory.
Non-phosphor only.
4d   0.20   0.25
First Day Cover   6.00

Jodrell Bank Radio Telescope (**4d**)
Jaguar 'E' type and Mini cars (**6d**)
Hovercraft (**1/3**)
Windscale Nuclear Reactor (**1/6**)

1966, September 19. British Technology.
Des: D. and A. Gillespie (**4d, 6d**), A. Restall (**1/3, 1/6**).
i) Non-phosphor issue.
4d, 6d, 1/3, 1/6
Set   0.40   0.45
First Day Cover   1.75

ii) Phosphor issue – three bands.
4d, 6d, 1/3, 1/6
Set   0.45   0.50
First Day Cover   1.75

Scenes of the Battle of Hastings based on the Bayeux Tapestry
(six different designs) (**4d**)
A Norman Ship (**6d**)

Norman horseman attacking Harold's troops (1/3)

1966, October 14. 900th Anniversary of the Battle of Hastings.
Des: D. Gentleman. Wmk: sideways on 1/3. All multi-coloured.
i) Non-phosphor issue.
4d, 4d, 4d, 4d, 4d, 4d (se-tenant), **6d, 1/3**

Set	1.00	1.25
First Day Cover		2.25

ii) Phosphor issue: **4d, 6d** – three bands; **1/3** – four bands.
4d, 4d, 4d, 4d, 4d, 4d (se-tenant), **6d, 1/3**

Set	1.00	1.25
First Day Cover		2.75

King of the Orient (**3d**)
Snowman (**1/6**)

1966, December 1. Christmas.
Des: Miss T. Shemza (**3d**), J. Berry (**1/6**): both designers were six year old children. Wmk: upright on **1/6**.
i) Non-phosphor issue.
3d, 1/6

Set	0.15	0.20
First Day Cover		1.00

ii) Phosphor issue: **3d** – one band; **1/6** – two bands.
3d (band at left), **3d** (band at right), **1/6**

Set (one **3d**)	0.15	0.20
First Day Cover		0.90

Loading freight on a ship (**9d**)
Loading freight on an aeroplane (**1/6**)

1967, February 20. European Free Trade Association.
Des: C. Abbott.
i) Non-phosphor issue.

9d, 1/6

Set	0.15	0.20
First Day Cover		0.75

ii) Phosphor issue – three bands.
9d, 1/6

Set	0.15	0.20
First Day Cover		0.80

Hawthorn and Bramble (**4d**)
Bindweed and Viper's Bugloos (**4d**)
Daisy, Buttercup and Coltsfoot (**4d**)
Bluebell, Anemone and Red Campion (**4d**)
Dog Violet (**9d**)
Primrose (**1/9**)

1967, April 24. British Flowers.
Des: Keeble Martin (**4d**), Mary Grierson (**9d, 1/9**).
i) Non-phosphor issue.
4d, 4d, 4d, 4d (se-tenant), **9d, 1/9**

Set	0.60	0.75
First Day Cover		1.50

ii) Phosphor issue – three bands.
4d, 4d, 4d, 4d (se-tenant), **9d, 1/9**

Set	0.35	0.50
First Day Cover		1.50

'Master Lambton' by Lawrence (**4d**)
'Mares and Foals in a Landscape' by Stubbs (**9d**)
'Children coming Out of School' by Lowry (**1/6**)

1967, July 10. British Paintings.
No wmk.
4d, 9d, 1/6

Set	0.20	0.20
First Day Cover		1.50

Gipsy Moth IV (1/9)

1967, July 24. Sir Francis Chichester's Single-Handed Voyage Around the World.
Des: Michael and Sylvia Goaman. No watermark.
Three phosphor bands.

1/9 *2 will margin*	0.10	0.10
First Day Cover		0.50

Radar screen (**4d**)
Penicillin Mould (**1/-**)
Jet Engine (**1/6**)
Television Equipment (**1/9**)

1967, September 19. British Discoveries.
Des: C. Abbott (**4d, 1/-**), Negus and Sharland (**1/6,1/9**). Three phosphor bands on the **4d** value.

4d, 1/-, 1/6, 1/9		
Set	0.25	0.25
First Day Cover		0.75

All the following issues are printed only on paper without wmk.

'The Adoration of the Shepherds' by the School of Seville (**3d**)
'Madonna and Child' by Murillo (**4d**)
'The Adoration of the Shepherds' by Louis Le Nan (**1/6**)

1967. Christmas.
3d has one central phosphor band.
3d (November 27, 1967), 4d (October 18, 1967), 1/6

(November 27, 1967)		
Set	0.15	0.20
First Day Cover		0.75

(In conjunction with the release of the **3d** and **1/6** values of this issue, the Post Office put on sale a 'Gift Pack' containing the special issues of the year. This practice has since been continued each year and a full list of such packs will be found in the section of this book headed 'Presentation packs').

1967. Castle High Values on unwatermarked paper see page 68.

Unless otherwise stated, all the following issues have colourless polyvinyl alcohol (PVA) gum.

Tarr Steps (**4d**)
Aberfeldy Bridge (**9d**)
Menai Bridge (**1/6**)
M4 Viaduct (**1/9**)

1968, April 29. British Bridges.
Des: J. Matthews (**4d, 1/9**), A. Restall (**9d**), L. Rosoman (**1/6**).

4d, 9d, 1/6, 1/9		
Set	0.25	0.30
First Day Cover		0.75

Letters 'TUC' (**4d**)
Mrs. Emmeline Pankhurst (**9d**)
'Sopwith Camel' (**1/-**)
James Cook Signature and 'Endeavour' (**1/9**)

1968, May 29. Anniversaries.
Des: D. Gentleman (**4d**), C. Abbott (**others**).

4d, 9d, 1/-, 1/9		
Set	0.25	0.30
First Day Cover		2.25

Commemorated are the centenary of the Trades Union Congress, the 50th anniversary of Votes for Women, the 50th anniversary of the Royal Air Force and the bicentenary of Captain Cook's first voyage of discovery.

'Queen Elizabeth I' (artist unknown) **(4d)**
'Pinkie' by Lawrence **(1/-)**
'Ruins of St Mary le Port' by Piper **(1/6)**
'The Hay Wain' by Constable **(1/9)**

1968, August 12. British Painters.
4d, 1/-, 1/6, 1/9

Set	0.25	0.30
First Day Cover		0.60

Boy and Girl and Rocking Horse **(4d)**
Girl and Doll's House **(9d)**
Boy and Train Set **(1/6)**

} 6 with ribbon
platin.

1968, November 25. Christmas.
Des: Rosalind Dease.
i) Printed on a Rembrandt machine.
4d (one phosphor band), **9d, 1/6**

Set	0.20	0.20
First Day Cover		3.50

ii) Printed on a Thrissell machine.
4d multicoloured   0.15   0.20
NB – the Thrissell printing can be distinguished by the boy's
pullover having a more mottled appearance.

'Queen Elizabeth 2' **(5d)**
Elizabethan Galleon **(9d)**
East Indiaman **(9d)**
'Cutty Sark' **(9d)**
SS 'Great Britain' **(1/-)**
RMS 'Mauretania' **(1/-)**

1969, January 15. British Ships.
Des: D. Gentleman.
5d (one horizontal phosphor band), **9d** (in se-tenant strip),
1/- (in se-tenant pair)

Set	0.75	1.00
First Day Cover		1.75

'Concorde' over Great Britain and France **(4d)**
Silhouettes of 'Concorde' **(9d)**
Nose and Tail of 'Concorde' **(1/6)**

1969, March 3. Flight of 'Concorde'.
Des: Michael and Sylvia Goaman **(4d)**, D. Gentleman
(9d, 1/6).
4d, 9d, 1/6

Set	0.45	0.50
First Day Cover		1.75

Vickers 'Vimy' and Alcock and Brown **(5d)**
Europa/CEPT **(9d)**
Hand holding wrench **(1/-)**
NATO Flags **(1/6)**
Vickers 'Vimy' and globe showing route **(1/9)**

1969, April 2. Anniversaries.
Des: P. Sharland **(5d, 1/-, 1/6)**, Michael and Sylvia Goaman **(9d, 1/9)**.
5d, 9d, 1/-, 1/6, 1/9

Set	0.30	0.50
First Day Cover		1.10

Durham Cathedral **(5d)**
York Minster **(5d)**
St Giles' Cathedral, Edinburgh **(5d)**
Canterbury Cathedral **(5d)**

PRE-DECIMAL QEII

St Paul's Cathedral (**9d**)
Liverpool Metropolitan Cathedral (**1/6**)

1969, May 28. British Cathedrals.
Des: P. Gauld.
5d, 5d, 5d, 5d (se-tenant), **9d , 1/6**

Set	0.60	0.75
First Day Cover		1.20

The King's Gate, Caernarvon Castle (**5d**)
The Eagle Tower, Caernarvon Castle (**5d**)
queen Eleanor's Gate, Caernarvon Castle (**5d**)
Celtic Cross, Margam Abbey (**9d**)
The Prince of Wales (**1/-**)

1969, July 1. Investiture of the Prince of Wales.
Des: D. Gentleman.
5d, 5d, 5d (se-tenant), **9d, 1/-**

Set	0.30	0.50
First Day Cover		0.90

Gandhi and Flag of India (**1/6**)

1969, August 13. Gandhi Centenary Year.
Des: Biman Mullick.
1/6

	0.10	0.15
First Day Cover		0.50

National Giro symbol (**5d**)
Telephone Dials (**9d**)
Pulse Code Modulation (**1/-**)
Automatic Sorting (**1/6**)

1969, October 1. Post Office Technology.
Des: D. Gentleman. Printed in litho by De La Rue.
Perf: 13½ x 14.
5d, 9d, 1/-, 1/9

Set	0.25	0.30
First Day Cover		0.60

The Herald Angel (**4d**)
The Three Shepherds (**5d**)
The Three Kings (**1/6**)

1969, November 26. Christmas.
Des: F. Wegner.
4d (one centre phosphor band), **5d, 1/6**

Set	0.15	0.20
First Day Cover		0.50

Fife Harling (**5d**)
Cotswold Limestone (**9d**)
Welsh Stucco (**1/-**)
Ulster Thatch (**1/6**)

1970, February 11. Rural Architecture.
Des: D. Gentleman (**5d, 9d**), Sheila Robinson (**1/-, 1/6**).
5d, 9d, 1/-, 1/6

Set	0.30	0.40
First Day Cover		0.65

Signing the Declaration of Arbroath (**5d**)
Florence Nightingale and patients (**9d**)
Signing the International Co-Operative Alliance (**1/-**)
Sailing of the 'Mayflower' (**1/6**)
Sir William and Sir John Herschel with Francis Bailey (**1/9**)

1970, April 1. Anniversaries.
Des: F. Wegner (**5d, 9d, 1/6**), Marjorie Seynor (**1/-, 1/9**).
5d, 9d, 1/-, 1/6, 1/9

Set	0.30	0.40
First Day Cover		1.00

Commemorating the signing of the Declaration of Arbroath 1320, Florence Nightingale 1820 – 1910, the International Co-operative Alliance founded in 1895, the sailing of the Mayflower in 1620 and the Royal Astronomical Society founded in 1820.

Mr Pickwick and Sam (**5d**)
Mr and Mrs Micawber (**5d**)
David Copperfield and Betsey Trotwood (**5d**)
Oliver Twist asking for more (**5d**)
Grasmere (**1/6**)

1970, June 3. Literary Anniversaries.
Des: Rosalind Dease.
5d, 5d, 5d, 5d (se-tenant), **1/6**

Set	0.50	0.60
First Day Cover		1.00

Runners (**5d**)
Swimmers (**1/6**)
Cyclists (**1/9**)

1970, July 15. British Commonwealth Games.
Des: A. Restall. Printed in litho by De La Rue. Perf: 13½ x 14.
5d, 1/6, 1/9

Set	0.40	0.45
First Day Cover		0.60

Penny Black (line engraved) (**5d**)
1/- Green (embossed) (**9d**)
4d Carmine (surface printed) (**1/6**)

1970, September 18. Philympia 1970 International Stamp Exhibition.
Des: D. Gentleman.
5d, 9d, 1/6

Set	0.30	0.40
First Day Cover		0.75

The Angel appearing to the Shepherds (**4d**)
Mary, Joseph and Jesus (**5d**)
The Wise Men bringing gifts (**1/6**)

1970, November 25. Christmas
Des: Sally Stiff (based on the De Lisle Psalter).
4d, 5d, 1/6

Set	0.25	0.25
First Day Cover		0.50

The Great Britain Hingeless Album in four beautiful volumes

The Lighthouse Great Britain Hingeless album is unmatched in detail, accuracy and quality. Using the Stanley Gibbons GB Concise catalogue for guidance, each stamp is represented by a photo image and necessary technical information. Commemoratives and definitives are mostly housed on separate pages, as are regionnal issues and postage dues. To keep your stamps safe and secure, they are held in place using Lighthouse mounts which are affixed over the corresponding image.

Each album comes complete with our titled padded binder and a matching slipcase. The binder has a massive 120 page capacity.

Volume 1 - (1840 - 1970) Commences with the birth of the postage stamp and continues through covering the four Kings and Queen Elizabeth 11 up to the commencement of the decimal period in 1970.
Contents: 103 pages £180.00

Volume 2 - (1971 - 1989) Continues with Queen Elizabeth 11 from the beginning of the decimal era. This volume gives exceptional detail to the Machin definitives and covers these issues from 1971 to 1993.
Contents: 89 pages. £165.00

Volume 3 - (1990 - 1999) The in-depth cover given to definitives continues and commences with the elliptical series from 1993.
Contents: 67 pages £130.00

Volume 4 - (2000 - 2004) Continues with the reign of Queen Elizabeth 11.
Contents: 54 pages £115.00

To receive our latest brochure featuring thousands of products, please contact us at the address below

THE DUNCANNON PARTNERSHIP
4 BEAUFORT ROAD, REIGATE, RH2 9DJ
TEL: 01737 244222   FAX: 01737 224743
Buy online at www.duncannon.co.uk

MACHIN DEFINITIVES

4d sepia Queen Elizabeth II (from a sculpture by Arnold Machin) (all values)

1967-1969. The Machin Definitives
Des: A. Machin. No wmk. Two phosphor bands except where stated
i) Gum Arabic. All head 1 except where stated.

3d violet (one band) August 8, 1967)	0.10	-
4d sepia (June 5, 1967)	0.60	-
a) head 2	£2,000	-
4d red (one band)	15.00	-
9d green (August 8, 1967)	0.50	-
1/- pale violet (June 5, 1967)	0.30	-
1/- deep violet	3.00	-
1/6 green, deep blue (August 8, 1967)	0.40	-
1/9 orange, black (June 5, 1967)	1.25	-
First Day Cover (4d, 1/-, 1/9)	1.50	
First Day Cover (3d, 9d, 1/6)	1.50	

Se-tenant coil (all head 2 and one band).
Issued August 27, 1969

1d olive	0.30	-
2d brown	0.35	0.30
3d violet	0.20	-
4d red	0.30	-
Se-tenant coil of two 2d, one 1d, one 3d, and one 4d (sold at 1/-)	1.25	2.50

(NB – used prices not applicable to gum differences)

Booklet panes

Pane of six 4d sepia (head 1)	15.00	
Pane of six 4d red (head 1)	£120	

Stamp booklets
6/- booklets
Purple plain cover (three panes of six 4d sepia, two bands)   25.00
(Examples of the 6/- booklets with cover illustrations of the Barn Owl and Jay (listed under PVA Gum) containing the 4d red – one centre band – exist with gum arabic)

'2d' away from left margin (setting 1)
'2d' close to left margin (setting 2)

---

i) PVA gum. All head 1 except where stated

½d orange (February 5, 1968)	0.10	0.10
1d olive (February 5, 1968)	0.40	0.10
a) head 2	0.10	0.10
b) head 2 (one centre band)	0.60	0.50
2d brown (setting 1)		
(February 5, 1968)	0.15	0.10
a) (setting 2)	0.15	0.10
3d violet (one centre band)	0.10	0.10
a) head 2 (one centre band)	2.00	0.10
3d violet	0.20	0.10
a) head 2	0.50	0.10
4d sepia (shades)	0.15	0.10
a) head 2	0.10	0.10
4d sepia (one centre band)	0.15	0.10
a) head 2 (one centre band)	0.10	0.10
4d red (one centre band)		
(January 6, 1969)	0.10	0.10
a) head 2 (one centre band)	0.10	0.10
b) head 2 (one band at left)	1.00	1.00
c) head 2 (one band at right)	1.50	3.00
5d blue (July 1, 1968)	0.15	0.10
a) head 2	0.15	0.10
b) head 2 (two bands on 'all over' phosphor)	£250	-
6d purple (shades)		
(February 5, 1968)	0.15	0.10
a) head 2	8.00	3.00
7d green (July 1, 1968) – head 2	0.50	0.30
8d red (July 1, 1968)	0.10	0.25
8d light-blue – head 2 (January 6, 1969)	0.30	0.40
9d green	0.30	0.20
10d brown (July 1, 1968)	0.30	0.40
1/- deep violet	0.40	0.15
1/6 green, deep blue	0.50	0.50
a) 'All-over' phosphor	0.50	0.60
1/9 orange, black	1.00	0.40
Set (one of each value)	2.00	2.00
First Day Cover (½d, 1d, 2d, 6d)	1.50	
First Day Cover (5d, 7d, 8d, 10d)	1.50	
First Day Cover (4d red, 8d light blue)	1.50	

Booklet panes
Panes of four:

Four 4d sepia – head 2 (two bands)	0.90
Four 4d sepia – head 2 (one centre band)	1.00
Four 4d red – head 2 (one centre band)	1.00
Two 1d se-tenant with two 3d – head 2 (two bands)	
a) 1d to left of 3d	1.20
b) 1d to right of 3d	1.20
Two 4d sepia – head 2 (one centre band) se-tenant With two labels reading '£4,315 FOR YOU AT AGE 55' and 'SEE OTHER PAGES'	1.00
Two 4d red – head 2 (one centre band) se-tenant with two labels as above	1.00

Panes of six:
Six **1d** olive – head 2 (two bands)   1.00
Six **3d** violet – head (one centre band) 12.00
Six **4d** sepia – head 1 (two bands)   1.00
Six **4d** sepia – head 1 (one centre band) 1.00
Six **4d** red – head 1 (one centre band) 0.95
Six 4d red – head 2 (one centre band) 0.95
Six **5d** blue – head 2 (two bands)   1.00
Four **1d** olive (one centre band) se-tenant with two **4d** sepia
– head 2 (one centre band)   2.00
Four **1d** olive (two bands) se-tenant with two **4d** red
– head 2(one left band)   4.00

Panes of 15

These panes come from the £1 'Stamps for Cooks' booklet and can be found with just four holes in the binding margin (from booklets which were stapled together) or with a larger number of equally spaced holes (from booklets which were stitched). All head 2

Six **1d** olive (two bands) se-tenant with three **4d** red (one band at left), three **4d** (one band at right) and three **5d** blue, arranged in three rows of **4d** (right band) **1d/5d/1d/4d** (left band), all attached to recipe label   12.00
Fifteen **4d** red (one centre band) attached to a label
for 'Stuffed Cucumber'   3.00
Fifteen **4d** red (one centre band) attached to a label
headed 'Method'   3.00
Fifteen **5d** blue (two bands) attached to a recipe
label   3.00

5/- brown-red

1969, March 5. High values.
Des: A. Machin. Printed in recess by Bradbury, Wilkinson. Perf: 12.

2/6 brown	0.20	0.25
5/- brown-red	1.00	0.50
10/- deep blue	3.00	3.50
£1 black	2.00	1.00
Set	5.00	4.50
First Day Cover		15.00

STAMP BOOKLETS
2/- Booklets
Yellow cover (one pane of four **4d** sepia – two bands – and

one se-tenant pane of two **1d** with two **3d** (two bands)
     1.00
Grey cover (one pane of four **4d** sepia (two bands) and
one se-tenant pane of two **4d** sepia – one centre band – with
two labels)   1.00
Grey cover (one pane of four **4d** sepia – one centre
band – and one se-tenant pane as above)   1.00
Grey cover (one pane of four **4d** red – one centre
band – and one se-tenant pane of two **4d** red – one
centre band – with two labels)   1.50

4/6 Booklets
Blue plain cover (two panes of six **4d** sepia – two
bands – and one pane of six **1d**)   5.00
Blue cover showing Cutty Sark (contents as above) 1.00
Blue cover showing Golden Hind (contents as above
but **4d** with one centre band)   1.25
Blue cover showing Discovery (contents as above) 1.25
Prices: see the notes on page 37

Blue covers (illustrations as below) with two panes of six **4d**
red (one centre band) and one pane of six **1d**
Queen Elizabeth 2   1.50
Sirius   2.50
Dreadnought   2.50
Mauretania   2.00
Victory   2.00
Sovereign on the Seas   2.00

5/- Booklets
Bistre covers (illustrations as below) with two panes
of six **5d**:
Ightham House   1.75
Little Moreton Hall   1.50
Long Melford Hall   2.00
Mompesson House   1.75
Cumberland Terrace   2.00
The Vineyard, Saffron Walden   2.50
Mereworth Castle   2.00
Philympia 1970 London   1.50

6/- Booklets
Purple plain cover (three panes of six **4d** sepia
– two bands)   £150
Orange covers (illustrations as below) (contents as above):
Kingfisher   1.50
Peregrine Falcon   1.50
Orange covers (illustrations as below) (contents as
above but with **4d** sepia (one centre band)
Peregrine Falcon   1.50
Pied Woodpecker   1.50
Great Crested Grebe   1.50
Barn Owl   2.00
Orange covers (illustrations as below) (contents as
above but with **4d** red (one centre band)
Barn Owl (*)   2.50
Jay (*)   2.50
Puffin   2.50

Cormorant	2.50
Wren	2.50
Golden Eagle	2.50

(* - these booklets also exist with panes with gum arabic as well as with PVA gum).

10/- booklets

Purple cover showing Livingstone (four panes of six **4d** sepia – two bands – one pane of six **3d** and one pane of six **1d**)   3.50

Green cover showing Scott (two panes of six **5d**, two panes of six **4d** sepia – one centre band – and one se-tenant pane of four **1d** with two **4d** sepia – one band)   3.50

Green covers (illustrations as below) (contents as above but **4d** red):

Mary Kingsley	2.50
Shackleton	2.50
Frobisher	4.00
Captain Cook	4.00

£1 'Stamps for Cooks' booklets

Multicoloured cover showing Stuffed Baked Haddock Containing one of each of the four panes of 15 Listed under 'Booklet panes'   10.00

DECIMAL MACHINS

1971, February 15 onwards. Machin Decimal Definitives

Designed by Arnold Machin. Printed in photogravure by Harrisons, with no watermark and perforation 15 x 14, except where stated.

In view of the complexity of the Machin Decimal Definitive series, this listing is divided into several sections. In relation to the releases to the introduction of elliptical perforations, for each value the denomination and colour is given first, followed by the date of issue of the basic stamp. There is then recorded all the variations found on the particular value – including differences in gum, paper, phosphor, printer and printing method – followed by the source of such variations.

The following notes should help in understanding the differences.

Gums

These stamps can be found with three different gums.
Gum Arabic is either colourless or yellow in appearance and is very shiny.
Polyvinyl alcohol gum (PVA) is likewise colourless but has a matt appearance.
Polyvinyl alcohol with dextrin gum (PVAD) is also matt, but has a blueish or greenish tinge.
In more recent times self-adhesive stamps have become more common.

Paper

At first these stamps were printed on what is known as 'original coated paper' – this gives a dull violet reaction when the front of the stamp is viewed ultra-violet light.

This was replaced by 'fluorescent coated paper', which gives a bright reaction under ultra-violet light.

With the advent of 'phosphor coated paper' (see below), not only does one find the bright reaction of fluorescent coated paper, but also the after-glow produced by the phosphor.

Some stamps have been found with the 'fluorescent brightener omitted' (with phosphor coated paper): these still give the phosphor afterglow, but the paper gives a dull violet reaction similar to that found with original coated paper.

Phosphor

As with the earlier Wilding and Machin '£sd' definitives and special issues, the phosphor at first was applied in the form of 'bands'. These phosphor bands may be seen by holding the stamp up to the light so as to look along the surface. The stamp paper itself appears shiny, while the phosphor bands have a dull appearance. Most stamps have two phosphor bands, placed down the two vertical edges of the stamp others have just one phosphor band, which is either placed centrally, down the left vertical edge, or down the right vertical edge

The width of the phosphor bands can vary, as can the size of the printing screen used to apply the phosphor bands, but both these differences are beyond the scope of this publication.

In recent times, se-tenant booklet panes, where stamps of the second-class rate (requiring a single phosphor band) have been printed adjacent to other stamps (needing two phosphor bands), have been found with the phosphor printed as bars rather than bands. The difference is that phosphor bands extend across the perforations to the next stamp, whereas phosphor bars stop at the edge of the stamp design, and are not printed on the perforations. When recording individual stamps, we make no distinction between phosphor bands and bars in this volume, although of course the booklet panes on which phosphor bars are found are listed in their own right.

'All over' phosphor – this term was at first taken to mean that the phosphor was printed over the entire surface of the stamp, rather than in the form of 'bands' as described above. This means that the entire stamp has the dull appearance associated with phosphor bands. Sometimes the phosphor was printed on to the paper before the stamp design was printed: in other cases the phosphor was printed above the stamp design. One way of identifying positively 'all-over phosphor' is to examine certain marginal copies of such stamps, where the phosphor will be seen to end in the sheet margin.

Phosphor coated paper – in these cases the phosphor is included with the coating of the surface of the paper on which the stamps are printed. Such stamps appear uniformly shiny. It should be noted that most stamps intended to have phosphor bands have been found with the phosphor omitted, equally producing stamps with a uniformly shiny surface. Stamps with phosphor coated paper can thus only be positively identified by their reaction under ultra-violet light.

It has been found that the appearance of stamps with phosphor coated paper can differ considerably, due, it has been discovered, to differences in the drying time of the stamps. The differences range from dull to very shiny. Although a range of 'shine' can be detected, collectors have basically put these stamps into two categories:

Dull appearance know as phosphor coated paper I (PCPI).

Highly glazed appearance known as phosphor coated paper II (PCII).

The Post Office and stamp printers have been trying to standardise the paper, producing what has become known as Advanced Coated Paper (ACP). So far this paper has been used for a number of 'National' and 'Country' definitives. The visual difference between ACP and PCPI is slight, but the values affected are recorded in this volume. ACP gives a brighter reaction under ultra-violet light compared with PCPI.

No phosphor – when phosphor bands were the norm, most stamps were discovered with the phosphor omitted in error; such missing phosphor varieties vary considerably in price and are outside the scope of this publication. However, two values have been printed without phosphor in the normal course of events. These are the 50p and 75p, both with PVAD gum.

Printers and processes
Many of the Machin Decimal Definitives have been printed in photogravure by Harrisons. However, over the years, as the Post Office opened its contracts to competition, the work has been undertaken by John Waddington, The House of Questa, Walsall Security Printers, Enschedé (based in The Netherlands), and De La Rue, who took over both Harrisons and Questa. For a time lithography was used, but Royal Mail then decided that it preferred photogravure (or more strictly gravure since the advent of computer technology).

Chambon press – in 1979 the 10p definitive was printed on a Chambon press at Harrisons which produced sheets of 200 stamps comprising two panes of 100 stamps separated by a horizontal gutter. Stamps from this printing have either two phosphor bands on top of phosphor coated paper or two phosphor bands on top of fluorescent coated paper.

Booklet panes
The stamps which are found in stamp booklets are said to be in form of booklet panes. At first booklets were kept together by stitching, so that a number of small holes can be found in the binding margin on the left hand side of booklet panes. Later booklet panes were stuck into booklet covers by the binding margins: in many such cases panes can be found with the binding margin to the left or to the right of the stamps. When booklets were stitched, a number of variations were found in the way in which the binding margin was perforated: such differences are beyond the scope of this publication.

Many of the early decimal booklet panes included labels se-tenant with the stamps in the pane. These labels ere adjacent to the binding margin, and at first were perforated between the labels and the margin. Later the labels were imperforate with the binding margin.

Booklet panes intended to be stuck within card covers have often been found to be guillotined in the wrong place,

giving rise to mis-cut panes. Obviously if the panes are of just one value stamp, little difference will be noted, but if a se-tenant pane is involved, the difference can be quite dramatic. However, we do not record individual cases of mis-cut panes in this publication.

In 1987, as an experiment, two booklet panes were produced with imperforate sides (to counter complaints from collectors about poor guillotining of panes). These panes produce stamps in either the left or right-hand edge imperforate but these are not separately listed as individual stamps.

A further experiment of 1987 was to introduce booklets with 'bar codes' on the back cover, and with a 'window' in the front cover, so that the stamp content could be ascertained. The panes in these booklets have a margin surrounding the stamps, and as such are listed separately.

In the case of stitched booklets, the booklet panes are recorded separately. However, where the panes are stuck into the covers, most collectors prefer these as complete booklets, so the separate panes are not recorded.

Coils
There are basically two types of coils from which stamps may be found. First there are those coils that contain just one value: the stamps in such coils are joined either horizontally or vertically. These days such coils are usually prepared of the basic first and second class letter rate stamps for use by businesses. They are not separately listed, except that where the source of a particular stamp is given as 'coils', this refers to the single value version.

Other coils contain a mixture of values joined as a se-tenant strip. These have basically been produced for sale through vending machines, although two cases are so far known of coils specially produced for a commercial mailing shot. Under 'source' these are referred to a 'se-tenant coils' and they are also separately listed.

Value position and portrait types
Changes can be noted in many cases in both the position of the value in relation to the Queen's portrait, and the portrait in relation to the base of the stamp. Frequently the differences are particularly striking, they have been recorded in this volume.

Cartons
In 1976/8 an experiment was staged in Scotland whereby first and second-class definitives were sold in cartons from vending machines. Both Scottish 'Country' stamps and normal definitives were used. These cartons were sold at 30p or 60p and contained either 6½p and 8½p, or 7p and 9p stamps. Different styles of carton and the attached inscription label are known, but these items are beyond the scope of this publication.

IN THE MAIN LISTING

If no price is given in the 'used' column it is because the stamp exists with different gums which cannot be distinguished in used condition: a price for the basic used stamp will be found in the section under PVAD gum.

MACHINS

Value and description	MarketValue		Sources
(Note: all stamps have fluorescent coated paper unless otherwise stated)			
½p turquoise – February 15, 1971			
a) gum Arabic – two phosphor bands			
i – original coated paper	0.30	-	se-tenant coils
ii - original coated paper with silicone	35.00	-	se-tenant coils
iii – fluorescent coated paper	0.30	-	sheets
iv – fluorescent coated paper with silicone	0.40	-	se-tenant coils
b) PVA gum – two phosphor bands			
i – original coated paper	0.30	-	sheets, se-tenant coils, booklets
ii – fluorescent coated paper	0.50	-	sheets, booklets
c) PVA gum – one band at left	40.00	25.00	£1 Wedgwood booklet
d) PVAD gum – two phosphor bands	0.25	0.20	sheets, se-tenant coils, booklets
e) PVAD gum – one centre band	0.25	0.20	se-tenant coils, booklets
f) PVAD gum – phosphor coated paper			
i – PCPI	0.25	0.20	sheets, se-tenant coils
ii – PCPII	0.30	0.20	sheets
iii – fluorescent brightener omitted	50.00	17.50	se-tenant coils – poor gum –
	£800	-	good perfs and gum

Left: portrait above bottom margin
Right: portrait closer to bottom margin

1p purple – February 15, 1971			
a) gum Arabic – two phosphor bands			
i – original coated paper	0.30	-	se-tenant coils
ii - original coated paper with silicone	35.00	-	se-tenant coils
iii – fluorescent coated paper	0.50	-	coils
iv – fluorescent coated paper with silicone	0.40	-	se-tenant coils
b) PVA gum – two phosphor bands			
i – original coated paper	0.40	-	sheets
ii – fluorescent coated paper	1.25	-	sheets, booklets
c) PVAD gum – two phosphor bands			
i – value low	0.45	0.20	10p booklets
ii – value in middle position	0.30	0.20	50p booklets, 10p se-tenant coils
iii – value high	0.45	0.20	sheets, 5p se-tenant coils
d) PVAD gum – one centre band			
i – portrait above bottom margin	0.30	0.20	se-tenant coils (½p, 1p, 7p)
ii – portrait closer to bottom margin	0.30	0.20	10p, 50p booklets, se-tenant
coils (1p, 8p)			
e) PVAD gum – 'all over' phosphor	0.30	0.20	sheets
f) PVAD gum – phosphor coated paper			
i – PCPI – portrait above bottom margin	0.30	0.20	sheets
ii – PCPI – portrait closer to bottom margin	0.30	0.20	sheets, se-tenant coils (1p, 4p, 4p, 4p)
iii – PCPII	0.40	0.25	sheets

iv – advanced coated paper	0.25	0.20	sheets
g) PVAD gum – one band at left	0.75	0.75	50p booklet
h) PVAD gum – one band at right	2.00	2.25	£5 'P&O' booklet

Value and description	MarketValue		Sources
(Note: all stamps have fluorescent coated paper unless otherwise stated)			
1½p black – February 15, 1971			
a) PVA gum – two phosphor bands			
i – original coated paper	0.30	-	sheets, booklets
ii – fluorescent coated paper	1.00	-	sheets, booklets
b) PVAD gum – two phosphor bands	0.50	0.20	sheets, booklets
2p green – February 15, 1971			
a) gum arabic – two phosphor bands			
i – original coated paper	2.25	-	se-tenant coils
ii - original coated paper with silicone	125.00	-	se-tenant coils
iii – fluorescent coated paper with silicone	2.00	-	se-tenant coils
b) PVA gum – two phosphor bands			
i – original coated paper	0.25	-	sheets, booklets
ii – fluorescent coated paper	1.25	-	sheets, booklets
c) PVAD gum – two phosphor bands			
i – portrait above bottom margin	0.30	0.20	sheets, se-tenant coils, booklets
ii – portrait closer to bottom margin	0.30	0.20	booklets
d) PVAD gum – 'all over' phosphor	0.30	0.20	sheets
e) PVAD gum – phosphor coated paper			
i – PCPI	0.30	0.20	sheets
ii – PCPII	0.35	0.20	sheets
f) PVAD gum – phosphor coated paper			
printed in litho by Questa: perf 13½ x 14	0.25	0.25	sheets
g) as f) but perf 15 x 14	0.30	0.25	sheets
h) as g) but advanced coated paper	0.30	0.25	sheets
2p deep green – February 23, 1988			
a) PVAD gum – phosphor paper	0.25	0.20	sheets and booklets
b) PVAD gum – phosphor paper,			
printed in litho by Walsall	0.75	0.75	booklets
2½p pink – February 15, 1971			
a) gum arabic – one centre band	0.30	-	sheets, coils
b) PVA gum – one centre band			
i – original coated paper	0.30	0.20	sheets, coils, booklets,
ii – fluorescent coated paper	0.60	0.25	sheets, booklets
c) PVA gum – one band at left			
i – original coated paper	5.00	1.00	50p booklets,
ii – fluorescent coated paper	1.75	1.00	50p and £1 Wedgwood booklets
d) PVA gum – one band at right	1.70	1.70	£1 Wedgwood booklet
e) PVAD gum – two phosphor bands	0.40	0.25	sheets
f) PVAD gum – one centre band	0.30	0.20	sheets
2½p rose – January 14, 1981			
a) PVAD gum – phosphor coated paper			
i – PCPI	0.50	0.20	sheets, se-tenant coils
ii – PCPII	0.30	0.20	sheets,
iii – fluorescent brightener omitted	35.00	35.00	se-tenant coils
b) PVAD gum – two phosphor bands	0.40	0.25	50p booklets

Value and description	MarketValue		Sources
(Note: all stamps have fluorescent coated paper unless otherwise stated)			
3p blue – February 15, 1971			
a) gum arabic – two phosphor bands			
i – original coated paper	45.00	-	coils
ii – fluorescent coated paper	0.50	-	sheets, coils
b) gum arabic – one centre band	0.40	-	sheets
c) PVA gum two phosphor bands			
i – original coated paper	0.30	0.20	sheets, coils, booklets
ii –fluorescent coated paper	0.60	0.25	sheets, booklets
iii – on phosphor coated paper	-	-	two examples are known
d) PVA gum – one centre band	0.60	-	sheets, booklets
e) PVAD gum – one centre band	0.30	0.20	sheets, coils, booklets
3p pink – October 22, 1980			
a) PVAD gum – phosphor coated paper			
i – PCPI	0.30	0.25	sheets, se-tenant coils
ii – PCPII	0.35	0.25	
iii – fluorescent brightener omitted	4.00	4.00	se-tenant coils
iv – advanced coated paper	0.30	0.20	sheets, £4 'Royal Mint' booklet
b) PVAD gum – two phosphor bands	0.30	0.25	50p and £4 'SG' booklets
3½p olive green – February 15, 1971			
a) PVA gum – two phosphor bands			
i – original coated paper	0.50	0.25	sheets
ii – fluorescent coated paper	1.50	-	sheets, 35p booklets
b) PVAD gum – two phosphor bands			
i – original coated paper	£150	35.00	sheets
ii – fluorescent coated paper	0.50	0.20	sheets, coils, 35p and 50p booklets
c) PVAD gum – one centre band	0.35	0.25	sheets, coils, 35p and 85p booklets
3½p light red-brown – March 30, 1983			
i – PCPI	0.50	0.40	sheets,
ii – advanced coated paper	0.65	0.65	sheets, £4 'Royal Mint' booklet
b) PVAD gum – one centre band	1.50	0.75	50p booklets
4p bistre – February 15, 1971			
a) gum arabic – two phosphor bands	0.30	-	sheets
b) PVA gum – two phosphor bands			
i – original coated paper	0.30	0.25	sheets
ii – fluorescent coated paper	3.00	-	sheets
c) PVAD gum – two phosphor bands	0.30	0.20	sheets
4p blue – January 30, 1980			
a) PVA gum – two phosphor bands: printed in litho by Waddingtons	0.30	0.20	sheets
b) PVAD gum – phosphor coated paper: printed by Waddingtons	0.30	0.20	sheets
b) as b) but printed in litho by Questa, perf. 15 X 14	0.50	0.45	sheets
d) PVAD gum – two phosphor bands	0.90	0.75	50p booklets
e) PVAD gum – phosphor coated paper			
i – PCPI	0.35	0.30	se-tenant coils
ii – fluorescent brightener omitted	£400	-	se-tenant coils – perfect gum
iii – PCPI – value higher	0.35	0.30	se-tenant coils
f) PVAD gum – one centre band	0.75	0.70	50p booklets
g) PVAD gum – one band at left	1.50	1.25	£5 booklet
h) PVAD gum – one band at right	1.50	1.25	£5 booklet

Value and description	MarketValue		Sources
(Note: all stamps have fluorescent coated paper unless otherwise stated)			
4p bright blue – July 26, 1988			
a) PVAD gum – phosphor paper			
printed in litho by Questa	0.45	0.50	sheets
a) PVAD gum – phosphor paper	0.30	0.25	sheets and coils
4½p grey-blue – October 24, 1973			
a) PVAD gum – two phosphor bands	0.50	0.20	sheets, coils, 45p and 85p booklets
b) PVAD gum – two phosphor bands			
on 'all-over' phosphor	0.65	-	sheets
5p violet – February 15, 1971			
a) PVA gum – two phosphor bands			
i – original coated paper	0.30	0.25	sheets
ii – fluorescent coated paper	3.00	-	sheets
b) PVAD gum – two phosphor bands	0.40	0.20	sheets
c) PVAD gum – phosphor coated paper			
i – PCPI	0.35	0.25	sheets
ii – PCPI – value higher	0.40	0.35	sheets
d) PVAD gum – phosphor coated paper:			
printed in litho by Questa	0.30	0.25	sheets
e) PVA gum – phosphor coated paper:			
printed in litho by Questa	0.50	0.25	sheets
5p red-brown – January 27. 1982			
a) PVAD gum – phosphor coated paper:			
printed in litho by Questa: perf 13½ X 14	0.40	0.30	sheets
b) as a) but 15 X 14	0.50	0.40	sheets
c) as b) but advanced coated paper	0.45	0.40	sheets
d) PVAD gum – one centre band	1.00	1.10	50p booklet
5½p deep purple – October 24, 1973			
a) PVAD gum – two phosphor bands	60	40	sheets
b) PVAD gum – one centre band	40	35	sheets
6p light green – February 15, 1971			
a) gum arabic – two phosphor bands	2.00	-	sheets
b) PVA gum – two phosphor bands			
i – original coated paper	0.35	-	sheets, se-tenant coils
ii – fluorescent coated paper	20.00	-	sheets
c) PVAD gum – two phosphor bands	0.30	0.25	sheets, se-tenant coils, 10p booklet
6p olive – September 10, 1991			
a) PVAD gum – phosphor paper	0.30	0.30	sheets
6½p green-blue – September 7, 1974			
a) PVA gum – two phosphor bands	22..50	-	sheets
b) PVAD gum – two phosphor bands	0.75	0.30	sheets
c) PVAD gum – one centre band			
i - portrait above bottom margin	0.30	0.25	sheets
ii - portrait closer to bottom margin	0.30	0.25	sheets, coils, 65p booklets
d) PVAD gum – one band at left	0.70	0.70	50p booklets
e) PVAD gum – one band at right	0.80	0.80	50p booklets

Value and description	MarketValue		Sources
(Note: all stamps have fluorescent coated paper unless otherwise stated)			
7p red-brown – January 15, 1975			
a) PVAD gum – two phosphor bands	0.40	0.25	sheets
b) PVAD gum – one centre band			
i – portrait above bottom margin	0.35	0.25	sheets, coils
ii – portrait closer to bottom margin	0.35	0.25	sheets, coils, booklets, se-tenants coils
c) PVAD gum – one band at left	0.45	0.45	50p booklets
d) PVAD gum – one band at right	0.60	0.60	50p booklets
7p brick-red – October 29, 1985			
a) PVAD gum – phosphor coated paper	1.20	1.20	sheets
7½p brown – February 15, 1971			
a) PVA gum – two phosphor bands			
i – original coated paper	0.40	0.25	sheets
ii – fluorescent coated paper	2.50	-	sheets
b) PVAD gum – two phosphor bands	0.30	0.25	sheets
8p red – October 24, 1973			
a) PVAD gum – two phosphor bands	0.35	0.25	sheets
b) PVAD gum – one centre band:			
printed by Harrisons			
i – portrait high, value low	0.35	0.25	sheets
ii – portrait low, value high	0.45	0.25	sheets, booklets, coils
c) PVAD gum – one centre band:			
printed by Enschedé	0.35	0.25	sheets
d) PVAD gum – one band at left	0.50	0.30	50p booklets
e) PVAD gum – one band at right	0.50	0.30	50p booklets
8½p line green – September 24, 1975			
a) PVAD gum – two phosphor bands			
i – value high	0.40	0.25	sheets, coils, 85p booklets
ii – value low	0.45	0.35	50p booklets
b) PVAD gum – phosphor coated paper	0.55	0.40	sheets
9p orange and black – February 15, 1971			
a) PVA gum – two phosphor bands			
i – original coated paper	0.90	0.40	sheets
ii – fluorescent coated paper	2.75	-	sheets
b) PVAD gum – two phosphor bands	0.75	0.25	sheets
9p violet – February 25, 1976			
a) PVAD gum – two phosphor bands	0.45	0.25	sheets, coils, 50p, 90p and £1.60
9½p purple – February 25, 1976			
a) PVAD gum – two phosphor bands	0.35	0.30	sheets
10p yellow and orange – August 11, 1971			
a) PVA gum – two phosphor bands	0.50	-	sheets
b) PVAD gum – two phosphor bands	0.75	0.35	sheets
10p orange – February 25, 1976			
a) PVA gum – two phosphor bands			
i – base of value above edge of bus	0.30	0.20	sheets, £1.80 booklets
ii – base of value edge of bust	0.35	0.25	50p booklets
iii – re-drawn (narrower) value	17.50	12.50	£4 'Heritage' booklet
b) PVAD gum – 'all-over' phosphor	0.40	0.25	sheets, £1 booklets

c) PVAD gum – phosphor coated paper (PCPI)	0.50	0.25	sheets
d) PVAD gum advanced coated paper	0.40	0.25	sheets
e) PVAD gum – one centre band	0.35	0.20	sheets, £1, £2.20 and £3 booklets
f) PVAD gum – one band at left	0.60	0.50	50p and £3 booklets
g) PVAD gum – one band at right	0.60	0.50	50p booklets
h) PVAD gum – two phosphor bands on phosphor coated paper (PCPI): printed on Chambon press	0.50	-	sheets
i) gutter pair of above	1.25	-	sheets
j) PVAD gum – two phosphor bands on fluorescent coated paper: printed on Chambon press	0.40	0.35	sheets
k) gutter pair of above	1.00	1.50	sheets
l) PVAD gum – one centre band on phosphor coated paper (PCPI)	1.00	-	sheets

10½p yellow – February 25, 1976

a) PVAD gum – two phosphor bands	0.40	0.35	sheets

10½p blue – Aril 26, 1978

a) PVAD gum – two phosphor bands	0.50	0.50	sheets

11p orange-pink – February 25, 1976

a) PVAD gum – two phosphor bands	0.50	0.30	sheets
b) PVAD gum – phosphor coated paper (PCPI)	0.60	0.50	sheets

11½p sepia – August 15, 1979

a) PVAD gum – phosphor coated paper (PCPI)	0.60	0.30	sheets

11½p mushroom – January 14, 1981

a) PVAD gum – one centre band	0.50	0.25	sheets, coils, £1.15 and £2.55 booklets
b) PVAD gum – one band at left	0.50	0.30	50p and £1.30 booklets
c) PVAD gum- one band at right	0.50	0.30	50p and £1.30 booklets

12p yellow-green – January 30, 1980

a) PVAD gum – phosphor coated paper			
i – PCPI	0.50	0.25	sheets, coils, £1.20 booklet
ii – PCPII	0.80	0.25	sheets
b) PVAD gum – two phosphor bands	0.50	0.35	50p, £2.20 and £3 booklets

12p emerald-green – October 29, 1985

a) PVAD gum – one centre band	50	25	sheets, 50p, £1.20 and £5 booklets
b) PVAD gum – one centre band, with blue star printed on the gummed side	50	-	sheets
c) PVAD gum – one centre band in ACP-type phosphor	50	30	sheets
d) PVAD gum – one band at left	60	50	£1.50 and £5 booklets
e) PVAD gum – one band at right	60	50	£1.50 and £5 booklets

12½p light green – January 27, 1982

a) PVAD gum – one centre band	50	25	sheets, coils, 50p, £1.25 and £4 'SG' booklets
b) PVAD gum – one centre band, on phosphor coated paper (PCPI)	5.00	-	sheets
c) PVAD gum – one band at left	60	50	50p, £1.43, £1.46 and £4 booklets

MACHINS

Value and description	MarketValue		Sources
(Note: all stamps have fluorescent coated paper unless otherwise stated)			
d) PVAD gum – one band at right	60	50	50p, £1.43, £1.46 and £4 booklets
e) PVAD gum – one centre band			
and blue star printed on gummed side	50	50	£2.50 booklet
f) PVAD gum – one centre band and			
simple blue star printed on gummed side	45	40	£2.20 booklet

13p olive – August 15, 1979
a) PVAD gum – phosphor coated paper			
(PCPI)	50	30	sheets

13p light brown – August 28, 1984
a) PVAD gum – one centre band	50	25	sheets, 50p, £1.30 and £5 booklets
b) PVAD gum – one centre band, with a			
blue star printed on the gummed side	60	-	£1.20 booklet
c) PVAD gum – one centre band in			
ACP-type phosphor	60	30	sheets
d) PVAD gum – one band at left	60	35	50p, £1.54, £4 'Heritage' and £5
booklets			
e) PVAD gum – one bad at right	60	35	£1, £1.54, £4 'Heritage' and £5
booklets			
f) PVAD gum – one centre band, printed			
in litho by Questa	0.60	0.50	booklets
g) PVAD gum – one band at left, printed in			
litho by Questa	0.70	0.70	booklets
h) PVAD gum – one band at right, printed in			
litho by Questa	0.70	0.70	booklets

13½p red-brown – January 30, 1980
a) PVAD gum – phosphor coated paper			
(PCPI)	60	35	sheets

14p grey-blue – January 14, 1981
a) PVAD gum – phosphor coated paper			
i - PCPI	45	30	sheets, £1.40 booklets, coils
ii - PCPI I	50	30	sheets, £1.40 booklets, coils
iii - fluorescent brightener omitted	1.50	-	£1.40 booklets
b) PVAD gum – two phosphor bands	75	50	50p, £1.30 and £2.55 booklets

14p deep blue – August 23, 1988
a) PVAD gum – one centre band	0.45	0.25	sheets and booklets
b) PVAD gum – one band at right	2.25	2.30	booklets
c) PVAD gum – one centre band,			
printed in litho by Questa	1.50	1.50	booklets
d) PVAD gum – one band at right,			
printed in litho by Walsall	2.15	2.25	booklets

15p blue – August 15, 1979
a) PVAD gum – phosphor coated paper			
i - PCPI	0.50	0.30	sheets
ii - PCPI	0.55	0.55	sheets

15½p pale purple – January 14, 1981
a) PVAD gum – phosphor coated paper			
i – PCPI	0.60	0.25	sheets, £1.55 booklets, coils
ii – PCPI	0.60	0.25	sheets

MACHINS

iii – fluorescent brightener omitted	15.00	-	sheets
iv – advanced coated paper	3.00	3.00	£1.55 booklets
b) PVAD gum – two phosphor bands	0.60	0.40	£1.43 and £4 'SG' booklets
c) PVAD gum – two phosphor bands and			
blue star printed on the gummed side	0.55	0.55	£2.50 booklets

16p light mushroom – March 30, 1983

a) PVAD gum – phosphor coated paper			
(PCPI)	0.60	0.35	sheets, £1.60 and £4 'Mint' booklets
b) PVAD gum – phosphor coated paper (PCPI)			
and 'D' printed on the gummed side	0.70	0.70	£1.45 booklet
c) PVAD gum – advanced coated paper	0.60	0.50	sheets
d) PVAD gum – two phosphor bands	1.00	1.00	£1.46 booklet

16½p light brown – January 27 1982

a) PVAD gum – phosphor coated paper			
i – PCPI	0.75	0.50	sheets
ii – PCPII	3.50	2.00	sheets

17p sage green – January 30, 1980

a) PVAD gum – phosphor coated paper			
i – PCPI	0.70	0.70	sheets
ii – PCPII	3.00	2.00	sheets
iii – fluorescent brightener omitted	1.50	-	sheets

17p steel blue – March 30, 1983

a) PVAD gum – phosphor coated paper (PCPI)	0.70	0.40	sheets, £1/.70 and £4 'Heritage' booklets
b) PVAD gum – phosphor coated paper (PCPI)			
and 'D' on the gummed side	0.80	-	£1.55 booklet
c) PVAD gum – advanced coated paper	0.60	0.40	sheets, £1.70 and £5 booklets
d) PVAD gum - two phosphor bands	0.60	0.30	50p, £1.50, £1.54, £4 'Heritage' and £5 booklets
e) as d) but with stars on gummed side	0.70	-	50p booklet

17p deep blue – September 4, 1990

a) PVAD gum – one centre band	0.50	0.25	sheets
b) PVAD gum – one band at left	0.80	0.80	booklets
c) PVAD gum – one band at right	1.50	1.60	booklets
d) PVAD gum – one centre band,			
printed in litho by Questa	0.70	0.75	booklets

17½p light brown – January 30, 1979

a) PVAD gum – phosphor coated paper			
i – PCPI	0.75	0.40	sheets
ii – PCPII	1.75	1.75	sheets

18p violet – January 14, 1981

a) PVAD gum – phosphor coated paper			
i – PCPI	0.65	0.40	sheets
ii – PCPII	0.70	0.40	sheets

18p grey-green – August 28, 1984

a) PVAD gum – advanced coated paper	0.65	0.30	sheets
b) PVAD gum – two phosphor bands	0.80	0.40	50p, £1 booklets
c) PVAD gum – phosphor coated paper	0.80	0.60	£1.80 booklet
d) PVAD gum – phosphor paper,			
printed in litho by Questa	0.75	0.75	booklets

MACHINS

Value and description	MarketValue		Sources
(Note: all stamps have fluorescent coated paper unless otherwise stated)			
e) PVAD gum – two phosphor bands,			
printed in litho by Questa	3.50	3.60	booklets
18p bright green – September 10, 1991			
a) PVAD gum – one centre band	0.50	0.30	sheets
b) PVAD gum – one centre band paper,			
printed in litho by Questa	0.90	0.95	booklets
c) PVAD gum – one band at left,			
printed in litho by Questa	1.30	1.35	booklets
d) PVAD gum – one band at right,			
printed in litho by Questa	1.00	1.05	booklets
19p orange-red – August 23, 1988			
a) PVAD gum – phosphor paper	0.50	0.30	sheets and booklets
b) PVAD gum – phosphor paper,			
printed in litho by Questa	1.50	1.50	booklets
c) PVAD gum – two phosphor bands,			
printed in litho by Walsall	1.50	1.60	booklets
19½p – January 27, 1982			
a) PVAD gum – phosphor coated paper (PCPI	1.25	1.25	sheets
20p dull purple – February 25, 1976			
a) PVA gum – two phosphor bands; printed in			
litho by Waddingtons	0.80	0.70	sheets
b) PVAD gum – phosphor coated paper:			
printed in litho by Waddingtons	1.00	0.80	sheets
c) as d) but dull purple and sepia	2.00	1.40	sheets
d) as c) but printed in litho			
by Questa, perf 15 X 14	1.00	0.90	sheets
e) PVAD gum – two phosphor bands	0.70	0.30	sheets
f) PVAD gum – phosphor coated			
paper			
i – PCPI	0.75	0.50	sheets
ii – PCPII	0.75	0.60	sheets
20p turquoise – August 23, 1988			
a) PVAD gum – phosphor paper	0.40	0.30	sheets
20p brownish-black - September 26, 1989			
a) PVAD gum – phosphor paper	0.40	0.30	sheets and booklets
b) PVAD gum – two phosphor bands	1.50	1.50	sheets
20½p bright blue – March 30, 1983			
a) PVAD gum – phosphor coated			
paper (PCPI)	1.25	1.25	sheets
22p deep blue – October 22, 1980			
a) PVAD gum – phosphor coated paper			
i – PCPI	0.70	0.50	sheets
ii – PCPII	0.70	0.50	sheets
b) PVAD gum – experimental coated paper	2.75	2.75	sheets
22p yellow-green – August 28, 1984			
a) PVAD gum – advanced coated paper	0.60	0.45	sheets
b) PVAD gum – two phosphor bands,			

printed in litho by Questa	4.50	4.50	booklets

22p orange-red – September 4, 1990
a) PVAD gum – two phosphor bands	0.80	0.90	sheets
b) PVAD gum – phosphor paper	0.60	0.70	sheets
c) PVAD gum – phosphor paper,			
printed in litho by Questa	0.70	0.75	booklets

23p rose – March 30, 1983
a) PVAD gum – phosphor coated paper (PCPI)	1.20	1.00	sheets

23p bright green – August 23, 1988
a) PVAD gum – phosphor paper	0.75	0.75	sheets

24p light purple – August 28, 1984
a) PVAD gum – advanced coated paper	1.40	1.10	sheets

24p red – September 26, 1989
a) PVAD gum – phosphor paper	1.10	1.15	sheets

24p chestnut – September 10, 1991
a) PVAD gum – phosphor paper	0.50	0.30	sheets
b) PVAD gum – phosphor paper,			
printed in litho by Questa	0.70	0.70	booklets
c) PVAD gum – two phosphor bands,			
printed in litho by Questa	1.10	1.10	booklets
d) PVAD gum – phosphor paper,			
printed in litho by Walsall	0.90	0.90	booklets

25p purple – January 14, 1981
a) PVAD gum – phosphor coated paper			
i – PCPI	1.75	1.75	sheets
ii – PCPII	0.75	0.50	sheets

25p red – February 6, 1996
a) PVAD gum – two phosphor bands	4.25	4.25	sheets

26p red – January 27, 1982
a) PVAD gum – phosphor coated paper (PCPI)	0.75	0.50	sheets
b) PVAD gum – advanced coated paper	0.75	0.50	sheets
c) PVAD gum – two phosphor bands	5.50	5.00	£5 'P&O' booklet
d) as b) but narrow value	3.50	3.00	£1.04 booklet

26p drab – September 4, 1990
a) PVAD gum – phosphor paper	1.00	1.05	sheets

27p chestnut – August 23, 1988
a) PVAD gum – phosphor paper	0.90	0.95	sheets and booklets

27p violet – September 4, 1990
a) PVAD gum – phosphor paper	1.00	1.05	sheets

28p blue – March 30, 1983
a) PVAD gum – phosphor coated paper (PCPI)	0.90	0.90	sheets
b) PVAD gum – advanced coated paper	1.10	1.10	sheets

28p ochre – August 23, 1988
a) PVAD gum – phosphor paper	0.95	0.95	sheets

Value and description	MarketValue		Sources
(Note: all stamps have fluorescent coated paper unless otherwise stated)			
28p blue-grey – September 10, 1991			
a) PVAD gum – phosphor paper	0.65	0.65	sheets
29p sepia – January 27, 1982			
a) PVAD gum – phosphor coated paper			
i – PCPI	2.25	2.25	sheets
ii – PCPII	5.00	3.50	sheets
29p mauve – September 26, 1989			
a) PVAD gum – phosphor paper	1.50	1.50	sheets
b) PVAD gum – two phosphor bands,			
printed in litho by Walsall	2.50	2.50	booklets
c) PVAD gum – phosphor paper,			
printed in litho by Walsall	2.70	2.70	booklets
30p olive – September 26, 1989			
a) PVAD gum – phosphor paper	0.80	0.80	sheets
31p purple – March 30, 1983			
a) PVAD gum – phosphor coated paper (PCPI)	1.20	1.25	sheets
b) PVAD gum – advanced coated paper	1.10	0.75	sheets
c) PVAD gum – two phosphor bands	7.50	7.50	£5 'British Rail' Booklet
31p ultramarine – September 4, 1990			
a) PVAD gum – phosphor paper	1.00	1.00	sheets
b) PVAD gum – phosphor paper,			
printed in litho by Walsall	1.10	1.10	booklets
32p green-blue – August 23, 1988			
a) PVAD gum – phosphor paper	1.00	1.00	sheets
33p emerald – September 4, 1990			
a) PVAD gum – phosphor paper	0.90	0.90	sheets
b) PVAD gum – phosphor paper,			
printed in litho by Questa	1.40	1.40	booklets
c) PVAD gum – two phosphor bands,			
printed in litho by Questa	1.00	1.00	booklets
d) PVAD gum – phosphor paper,			
printed in litho by Walsall	1.00	1.00	booklets
34p sepia – August 28, 1984			
a) PVAD gum – phosphor coated paper	1.00	1.00	sheets
b) PVAD gum – two phosphor bands	5.00	5.00	£5 'Times' booklet
c) PVAD gum – advanced coated paper	1.25	1.25	sheets
d) PVAD gum – two phosphor bands,			
printed in litho by Questa	4.40	4.40	booklets
34p blue-grey – September 26, 1989			
a) PVAD gum – phosphor paper	1.00	1.00	sheets
34p mauve – September 10, 1991			
a) PVAD gum – phosphor paper	1.10	1.10	sheets
35p sepia – August 23, 1988			
a) PVAD gum – phosphor paper	1.20	1.25	sheets

35p yellow – September 10, 1991
a) PVAD gum – phosphor paper	0.95	0.95	sheets

37p rosine – September 26, 1989
a) PVAD gum – phosphor paper	1.25	1.25	sheets

39p mauve – September 10, 1991
a) PVAD gum – phosphor paper	1.15	1.15	sheets
b) PVAD gum – two phosphor bands, printed in litho by Questa	1.25	1.30	booklets
c) PVAD gum – phosphor paper, printed in litho by Walsall	1.10	1.10	booklets

50p dull brown – February 2, 1977
a) PVAD gum – two phosphor bands	1.50	0.50	sheets
b) PVAD gum – no phosphor	1.50	0.70	sheets

50p ochre – March 13, 1990
a) PVAD gum – phosphor paper	1.50	1.25	sheets
b) PVAD gum – two phosphor bands	3.00	3.00	sheets

75p deep grey – January 30, 1980
a) PVAD gum – no phosphor: printed in litho by Questa: perf 13½ x 14	3.00	70	sheets
b) as a) but perf 15 x 14 and PVA gum	3.00	90	sheets
c) as b) but PVAD gum	3.75	-	sheets
d) as b) but on paper supplied by Coated Paper Ltd	3.00	-	sheets

75p grey and black – February 23, 1988
a) PVAD gum – printed in litho by Questa	6.50	6.50	sheets

MACHINS

Booklet panes

Panes listed are those from stitched booklets only. Those from the Prestige stamp books are listed with their respective books.

a) Polyvinyl alcohol gum

Panes of four

Two 2p se-tenant with two ½p
a) vertically se-tenant	5.00
b) horizontally se-tenant	
i) original coated paper	9.00
ii) fluorescent coated paper	4.00

Two 1p se-tenant with two ½p
a) vertically se-tenant	5.00
b) horizontally se-tenant	
i) original coated paper	6.00
ii) fluorescent coated paper	3.00

Panes of six

Five ½p se-tenant with label 'B. ALAN LTD for G.B. STAMPS…'
a) perforated label	4.00
b) imperforate label	7.50

Five ½p se-tenant with label 'LICK battery failure…'
a) perforated label	4.00
b) imperforate label	10.00

Five ½p se-tenant with label 'MAKE YOUR LUCKY FIND PAY…'
imperforate label only	1.75

Four 2½p (one centre band) se-tenant with two labels reading 'UNIFLO STAMPS…' and 'STICK FIRMLY…'
a) perforated label	4.00
b) imperforate label	9.00

Five 2½p (one centre band) se-tenant with label 'STICK FIRMLY…'
a) perforated label	4.50
b) imperforate label	9.00

Five 2½p (one centre band) se-tenant with label 'TEAR OFF to ESSO…'
a) perforated label	4.50
b) imperforate label	9.00

Five 2½p (one centre band) se-tenant with label 'STAMP COLLECTIONS…'
imperforate label only	3.50

Four 2½p (one centre band) se-tenant with two labels reading 'DO YOU COLLECT G.B. STAMPS…' and 'BUYING or SELLING…'
imperforate label only	3.50

Five 2½p (one centre band) se-tenant with label 'B ALAN for…'
imperforate label only	3.75

Five 3p (two bands) se-tenant with label '£4,315 FOR YOU…'
a) perforated label	3.00
b) imperforate label, OCP	10.00
c) imperforate label, FCP	1.50

Four 3p (two bands) se-tenant with two 2½p

(one band at left)
a) OCP	10.00
b) FCP	5.00

Six 3p (two bands)
a) OCP	5.00
b) FCP	2.50

Five 3p (one centre band) se-tenant with blank imperforate label	12.50
Five 3½p (two bands) se-tenant with blank imperforate label	7.50

b) Polyvinyl alcohol gum with dextrin

Panes of four
Two 2p horizontally se-tenant with two ½p	2.00
Two 1p horizontally se-tenant with two 1½p	2.00

Panes of six
Five 3p (one centre band) se-tenant with blank imperforate label	10.00
Five 3½p (two bands) se-tenant with blank imperforate label	2.50
Five 3½p (one centre band) se-tenant with blank imperforate label (*)	2.50

(*- while this pane is normally found with the label in the lower row, miss-cut panes with the label in the upper row also exist.)
Five 4½p (two bands) se-tenant with blank imperforate label	3.00

Stamp booklets

This listing makes no distinction between booklets containing panes with PVA gum or PVAD gum.

10p booklets (containing two ½p, two 1p and two 1½p and two 2p): yellow covers with the following illustrations
London's first pillar box	2.00
Pillar box of 1856	2.00
Urban pillar box 1857	4.00
Penfold type 1866	3.00
Double aperture type 1899	2.00
Mellor type 1968	2.00
King Edward VIII type 1936	2.00
Queen Elizabeth II type 1952	2.00
Double aperture type 1973	2.75
Philatelic Posting Box	1.50
General Letter Carrier 1793	1.50
Letter Carrier 1837	1.25
Letter Carrier 1855	0.75

25p booklets (containing five ½p, nine 2½p): violet covers with the following illustrations
Knifeboard Omnibus	3.00
80 Years of British Stamp Books	3.75
B-type Omnibus	3.75
Showman's Engine	7.50
Royal Mail Van 1913	4.25
Motor Wagonette 1901	4.50
London Taxi Cab 1931	5.00

Norwich Electric Tramway	6.00
Help Children… Save the Children	5.50

30p booklets (containing ten at **3p**): purple covers
with the following illustrations

Curlew	3.25
80 Years of British Stamp Books	3.50
Lapwing	3.50
Robin	3.50
Pied Wagtail	3.75
Kestrel	4.00
Black Grouse	5.00
Skylark	4.00
Oyster-catcher	4.00
Oyster-catcher (bistre cover)	5.00
Help Children…. Save the Children (red cover)	4.00
The Canada Life Assurance Group (red cover)	4.00

35p booklets (containing ten at **3½p**): blue covers
with the following illustrations

Cuthred Penny	3.00
Edward I Silver Groat	3.00
The Canada Life Assurance Group	2.50

45p booklet (containing ten at **4½p**): brown cover

Elizabeth Gold Crown	3.75

50p booklets (containing five **½p**, seven **2½p**, ten **3p**):
blue-green covers with the following illustrations:

Large Bindweed	5.50
Primrose	6.50
Honey Suckle	6.50
Hop	7.00
Common Violet	7.00
Lords-and-Ladies	7.00
Wood Anemone	7.00
Deadly Nightshade	6.50
The Canada Life Assurance Group	6.50

As above, but contents changed to five **3p** and ten
3½p with deeper green cover:

The Canada Life Assurance Group	3.50

85p booklet (containing five **3½p** and fifteen **4½p**):
purple cover:

The Canada Life Assurance Group	6.00

**The following booklets consist of card covers into
which the stamps are stuck by the margin**

10p (containing two **½p**, and three **1p**, one **6p**): cover
design of '**10p**' made up of red dots

10p (containing two **½p**, two **1p**, one **7p**): comes with
the following illustrations (farm buildings):

Kent	0.75
Northern Ireland	0.75
Yorkshire	0.75
Wales	0.75

Scotland	0.75
Sussex	0.75

10p (containing two **1p**, one **8p**): cover illustrates
Post Office stand at LONDON 1980 International
Stamp Exhibition   0.70
(NB: this booklet exists with differing postal rates
printed on the inner covers.)

50p (containing two **½p**, two **1p**, two **6½p**, four **8½p**): cover
lists contents with bold '50p'

a) **6½p** with one phosphor band at left	2.50
b) **6½p** with one phosphor band at right	2.50

50p (containing two **1p**, three **7p**, three **9p**): cover
design as above

a) **7p** with one phosphor band at left	3.00
b) **7p** with one band at right	5.00

50p (contents as before); covers with the following
illustrations:
The following six booklets exist with the **7p** stamp
with either one phosphor band on the left or one
phosphor band of the right.

	Left Band	Right Band
Clement Talbot Van	2.75	4.50
Austin Cape Taxi	3.00	4.50
Morris Royal Mail Van	3.25	5.00
Guy Electric Dustcart	3.75	5.00
Albion Van	5.50	6.50
Leyland Fire Engine	3.50	5.00

50p (containing two **2p**, two **8p**, three 10p): cover
with the following illustrations:

Leyland Fire Engine (**8p** band at left or right)	2.50

50p (containing two **2p**, two **8p**, three 10p): cover
with the following illustration:

Rolls Royce Silver Ghost (**8p** band at left or right)	2.50

50p (containing three **2p**, two **10p**, two **12p**): covers
with the following illustrations:

Grand Prix Austin (**10p** band at left or right)	2.50
1903-1905 Vauxhall car (**10p** band at left or right)	2.25
1900 Daimler (**10p** band at left or right)	2.25

50p (containing one **½p**, one **1p**, one **14p** and three
11½p): covers with the following illustrations:

Lanchester of 1896 (**11½p** band at left or right)	2.25
Bullnose Morris of 1913 (**11½p** band at left or right)	2.75
Mugdock Castle, Stirlingshire (**11½p** band at left or right)	2.25

50p (containing three **2½p**, two **4p** and three **11½p**);
covers with the following illustrations:
Mugdock Castle, Stirlingshire

a) **11½p** band at left	6.50

MACHINS

b) 11½p band at right   3.50
Mow Cop Castle
a) 11½p band at left   5.00
b) 11½p band at right   3.50

50p (containing one ½p, four 3p pink and three
12½p): covers with the following illustrations:
Paxton's Tower (12½p band at left or right)   2.00
Temple of the Winds, Northern Ireland
(12½p band at left or right)   2.00
Temple of the Sun, Stourhead, Wilts
(12½p band at left or right)   2.00
Water Garden, Cleveden, Bucks
(12½p band at left or right)   2.00
Bagot Goat
(12½p band at left or right)   2.50

50p (containing two 1p, three 3½p and three 12½p, all with
one centre band): covers with the following illustrations:
Gloucester Old Spot Pig   3.50
Toulouse Goose   3.50
Orkney Sheep   3.50

50p (containing three 1p, two 4p and three 13p, all with one
centre band): front cover with the following illustrations:
Orchids – Dendrobium nobile   2.50
Cyripedium calcedolus and ophrys apifera   2.50
Bifienasia and Vandatricolour   2.50
Cymbodium and Arpophyllum   2.50

50p (containing three 17p with two phosphor bands
and 'stars' printed on the gummed side): front cover
with the following illustrations:
Pillar box   2.50
Emperor dragonfly   2.00
Common frog   3.00

50p (containing three 17p with two phosphor bands
but without 'stars' printed on the gummed side):
front cover with the following illustration:
Common frog   2.00

50p (containing two 1p with one centre band and
four 12p emerald-green with one centre band): front
cover with the following illustration:
Hadrian's Wall   6.50

50p (containing one 1p right band, one 13p left band
and two 18p – two bands): front cover with the
following illustrations:
Roman Theatre at St Albans   2.50
Portchester Castle, Hampshire   2.50
Weather Vane at Thomas Lord's original
cricket ground   2.00
The Ashes Urn   2.25
The present Lord's pavilion   2.25
The New Stand   2.25

50p (containing one 1p, two 5p and three 13p, all with one
centre band): front cover with the following illustrations:
Moorhen and Dabchicks   4.00
Great Pond Snail   3.75
Bondnant Gardens, Colwyn Bay   3.00
Botanical Gardens, Edinburgh   3.00
Mount Stuart Gardens, Northern Ireland (the stamp pane in
this booklet has the side edges imperforate)   3.00
Mount Stewart (corrected spelling)   3.00
Kew Gardens   2.50
Common whelk and jellyfish   2.75

50p (containing one 1p, one 13p, two 18p):
Pigs   2.75
Birds   2.50
Elephants   2.50

50p (containing one 14p, two 19p):
The Yeomen of the Guard   3.75
The Pirates of Penzance   3.75
The Mikado   3.75
Hermit crab, bladder wrack and laver spire shell   3.50

50p (containing two 15p, one 20p):
Armstrong Whitworth Atalanta and De Havilland
Dragon Rapide   6.50
Vickers Viscount 806 and De Havilland Comet 4 (this book
contains the Penny Black Anniversary definitives)   5.50
BAC 1-11 and VC10   3.50
BAe ATP, BAe 146 and Concorde   3.50

50p (containing two 1p, two 24p):
Sir Arthur Evans at Crete   2.00
Howard Carter of the tomb of Tutankhamun   2.00
Sir Austen Layard in Assyria   1.75
Sir Flinders Petrie at Giza   2.25
Sheriff's Millennium 1992   1.75
Airmail markings   1.75
Ship mail markings   1.75
Registered mail   1.75

50p (containing two 25p):
'Paid' marking   1.75
Swan with Two Necks   1.75
Bull and Mouth   1.75
Golden Cross   1.75
Pheasant Inn   1.75
John O'Groats   1.75
Land's End   1.75
St. David's Head   3.00
Giant's Causeway   3.00

£1 (containing six 17p advanced coated paper): cover
with the following illustration:
Violin   4.00

£1 (containing one 13p right band and five 18p two
bands): front cover with the following illustrations:

French horn	5.00
Bass Clarinet	4.50
A Study in Scarlet	5.00
The Hound of the Baskervilles	4.75
The Adventure of the Speckled Band (the stamp pane in this booklet has the side edges imperforate)	5.00
Bears	4.00
Oliver Twist	4.25
Nicholas Nickleby	4.50
David Copperfield	3.50
Great Expectations	8.00
Sea Urchin, starfish and crab	3.50

£1 (containing five 20p):

Wicken Fen	4.75
Wicken Fen (glossy cover) (this book contains the Penny Black Anniversary definitives)	7.50
Click Mill (this book contains the Penny Black Anniversary definitives)	6.00
Jack and Jill Mills	3.50
Howell Mill	4.00

£1 (containing two 2p, four 24p):

Punch illustrations by Richard Doyle and Hoffnung	3.00
Punch illustrations by Sir John Tenniel and Eric Burgin	3.00
Punch illustrations by Sir John Tenniel and Anton	3.00
Punch illustrations by Sir John Tenniel and Hewison	3.00
Sheriff's Millennium 1992	3.00
University of Wales	4.00
St. Hilda's College, Oxford	4.00
Marlborough College	4.00

£1 (containing four 25p):

Free Church of Scotland College	3.75
Herbert Asquith	3.00
David Lloyd-George	3.00
Winston Churchill	3.00
Clement Attlee	3.00
Violette Szabo	2.75
Dame Vera Lynn	2.75
R. J. Mitchell	2.75
Archibald McIndoe	3.25

The following booklets have a red cover featuring the Royal Mail cruciform.

£1 (four at 25p)	4.00
£1 (two 1p, one 20p, three 26p – stamps printed in litho)	3.00
£1 (two 1p, one 20p, three 26p – stamps printed in gravure)	15.00
£1 (one 1p, one 2p, one 19p, three 26p	3.00
£1 (one 2nd, three 1st)	3.00

The following booklets all have the panes with the margin at the left or right: the price is the same either way except where indicated.

65p (containing ten 6½p): cover lists contents with

bold '65p'	5.50
a) with left margin	12.00

70p (containing ten 7p): cover lists contents with

bold '70p'	4.50

70p (contents as above): coves with the following illustrations:

Horse-shoeing	4.00
a) with left margin	30.00
Thatching	4.00
a) with left margin	£140
Dry-stone Walling	4.00
a) with left margin	£150
Wheel making	4.00
a) with left margin	5.50
Wattle fence making	4.50
a) with left margin	12.50
Basket making	4.00
a) with left margin	6.00
Keddlestone Hall (Derby Postcode Publicity)	6.00

80p (containing ten 8p): cover with the following illustration:

1915 Vickers	3.75

85p booklets (containing ten 8½p): cover lists contents

with bold '85p'	6.50
a) with left margin	7.50

90p booklet (containing ten 9p): cover lists contents

with bold '90p'	4.00
a) with right margin	5.00

90p booklets (contents as above): covers with the following illustrations:

Grand Union Canal	4.50
a) with left margin	20.00
Llangollen Canal	4.00
a) with right margin	£275
Kennet and Avon Canal	7.00
a) with left margin	11.00
Caledonian Canal	4.50
a) with right margin	6.50
Regents Canal	7.00
a) with left margin	13.00
Leeds and Liverpool Canal	6.00
Tramway Museum, Crich (Derby Postcode Publicity)	6.00

£1 (containing ten 10p – all-over phosphor): cover with the following illustration:

Ironbridge, Telford, Shropshire	3.75

£1 (containing ten 10p – one centre band): covers with the following illustrations:

Sopwith Camel and Vickers Vimy	3.50

Hawker Fury and Handley Page Heyford	4.00
Wellington Bomber and Hurricane	3.50

£1.15 (containing ten 11½p – one centre band): covers with the following illustrations:

Spitfire and Lancaster	3.75
Lightning and Vulcan	4.00
Natural History Museum, London	3.75
National Museum of Antiquities of Scotland	3.75

£1.20 (containing ten 12p yellow-green): covers with the following illustrations:

Beetle Mill, Ireland	4.00
Tin mines in Cornwall	4.00
Bottle Kilns, Stoke	4.00

£1.20 (containing ten 12p emerald-green – one centre band): coves with the following illustrations:

Pillar box	4.00
National Gallery	3.75
'Maybe'	3.75

£1.25 (containing ten 12½p – one centre band): covers with the following illustrations:

Ashmolean Museum, Oxford	3.75
National Museum of Wales	4.00
Ulster Museum, Belfast	3.75
Castle Museum, York	3.75
GWR Isambard Kingdom Brunel	4.50
LMS Class 4P Passenger Tank Engine	5.00
LNER Mallard	4.25
SR/BR Clan Line	4.25

£1.30 (containing ten 13p – on centre band): cover with the following illustrations:

Swansea/Mumbles Railway Car	3.25
The Glasgow Tram	4.00
Blackpool car No. 717	3.75
'D' Class London tram	3.50
The Three Bears starting the day	3.50
Keep in touch	3.50
Garden Scene	3.25
Brighter Writer	3.50
Jolly Postman	3.50
Linnean Society	3.75
Recipes (vegetables)	3.50
Children's Parties (balloons)	3.50

£1.30 (containing six 14p (two bands), two 11½p (band at left) and two 11½p (band at right): covers with the following illustrations:

Penny Black	3.50
a) with left margin	4.50
King George V ½d and 1d 'Downey Head'	5.00
a) with right margin	17.50

£1.40 (containing ten 14p – phosphor coated paper): covers with the following illustrations:

Preston Mill in Scotland	3.75
Talyllyn Railway, Tywyn	4.00
Costumes of 1860-1880	4.00
Costumes of 1815-1830	4.00
Legal Charge	3.75
Fox Talbot photographs	3.75

£1.43 containing six 15½p two bands, two 12½p band at left and two 12½p band at right: covers with the following illustrations:

James Chalmers portrait	4.00
Edmund Dulac (KGVI 5/- red)	4.00
Forces Postal Service	4.00
£5 orange of 1882	4.25
Postmark Collecting	4.25

£1.43 contents as above: cover illustration as follows:

Golden Hinde inscribed 'The Holiday Postcard Stamp Book'	3.75

£1.45 containing ten at 16p – phosphor coated paper – sold at a discount of 15p off the face value: stamps have a 'D' printed on the gummed side. Cover illustration as follows:

Lyme Regis, Dorset	5.00

£1.46 Containing six 16p two bands, two 12½p band at left and two 12 ½p band at right: panes have either the four 12½p followed by one 16p on the bottom row, or one 16p followed by four 12½p – prices are the same either way: covers have the following illustrations:

Seahorse high values	8.00
Parcel Post	7.50
Regional Stamps	7.50

£1.50 containing six 17p two bands, two 12p band at left and two 12p band at right: panes have either the four 12p followed by one 17p on the bottom row, or one 17p followed by four 12p – prices are the same either way: covers with the following illustrations:

Pillar box	4.00
National Gallery	4.00
'No'	4.50

£1.54 containing six 17p two bands, two 13p band at left and two 13p band at right: panes have either the four 13p followed by one 17p on the bottom row, or one 17p followed by four 13p – prices are the same either way. Covers with the following illustrations:

To Pay Labels	3.75
Embossed stamps	3.75
Surface printed stamps	3.75
350th Anniversary of The Post Office	3.75

£1.55 containing ten 15½p – phosphor coated paper: covers with the following illustrations:

Costumes of 1830-1850	3.75
Costumes of 1850-1860	3.75
Costumes of 1860-1880	4.00
Costumes of 1880-1900	4.25

MACHINS

£1.55 containing ten at 17p – phosphor coated paper – sold at a discount: stamps have a 'D' printed on the gummed side. Cover illustration as follows:
Paper boat and paper plane   5.50

£1.60 containing ten at 16p – phosphor coated paper: cover illustrations as follows.

Birthday Cake	5.25
Weavers Cottages, Bibury	4.50
Write It	4.25

£1.70 containing ten at 17p – phosphor coated paper: cover illustrations as follows:

Love Letters	4.50
Hands exchanging letters	4.00
Pillar box	4.25
National Gallery	4.50
'Yes'	4.25

£1.80 containing ten at 18p – phosphor coated paper: cover illustration as follows:

Rag, Tag and Bobtail	5.25
Keep in Touch	7.25
Garden Scene	5.25
Brighter Writer	5.25
Jolly Postman	5.00
Linnean Society	4.75
Recipes (fruits)	5.00
Children's Parties (balloons)	5.00

£1.90 (containing ten at 19p):

Pocket Planner	5.50
Fox Talbot photographs	5.50

£2 (containing eight at 25p):

Motorised cycle	3.75
Motor mail van	3.75
Electric mail van	3.75
Sir Rowland Hill (London and Brighton Railway)	3.75
Sir Rowland Hill (Hazlewood School)	3.75
Sir Rowland Hill (Secretary to the Post Office)	4.50
Sir Rowland Hill (Uniform Penny Postage)	4.50

The following booklets have a red cover featuring the Royal Mail cruciform.

£2 (eight 25p)	4.50
£2 (one 20p, seven 26p – stamps printed in litho)	4.00
£2 (one 20p, seven 26p – stamps printed in gravure)	15.00
£2 (one 19p, seven 26p)	4.50
£2 (two 2nd, six 1st)	4.25

Christmas booklets
The following booklets have panes with the margin at the left only

£1.60 containing ten 7p one band, ten 9p two bands: cover shows a decoration of holly with the legend 'Greetings Christmas 1978'   4.00

£1.80 containing ten 8p one band, ten 10p two bands: cover shows Christmas cracker with the legend 'Greetings Christmas 1979'   4.25

£2.20 containing ten 10p one band, ten 12p two bands: cover show Nativity Scene with the legend 'Greetings Christmas 1980'   4.50

£2.55 containing ten 14p two bands, ten 11½p one band: cover shows skating scene with legend 'Christmas Greetings 1981'   6.25

£2.50 containing ten 15½p, two bands, then 12½p one band – sold at a discount of 30p off the face value. Stamps have a blue star printed on the gummed side.
Cover shows Christmas mummers   6.50

£2.20 containing twenty 12½p, one band – sold at a discount of 30p off the face value. Stamps have a blue star printed on the gummed side. Cover shows a Pantomime Scene   6.00

£1.20 containing ten 13p light brown – one centre band – sold at a discount of 10p off the face value. Stamps with a blue star printed on the gummed side. Cover shows Cooking Shetland Yule cakes   5.50

These booklets contain the Christmas stamps of the relevant year.

1990, November 13. 20 at 17p	7.00
1991, November 12. 20 at 18p	6.25
1992, November 10. 20 at 18p	6.25
1993, November 9. 20 at 19p	7.00
1993, November 9. 10 at 25p	5.75
1994, November 1. 20 at 19p	6.75
1994, November 1. 10 at 25p	4.25
1995, October 30. 20 at 19p	7.00
1995, October 30. 10 at 25p	4.25
1995, October 30. 4 at 60p	4.25
1996, October 28. 20 at 2nd	7.00
1996, October 28. 10 at 1st	4.25
1997, October 27. 20 at 2nd	6.75
1997, October 27. 10 at 1st	5.00
1998, November 2. 20 at 20p	6.50
1998, November 2. 10 at 26p	4.50
1999, November 2. 20 at 19p	6.75
1999, November 2. 20 at 26p	4.75
2000, November 7. 20 at 2nd	6.25
2000, November 7. 10 at 1st	4.75
2001, November 6. 24 at 2nd	7.50
2001, November 6. 12 at 1st	5.50
2002, November 5. 24 at 2nd	7.50
2002, November 5. 12 at 1st	5.25
2003, November 4. 24 at 2nd	8.00
2003, November 4. 12 at 1st	5.50
2004, November 2. 24 at 2nd	7.00
2004, November 2. 12 at 1st	4.75
2005, November 1. 24 at 2nd	7.00
2005, November 1. 12 at 1st	4.75

MACHINS – DECIMAL HIGH VALUES

10p cerise (phosphor paper)

1970, June 17 – 1972. Machin decimal high values.
Des: Arnold Machin. Printed in recess by Bradbury, Wilkinson.
No wmk. Perf: 12.

10p cerise (phosphor paper)	0.40	0.25
20p olive-green	0.50	0.30
50p ultramarine	1.50	0.65
£1 black (December 6, 1972)	2.50	0.60

NB: Initially the £1 was identical to that issued on March 5, 1969, but was printed in sheets of 100 instead of sheets of 40. However, on December 6, 1972 the £1 was re-released with the denomination in a changed typeface, namely Perpetua.

£1 olive, deep green

1977, February 2 – 1987.
Machin photogravure decimal high values.
Des: Arnold Machin. Printed in photogravure by Harrison. Perf:
14 x 15.

£1 olive, deep green	1.75	0.50
£1.30 steel blue, buff (August 3, 1983)	3.00	3.50
£1.33 lilac, deep blue (August 28, 1984)	4.50	5.00
£1.41 deep blue, pale blue, green (September 17, 1985)	5.00	5.50
£1.50 rose-lilac, blue-black (September 2, 1986)	3.50	3.00
£1.60 buff, blue-green		

(September 15, 1987)	4.00	3.50
£2 emerald, deep purple	3.50	0.60
£5 pink, blue	8.00	2.00
Set	30.00	20.00
Gutter pairs	70.00	
Traffic light gutter pairs	80.00	
First Day Cover (£1, £2, £5)	8.00	
First Day Cover (£1.30)	3.00	
First Day Cover (£1.33)	4.00	
First Day Cover (£1.41)	5.00	
First Day Cover (£1.50)	5.00	
First Day Cover (£1.60)	5.00	

Carrickfergus Castle (£1)
Caernarfon Castle (£1.50)
Edinburgh Castle (£2)
Windsor Castle (£5)

1988, October 18. Castle high value definitives.
Engraved by C. Matthews from photographs by Prince Andrew.
Recess printed by Harrison.
£1, £1.50, £2, £5

Set	16.00	4.50
Gutter pairs	35.00	
Centre cross gutter blocks of four	75.00	
First Day Cover	20.00	

Caernarfon Castle (£1.50), silhouette head

1992, March 24. Castle definitives.
As issue of October 18, 1988, but Queen's head is in silhouette printed in optically variable ink which changes colour from gold to green depending on the angle at which it is viewed. In addition, an elliptical perforation is included along the side of each stamp.
£1, £1.50, £2, £5

MACHINS

Set	19.50	4.00
Gutter pairs	40.00	
Centre cross gutter blocks of four	85.00	
First Day Cover	15.00	
Stamp cards	10.00	40.00

NB: the £1.50, £2 and £5 exist with either blue tinted PVAD gum, or white PVA gum. The date of release of the stamp cards is not the day of issue of the stamps.

1995, August 22. Castle definitive: new value
As issue of March 24, 1992, but new value (the £1 was withdrawn).

£3

Single stamp	8.50	1.35
Gutter pair	18.00	
Centre cross gutter block of four	40.00	
First Day Cover	5.00	
Stamp card	7.00	20.00

NB: this stamp exists with either blue tinted PVAD gum, or white PVA gum.

1997, July 29. Castle definitives.
As £1.50, £2 and £5 of March 24, 1992, and £3 of August 8, 1995, but printed in recess and silk screen (for Queen's portrait) by Enschedé. Engraved by Inge Madlé.

£1.50, £2, £3, £5

Set	45.00	10.00
Gutter pairs	95.00	
Centre cross gutter blocks of four	200.00	
First Day Cover	25.00	

Britannia (£10)

1993, March 2. £10 Definitive.
Des: B. Craddock and Roundel Design Group. Printed in litho by Questa, also including die-stamping and embossing of Braille.

£10

Single stamp	16.50	7.50
First Day Cover	15.00	
Stamp card	4.00	27.50

March 9, 1999. Small format Machin portrait definitives.
Printed in intaglio by Enschedé. Engraved by C. Slania.

£1.50, £2, £3, £5

Set	20.00	10.00
First Day Cover	15.00	

April 11, 2000.
Printed in intaglio by De La Rue.

£1.50, £2, £3, £5

Set	18.50	10.00
First Day Cover	20.00	

July 1, 2003.
Printed in gravure by De La Rue.

£1.50, £2, £3, £5

Set	18.00	18.00
First Day Cover	20.00	

STOP PRESS!
Pictorial definitives
The follwoing designs are intended for use with Smilers sheets, but are also made avilable as a booklet. All are small-size pictorial definitives.

Guzmania splendens (1st)
Hello (1st)
LOVE (1st)
Union flag (1st)
Teddy bear (1st)
Robin looking through pillar box slit (1st)

2005, October 4. Pictorial definitives.
Printed in litho by Walsall. Self-adhesive. Issued in booklets containing one of each of teh six designs.

Booklet	2.50	
First Day Cover		4.00

QUEEN ELIZABETH II
DECIMAL SPECIAL ISSUES

'A Mountain Road' by Flanagan (3p)
'Deer's Meadow' by Carr (7½p)
'Slieve na brock' by Middleton (9p)

1971, June 16. Ulster Painstius
Des: S. Rose.

3p multicoloured	0.20	0.10
7½p mulitcoloured	0.50	0.60
9p multicoloured	0.60	0.60
Set	0.50	0.60
First Day Cover		1.00

John Keats (3p)
Thomas Gray (5p)
Sir Walter Scott (7½p)

1971, July 28. Literary Anniversaries
Des: Rosalind Dease

3p blue, black, gold	0.15	0.10
5p olive, black, gold	0.50	0.50
7½p brown, black, gold	0.60	0.60
Set	0.50	0.60
First Day Cover		1.00

Servicemen and a nurse (3p)
A Roman Centurion (7½p)
Ruby Players (9p)

1971, August 25. Anniversaries
Des: F. Wegner

3p multicoloured	0.20	0.10
7½p multicoloured	0.75	0.60
9p multicoloured	0.80	0.70
Set	0.50	0.60

First Day Cover		1.00

Commemorates the 50th anniversary of the British Legion, the 1900th anniversary of the City of York and the centenary of the Ruby Football Union.

University College, Aberystwyth (3p)
University of Southampton (5p)
University of Leicester (7½p)
University of Essex (9p)

1971, September 22. University Buildings
Des: N. Jenkins.

3p multicoloured	0.20	0.10
5p multicoloured	0.60	0.40
7½p multicoloured	0.75	0.75
9p multicoloured	1.00	1.00
Set	0.75	1.00
First Day Cover		1.10

'Dream of the Wise Men' (2½p)
'Adoration of the Magi' (3p)
'Ride of the Magi' (7½p)

1971, October 13. Christmas
Des: Clarke, Clement and Hughes based on stained glass windows at Canterbury Cathedral

2½p multicoloured	0.15	0.10
3p multicoloured	0.15	0.10
7½p multicoloured	1.00	0.90
Set	0.30	0.40
First Day Cover		1.00

(NB – a pack was produced by the Post Office for Heinz containing six 2½p stamps: price £18)

Sir James Clarke Ross (3p)
Sir Martin Frobisher (5p)

Henry Hudson (7½p)
Captain Scott (9p)

1972, February 16. Polar Explorers
Des: Marjorie Seynor

3p multicoloured	0.20	0.15
5p multicoloured	0.50	0.40
7½p multicoloured	0.60	0.60
9p multicoloured	0.75	0.75
Set	0.60	0.75
First Day Cover		1.10

Tutankhamun (3p)   *~ corner block of 6 w/traffic*
Coastguard (7½p)
Ralph Vaughan Williams (9p)

1972, April 26. Anniversaries
Des: Rosalind Dease **3p**, F. Wegner **7½p**, C. Abbott **9p**

3p multicoloured	0.10	0.10
7½p multicoloured	0.50	0.50
9p multicoloured	0.50	0.50
Set	0.50	0.60
First Day Cover		1.10

Commemorates the discovery of the tomb of Tutankhamun 1922, the 150th anniversary of HM Coastguards and Ralph Vaughan Williams 1872-1958

St. Andrew's, Greensted-juxta-Ongar, Essex (3p)
All Saints, Earls Barton, Northants (4p)
St. Andrew's, Lethringsett, Norfolk (5p)
St. Andrew's, Helpringham, Lincs (7½p)
St. Mary the Virgin, Huish Episcopi, Somerset (9p)

1972, June 21. Village Churches
Des: R. Maddox

3p multicoloured	0.15	0.15
4p multicoloured	0.60	0.60
5p multicoloured	0.60	0.60
7½p multicoloured	0.75	0.75
9p multicoloured	1.00	1.00
Set	0.75	1.00
First Day Cover		1.50

(NB – a Souvenir Pack was produced for sale at the

International Stamp Exhibition, Belgica 72, containing the Christmas 1971 and the Village Churches series of stamps: price £12)

Microphones (3p)
Horn Loudspeaker (5p)
Colour Television (7½p)
Oscillator and Spark Transmitter (9p)

1972, September 13. 50th Anniversary of the BBC
Des: D. Gentleman.

3p multicoloured	0.10	0.10
5p multicoloured	0.35	0.40
7½p multicoloured	0.50	0.50
9p multicoloured	0.75	0.75
Set	0.75	0.80
First Day Cover		1.10

(NB – a presentation pack containing the 3p, 5p and 7½p values was prepared by the BBC for distribution to its staff: price £21)

Angel with trumpet (2½p)
Angel with lute (3p)
Angel with harp (7½p)

1972, October 19. Christmas
Des: Sally Stiff.

2½p multicoloured (one phosphor band)	0.10	0.05
3p multicoloured	0.10	0.05
7½p multicoloured	0.50	0.40
Set	0.25	0.90
First Day Cover		0.60

From this time modern British stamps started appearing in sheets with gutters. Gutter pairs and traffic light gutter pairs are priced in complete sets where applicable and in unfolded condition.

QEII SPECIALS

Queen Elizabeth II and Prince Phillip (3p), (20p)

1972, November 20, Royal Silver Wedding
Des: J. Matthews from photograph by Norman Parkinson.
All-over phosphor 3p, no phosphor 20p
i) printed on a 'Rembrandt' machine

3p deep blue, brown, silver	0.15	0.15
20p deep purple, brown, silver	0.50	0.50
Set	0.50	0.60
First Day Cover		0.60

ii) Printed on the 'Jumelle' machine.

3p deep blue, brown, silver	0.20	0.20
Gutter Pair	0.30	
Traffic Light Gutter Pair	7.00	

(NB – the portraits tend to be lighter in shade on the Jumelle printing compared with the Rembrandt printing)

Jigsaw pieces representing Europe (3p), (5p)

1973, January 3, European Communities
Des: P. Murdoch. All multicoloured, but background colours given.

3p lilac	0.15	0.10
5p blue	0.40	0.40
5p light green	0.40	0.40
Se-tenant pair	1.00	1.75
Set	0.50	0.60
First Day Cover		0.80

Oak Tree (9p)

1973, February 28. British Trees
Des: D. Gentleman

9p multicoloured	0.25	0.25

First Day Cover	0.50

Unless otherwise stated, the following issues have 'all-over' phosphor.

David Livingstone (3p – 1)
H.M. Stanley (3p - 2)
Francis Drake (5p)
Walter Raleigh (7½p)
Charles Sturt (9p)

1973, April 18. British Explorers
Des: Marjorie Seynor. All-over phosphor

3p multicoloured design 1	0.25	0.15
3p multicoloured design 2	0.25	0.15
Se-Tenant Pair	0.60	1.00
5p multicoloured	0.60	0.60
7½p multicoloured	0.75	0.80
9p multicoloured	0.75	0.80
Set	0.80	1.00
First Day Cover		1.10

About to bat (3p)
Watching the ball (7½p)
Leaving the wicket (9p)

1973, May 16. County Cricket
Des: E Ripley, based on drawings by Harry Furniss of W.G. Grace

3p bistre, black, gold	0.10	0.15
7½p green, black, gold	0.75	0.70
9p blue, black, gold	0.75	0.75
Set	1.50	1.00
First Day Cover		1.25
Stamp card (of 3p design)	40.00	

Self portrait of Joshua Reynolds (3p)
Self portrait of Henry Raeburn (5p)
'Nelly O'Brien' by Reynolds (7½p)
'Rev. R. Walker' by Raeburn (9p)

1973, July. British Painters
Des: S. Rose.

3p multicoloured	0.10	0.15
5p multicoloured	0.25	0.25
7½p multicoloured	0.60	0.60
9p multicoloured	0.60	0.60
Set	0.55	0.65
First Day Cover		1.00

These stamps honour Sir Joshua Reynolds, 1723-1792, and Sir Henry Raeburn, 1756-1823.

Court Masque Costumes (3p-1)
St Paul's church, Covent Garden (3p-2)
Prince's Lodging, Newmarket (5p-1)
Court Masque Stage Scene (5p-2)

1973, August 15. 400th Anniversary of Birth of Inigo Jones
Des: Rosalind Dease. Printed in litho and typo by Bradbury, Wilkinson.

3p mauve, black, gold design 1	0.40	0.15
3p brown, black, gold design 2	0.40	0.15
Se-tenant pair	0.80	1.25
5p blue, black, gold design 1	0.50	0.40
5p olive, black, gold design 2	0.50	0.40
Se-tenant pair	1.00	1.50
Set	0.50	0.65
First Day Cover		0.90
Stamp card (of 3p, design 2)	50.00	£225

Palace of Westminster from Whitehall (8p)
Palace of Westminster from Millbank (10p)

1973, September 12. Commonwealth Parliamentary Conference
Des: R. Downer. Printed in recess and litho by Bradbury, Wilkinson.

8p yellow, brown, black	0.35	0.35
10p black, gold	0.40	0.40
Set	0.40	0.50
First Day Cover		0.75
Stamp card (of 8p design)	25.00	£150

Unless otherwise stated, the following stamps have blue-tinted polyvinyl alcohol dextrin (PVAD) gum.

Princess Anne and Captain Mark Phillips (3½p), (20p)

1973, November 14. Royal Wedding
Des: C. Clements and E. Hughes based on photograph by Lord Lichfield

3½p violet, silver	0.15	0.10
20p brown, silver	0.60	0.60
Set	0.50	0.55
Gutter Pairs		1.50
Traffic Light Gutter		
Pairs	50.00	
First Day Cover		0.60
Stamp card (of 3½p design)		5.00
30.00		

NB – the 3½p exists from sheets guillotined in the wrong place giving incorrect inscriptions within the gutter: price for a mis-cut gutter pair £30.

Good King Wenceslas five different designs representing the verses of this carol (3p)
Good King Wenceslas, the Page and the Peasant (3½p)

1973, November 28. Christmas
Des: D. Gentleman. 3p values have one phosphor band. All multicoloured. These stamps exist with either gum Arabic, PVA gum or dextrin gum as indicated.

	Gum Arabic		Dextrin Gum	
3p design 1	0.40	-	0.40	0.20
3p design 2	0.40	-	0.40	0.20
3p design 3	0.40	-	0.40	0.20
3p design 4	0.40	-	0.40	0.20

3p design 5	0.40	-	0.40	20
Se-tenant strip of five	1.75	-	1.75	2.00
	PVA gum		Dextrin gum	
3½p	30	-	30	15
Set	1.00	-	1.00	1.50
First Day Cover				1.20

Horse Chestnut (10p)

1974, February 27. British Trees
Des: D. Gentleman.

10p multicoloured	0.20	0.25
Gutter Pair	1.00	
Traffic Light Gutter Pair	21.00	
First Day Cover		0.50
Stamp card	75.00	75.00

First Motor Fire Engine 1904 (3½p)
Fire Engine 1863 (5½p)
Steam Fire Engine (8p)
Fire Engine 1766 (10p)

1974, April 24. Fire Engines
Des: D. Gentleman. Dextrin gum except where stated

3½p multicoloured	0.10	0.15
a) with PVA gum	9.00	-
5½p multicoloured	0.30	0.40
8p multicoloured	0.40	0.40
10p multicoloured	0.50	0.40
Set	0.75	0.80
Gutter Pairs	1,75	
Traffic Light Gutter Pairs	25.00	
First Day Cover		1.25
Stamp card (of 3½p design)	75.00	75.00

P&O Packet Steamer 'Peninsular' (3½p)
Coronation Airmail 1911 (5½p)

Blue Airmail Van (8p)
Imperial Airways Flying boat (10p)

1974, June 12. Centenary of the UPU
Des: Rosalind Dease.

3½p multicoloured	10	15
5½p multicoloured	35	30
8p multicoloured	45	40
10p multicoloured	50	50
Set	0.50	0.75
Gutter Pairs	1.50	
Traffic Light Gutter Pairs	20.00	
First Day Cover		0.75

Robert the Bruce (4½p)
Owain Glyndwr (5½p)
Henry V (8p)
The Black Prince (10p)

1974, July 10. Famous Britons
Des: F. Wegner.

4½p multicoloured	15	15
5½p multicoloured	50	40
8p multicoloured	75	60
10p multicoloured	75	60
Set	0.55	0.75
Gutter Pairs	1.60	
Traffic Light Gutter Pairs		7.00
First Day Cover		1.50
Stamp card (of each design)	16.00	50.00

Portrait of Sir Winston Churchill as Lord Warden of the Cinque Ports (4½p)
Prime Minister (5½p)
Secretary for War and Air (8p)
War Correspondent in South Africa (10p)

1974, October 9. Birth Centenary of Sir Winston Churchill
Des: C. Clements and E. Hughes. Dextrin gum except where stated.

4½p blue, turquoise, silver	0.10	0.15
5½p sepia, grey, silver	0.35	0.30
8p crimson, pink, silver	0.30	0.30
a) with PVA gum	1.25	-
10p brown, light brown, silver	0.30	0.30
Set	0.90	0.85
Gutter Pairs	1.75	
Traffic Light Gutter Pairs	16.50	
First Day Cover		1.00
Stamp card (of 5½p design)	3.50	17.00

'Adoration of the Magi' (3½p)
'The Nativity' (4½p)
'Virgin and Child' (8p)
'Virgin and Child' (10p)

1974, November 27. Christmas
Des: Peter Hatch Partnership based on church roof bosses.
All multicoloured

3½p one centre phosphor band	0.15	0.15
a) phosphor band to right of stamp	0.20	0.25
4½p	0.15	0.10
8p	0.40	0.50
10p	0.40	0.40
Set	0.50	0.60
Gutter Pairs	2.25	
Traffic Light Gutter Pairs	25.00	
First Day Cover		0.90

Invalid in Wheelchair (4½p + 1½p)

1975, January 22. Health and Handicap Charities
Des: P. Sharland

4½p + 1½p blue, grey-blue *cut blad* 0.15 ✓		0.15
Gutter Pair	0.30	
Traffic Light Gutter Pair	0.50	
First Day Cover		0.50

NB – the surcharge of 1½p was donated to Health and
Handicap Charities.

'Peace – Burial at Sea' (4½p)
'Snowstorm' (5½p)
'The Arsenal, Venice' (8p)
'St. Laurent' (10p)

1975, February 19. Bicentenary of the Birth of Turner
Des: S. Rose

4½p multicoloured	0.10	0.15
5½p multicoloured	0.15	0.15
8p multicoloured	0.25	0.25
10p multicoloured	0.30	0.35
Set	0.50	0.60
Gutter Pairs	1.25	
Traffic Light Gutter Pairs	2.70	
First Day Cover		1.25
Stamp card (of 5½p design)	22.00	17.00

Charlotte Square, Edinburgh (7p-1)
The Rows, Chester (7p-2)
Royal Observatory, Greenwich (8p)
St. George's Chapel, Windsor (10p)
National Theatre, London (12p)

1975, April 23. European Architectural Heritage Year.
Des: P Gauld

7p multicoloured design 1	0.15	0.15
7p multicoloured design 2	0.15	0.15
Se-tenant pair	0.30	1.25
8p multicoloured	0.20	0.35
10p multicoloured	0.30	0.40
12p multicoloured	40	40
Set	0.75	0.80
Gutter Pairs	2.25	
Traffic Light Gutter Pairs	12.00	
First Day Cover		1.00
Stamp card (of 7p and 8p designs)	6.00	22.00

Sailing Dinghies (7p)
Racing Keel Boats (8p)
Cruising Yachts (10p)
Multihulls (12p)

1975, June 11. Sailing
Des: A. Restall. Printed in photogravure and recess by Harrison

7p multicoloured	0.15	0.20
8p multicoloured	0.20	0.40
10p multicoloured	0.25	0.40
12p multicoloured	0.50	0.60
Set	0.50	0.60
Gutter Pairs	1.50	
Traffic Light Gutter Pairs	10.00	
First Day Cover		0.90
Stamp card (of 8p design)	4.00	15.00

NB – the 7p value exists from sheets guillotined in the wrong place giving gutter pairs with the wrong inscriptions: price for a mis-cut gutter pair £45.

Stephenson's 'Locomotion' (7p)
Waverley Class (8p)
Caerphilly Class (10p)
High Speed Train (12p)

1975, August 13. Railways
Des: B. Cracker

7p multicoloured	0.15	0.15
8p multicoloured	0.30	0.30
10p multicoloured	0.45	0.40
12p multicoloured	0.50	0.50
Set	0.80	0.75
Gutter Pairs	2.00	
Traffic Light Gutter Pairs	5.00	
First Day Cover		1.10
Stamp card (one of each design)	35.00	35.00

Palace of Westminster (12p)

1975, September 3. Inter-Parliamentary Union Conference
Des: R Downer

12p multicoloured	0.25	0.25
Gutter Pair	0.60	
Traffic Light Gutter Pair	1.00	
First Day Cover		0.50

Emma and Mr. Woodhouse (8½p)
Catherine Morland (10p)
Mr. Darcy (11p)
Mary and Henry Crawford (13p)

1975, October 22. Jane Austen Birth Bicentenary
Des: Barbara Brown.

8½p multicoloured	0.15	0.15
10p multicoloured	0.30	0.30
11p multicoloured	0.30	0.40
13p multicoloured	0.50	0.50
Set	0.65	0.60
Gutter Pairs	1.25	
Traffic Light Gutter Pairs	3.00	
First Day Cover		0.90
Stamp card one of each design	12.00	30.00

Angel with harp and lute (6½p)
Angel with mandolin (8½p)

Angel with horn (11p)
Angel with trumpet (13p)

1975, November 25. Christmas
Des: R. Downer. Dextrin gum except where stated. The 8½p
has the phosphor in the green printing ink

6½p multicoloured one phosphor band	0.15	0.10
a) with PVA gum	0.50	-
8½p multicoloured	0.30	0.15
11p multicoloured	0.40	0.50
13p multicoloured	0.50	0.30
Set	0.65	0.60
Gutter Pairs	1.40	
Traffic Light Gutter Pairs	2.75	
First Day Cover		0.75

Housewife with telephone (8½p)
Policeman with telephone (10p)
District Nurse with telephone (11p)
Industrialist with telephone (13p)

1976, March 10. Centenary of First Telephone Conversation
Des: P. Sharland

8½p multicoloured	0.15	0.10
10p multicoloured	0.30	0.20
11p multicoloured	0.40	0.25
13p multicoloured	50	30
Set	0.60	0.60
Gutter pairs	1.50	
Traffic Light Gutter Pairs	3.00	
First Day Cover		0.75

Mining coal – Thomas Hepburn (8½p)
Machinery – Robert Owen (10p)
Sweeping a chimney – Lord Shaftesbury (11p)
Prison Bars – Elizabeth Fry (13p)

1976, April 28. Social Reformers
Des: D. Gentleman

8½p multicoloured	0.15	0.10
10p multicoloured	0.30	0.20
11p multicoloured	0.40	0.25
13p multicoloured	0.50	0.30
Set	0.60	0.60
Gutter Pairs	1.50	
Traffic Light Gutter Pairs	3.00	
First Day Cover		0.75
Stamp card (of 8½p design)	6.00	4.50

Benjamin Franklin (11p)

1976, June 2. American Bicentennial
Des: P. Sharland

11p multicoloured	0.25	0.25
Gutter Pair	0.50	
Traffic Light Gutter Pair	0.75	
First Day Cover		0.50
Stamp card	3.50	12.00

**Unless otherwise stated, all issues listed on this
page are printed in photogravure by Harrison on
unwatermarked paper with "All-over" phosphor.
Perf: 15x14 (or 14x15 on vertical designs).**

■ **From this point, Stamp cards were released
for each new special stamp issue and in each
case cards were produced for each of the
stamp designs: prices quoted are for complete
sets of cards.**

QEII SPECIALS

Elizabeth of Glamis (8½p)
Grandpa Dickson (10p)
Rosa Mundi (11p)
Sweet Briar (13p)

1976, June 30. Roses
Des: Kristin Rosenberg

8½p multicoloured	0.15	0.10
10p multicoloured	0.30	0.25
11p multicoloured	0.30	0.30
13p multicoloured	0.40	0.40
Set	0.60	0.60
Gutter Pairs	1.50	
Traffic Light Gutter Pairs	4.00	
First Day Cover		0.90
Stamp card	17.00	25.00

Archdruid (Royal National Eisteddfod) (8½p)
Morris Dancing (10p)
Highland Gathering (11p)
Harpist (Royal National Eisteddfod) (13p)

1976, August 4. Cultural Traditions
Des: Marjorie Seynor

8½p multicoloured	0.15	0.10
10p multicoloured	0.30	0.25
11p multicoloured	0.35	0.30
13p multicoloured	0.45	0.30
Set	0.60	0.60
Gutter Pairs	1.50	
Traffic Light Gutter Pairs	4.00	
First Day Cover		0.75
Stamp card	9.00	17.00

'The Canterbury Tales' (8½p)
'The Tretyse of Love' (10p)
'The Game and Playe of Chesse (11p)
Printig Press (13p)

1976, September 29. William Caxton
Des: R. Gay.

8½p blue, black, gold	0.15	0.10
10p olive, black, gold	0.25	0.25
11p grey, black, gold	0.35	0.30
13p brown, black, gold	0.45	0.30
Set	0.60	0.60
Gutter Pairs	1.50	
Traffic Light Gutter Pairs	3.50	
First Day Cover		0.75
Stamp card	7.00	17.00

Virgin and Child (6½p)
Angel (8½p)
Angel with Shepherds (11p)
The Three Kings (13p)

1976, November 24. Christmas.
Des: Enid Marx (based on English embroideries)

6½p multicoloured one phosphor band	0.15	0.10
8½p multicoloured	0.20	0.10
11p multicoloured	0.30	0.30
13p multicoloured	0.50	0.35
Set	0.60	0.60
Gutter Pairs	1.50	
Traffic Light Gutter Pairs	2.75	
First Day Cover		0.75
Stamp card	2.50	15.00

Lawn Tennis (8½p)
Table Tennis (10p)
Squash (11p)
Badminton (13p)

1977, January 12. Racket Sports
Des: A. Restall

8½p multicoloured	0.15	0.10
10p multicoloured	0.20	0.25
11p multicoloured	0.30	0.30
13p multicoloured	0.40	0.30
Set	0.65	0.60
Gutter Pairs	1.75	
Traffic Light Gutter Pairs	3.00	
First Day Cover		0.80
Stamp card	4.00	15.00

Steroids (8½p)
Vitamin C (10p)
Starch Chromatography (11p)
Salt Crystallography (13p)

1977, March 2. Centenary of the Royal Institute of Chemistry
Des: J. Karo

8½p multicoloured	15	10
10p multicoloured	25	25
11p multicoloured	30	30
13p multicoloured	40	30
Set	0.65	0.60
Gutter Pairs	1.75	
Traffic Light Gutter Pairs	2.75	
First Day Cover		0.75
Stamp card	4.00	10.00

'ER' all values

1977, Silver Jubilee.
Des: Professor R. Guyatt. All multicoloured

8½p May 11, 1977	15	10
9p June 15, 1977	20	20
10p May 11, 1977	30	25
11p May, 1977	30	30
13p May11, 1977	40	30
Set	0.75	0.75
Gutter Pairs	1.80	
Traffic Light Gutter Pairs	2.50	

First Day Cover		
(8½p, 10p, 11p, 13p)		0.80
First Day Cover (9p)		0.80
Stamp card	7.00	11.00

Symbol of Pentagons (13p)

1977, June 8. Commonwealth Heads of Government Meeting
Des: P. Murdoch. Printed in photogravure and recess by Harrison

13p multicoloured	0.25	0.25
Gutter Pair	0.50	
Traffic Light Gutter Pair	0.60	
First Day Cover		0.50
Stamp card	3.00	4.00

Hedgehog (9p - 1)
Hare V (9p - 2)
Red Squirrel (9p – 3)
Otter (9p - 4)
Badger (9p – 5)

1977, October 5. Wildlife.
Des: P Oxenham. All multicoloured

9p design 1	0.25	0.20
9p design 2	0.25	0.20
9p design 3	0.25	0.20
9p design 4	0.25	0.20
9p design 5	0.25	0.20
Se-tenant strip of five	0.75	0.90
Gutter Strip (*)	1.25	
Traffic Light Gutter Strip (*)	2.50	
First Day Cover		1.00
Stamp card	1.75	5.00

QEII SPECIALS

(* = gutter strips normally comprise a strip of four designs separated from the fifth design by the gutter)

Three French Hens, two Turtle Doves and a Partridge and a Pear Tree (7p - 1)
Six Geese, five Gold Rings, four Colley Birds (7p - 2)
Eight Maids, seven Swans (7p - 3)
Ten Pipers, nine Drummers (7p - 4)
Twelve Lords, eleven Ladies (7p - 5)
A Partridge and Pears (9p)

1977, November 23. Christmas
Des: D. Gentleman based on the Christmas son 'The Twelve Days of Christmas'. All multicoloured. The 7p values have one phosphor band

7p (design 1)	0.15	0.15
7p (design 2)	0.15	0.15
7p (design 3)	0.15	0.15
7p (design 4)	0.15	0.15
7p (design 5)	0.15	0.15
Se-tenant strip of five	0.80	1.50
9p	0.20	0.25
Set	0.75	0.85
Gutter Pairs (*)	1.50	
Traffic Light Gutter Pairs	2.25	
First Day Cover		0.80
Stamp card	2.00	4.50

(* = the gutter pairs of the 7p values comprise two horizontal se-tenant strips of the stamps separated by a horizontal gutter)

North Sea Oil (9p)
Coal Pithead (10½p)
Natural Gas Flame (11p)
Electricity (13p)

1978, January 25. Energy
Des: P. Murdoch

9p multicoloured	0.15	0.15

10½p multicoloured	0.15	0.25
11p multicoloured	0.25	0.30
13p multicoloured	0.25	0.25
Set	0.65	0.75
Gutter Pairs	1.50	
Traffic Light Gutter Pairs	2.00	
First Day Cover		0.80
Stamp card	1.75	4.00

Tower of London (9p)
Holyroodhouse (10½p)
Caernarvon Castle (11p)
Hampton Court (13p)

1978, March 1. Historic Buildings
Des: R. Maddox

9p multicoloured	0.20	0.20
10½p multicoloured	0.25	0.25
11p multicoloured	0.30	0.30
13p multicoloured	0.30	0.25
Set	75	0.75
Gutter Pairs	1.60	
Traffic Light Gutter Pairs	2.00	
First Day Cover		0.80
Stamp card	2.00	3.00
Miniature Sheet		
(comprising one of each value) (*)	0.80	0.85
First Day Cover		1.00

(* = this sheet, designed by J. Matthews, was sold at 53½p, the extra 10p being donated to assist the finances of staging the International Stamp Exhibition. LONDON 1980, which the sheet itself publicised)

State Coach (9p)
St. Edward's Crown (10½p)
Sovereign's Orb (11p)

Imperial State Crown (13p)

1978, May 31. 25th Anniversary of the Coronation
Des: J. Matthews

9p blue, gold	0.20	0.20
10½p red, gold	0.20	0.20
11p green, gold	0.25	0.30
13p violet, gold	0.25	0.25
Set	0.75	0.75
Gutter Pairs	1.60	
Traffic Light Gutter Pairs	2.00	
First Day Cover		0.75
Souvenir Pack ✓ 2	1.75	
Stamp card	2.00	3.00

Shire Horse (9p)
Shetland Pony (10½p)
Welsh Pony (11p)
Thoroughbred (13p)

1978, July 5. Horses
Des: P. Oxenham.

	0.15	0.15
	0.20	0.20
	0.30	0.25
	0.40	0.30
	0.70	0.75
	1.50	
	2.00	
		0.75
	1.75	3.00

Penny Farthing and Safety Bicycle of 1884 (9p)
Touring bicycles (10½p)
Small-Wheel Bicycles (11p)
Road-racers (13p)

1978, August 2. Cycling
Des: F. Wegner

9p multicoloured	0.20	0.15

10½p multicoloured	0.20	0.25
11p multicoloured	0.20	0.30
13p multicoloured	0.25	0.25
Set	0.70	0.75
Gutter Pairs	1.60	
Traffic Light Gutter Pairs	2.25	
First Day Cover		1.00
Stamp card	1.50	3.00

(NB – a pack containing the Horses and Cycling sets was put on sale at the American Philatelic Society Convention at Indianapolis: price £5.)

Dancing around a Christmas Tree (7p)
The Waits (9p)
Carol Singers (11p)
Carrying the Boar's Head (13p)

1978, November 22. Christmas
Des: Faith Jacques

7p multicoloured one phosphor band	0.15	0.12
9p multicoloured	0.20	0.20
11p multicoloured	0.25	0.30
13p multicoloured	0.60	0.75
Set	1.25	
Traffic Light Gutter Pair	2.00	
First Day Cover		0.75
Stamp card	2.00	3.00

Old English Sheepdog (9p)
Welsh Springer Spaniel (10½p)
West Highland Terrier (11p)
Irish Setter (13p)

1979, February 7. British Dogs
Des: P. Barrett

9p multicoloured	0.15	0.15
10½p multicoloured	0.20	0.25
11p multicoloured	0.30	0.30
13p multicoloured	0.70	0.75

Set	1.50	
Gutter Pairs	2.00	
First Day Cover		0.75
Stamp card	1.75	3.00

Saddling Mahmoud for the Derby (9p)
The Liverpool Great National Steeple Chase (10½p)
The First Spring Meeting, Newmarket (11p)
Racing at Dorsett Ferry, Windsor (13p)

1979, June 6. Horse Racing
Des: S. Rose

Primrose (9p)
Daffodil (10½p)
Bluebell (11p)
Snowdrop (13p)

9p multicoloured	0.15	0.15
10½p multicoloured	0.20	0.25
11p multicoloured	0.25	0.30
13p multicoloured	0.30	0.30
Set	0.70	0.75
Gutter Pairs	1.50	
Traffic Light Gutter Pairs	2.00	
First Day Cover		0.75
Stamp card	1.50	3.00

1979, March 21. Spring Flowers
Des: P. Newcombe

9p multicoloured	0.15	0.15
10½p multicoloured	0.20	0.25
11p multicoloured	0.25	0.30
13p multicoloured	0.30	0.30
Set	0.80	0.85
Gutter Pairs	1.60	
Traffic Light Gutter Pairs	2.25	
First Day Cover		1.25
Stamp card	1.25	4.00

The Tale of Peter Rabbit (9p)
The Wind in the Willows (10½p)
Winnie the Pooh (11p)
Alice's Adventures in Wonderland (13p)

1979, July 11. International Year of the Child
Des: E. Hughes

9p multicoloured	0.25	0.15
10½p multicoloured	0.30	0.25
11p multicoloured	0.40	0.30
13p multicoloured	0.50	0.30
Set	0.75	0.70
Gutter Pairs	1.75	
Traffic Light Gutter Pairs	2.00	
First Day Cover		0.75
Stamp card	1.60	3.00

Hands placing 'flag' voting papers into ballot boxes (all values, but designs vary slightly)

1979, May 9. Direct Elections to the European Assembly
Des: S. Cliff

9p multicoloured	0.15	0.15
10½p multicoloured	0.20	0.25
11p multicoloured	0.25	0.30
13p multicoloured	0.30	0.30
Set	0.70	0.75
Gutter Pairs	1.50	
Traffic Light Gutter Pairs	2.00	
First Day Cover		0.75
Stamp card	1.50	3.00

Sir Rowland Hill (10p)
London Post (11½p)
General Post (13p)
Penny Post (15p)

1979, August 22. Centenary of Death of Sir Rowland Hill
Des: E Stemp

10p multicoloured	0.15	0.15
11½p multicoloured	0.20	0.25
13p multicoloured	0.30	0.30
15p multicoloured	0.30	0.30
Set	0.70	0.70
Gutter Pairs	1.60	
Traffic Light Gutter Pairs	2.00	
First Day Cover		0.75
Stamp card	1.50	3.00
Miniature Sheet		
comprising one of each value	0.75	0.70
First Day Cover		0.75

NB – this miniature sheet, designed by J. Matthews, was sold at 59½p, the extra 10p being donated towards the finances of staging the International Stamp Exhibition, LONDON 1980, which the sheet itself publicised; issued October 24, 1979.

Unless otherwise stated, all the following issues are printed on phosphor coated paper.

Policeman talking to two children (10p)
Street Patrol (11½p)
Policewoman on horseback (13p)
River police (15p)

1979, September 26. Metropolitan Police 150th Anniversary
Des: B. Sanders

10p multicoloured	0.20	0.15

11½p multicoloured	0.20	0.25
13p multicoloured	0.25	0.30
15p multicoloured	0.30	0.35
Set	0.70	0.75
Gutter Pairs	1.60	
Traffic Light Gutter Pairs	2.00	
First Day Cover		0.80
Stamp card	1.50	3.00

The Kings following the Star (8p)
The Angel appearing to the Shepherd (10p)
The Manger Scene (11½p)
Joseph and Mary travelling to Bethlehem (13p)
The Annunciation (15p)

1979, November 21. Christmas
Des: F. Wegner

8p multicoloured (one phosphor band)	0.12	0.10
10p multicoloured	0.15	0.10
11½p multicoloured	0.20	0.25
13p multicoloured	0.25	0.30
15p multicoloured	0.30	0.35
Set	0.90	0.90
Gutter Pairs	1.80	
Traffic Light Gutter Pairs	2.00	
First Day Cover		0.90
Stamp card	1.50	3.00

■ **Starting with the Water Birds issue of January 16, 1980, the Post Office ceased to include the 'traffic lights' within the gutter margin. Therefore, while gutter pairs are still available, traffic light gutter pairs no longer exist.**

Kingfisher (10p)
Dipper (11½p)

Moorhen (13p)
Yellow Wagtail (15p)

1980, January 16. Water Birds
Des: Michael Warren

10p multicoloured	0.15	0.15
11½p multicoloured	0.20	0.25
13p multicoloured	0.30	0.30
15p multicoloured	0.30	0.25
Set	0.80	0.80
Gutter Pairs	1.75	
First Day Cover		0.90
Stamp card ✓	1.50	3.00

The Rocket (12p - 1)
First and second class carriages (12p - 2)
Third class carriage and cattle truck (12p - 3)
Open coach on truck and horsebox (12p - 4)
Goods wagon and mail coach (12p - 5)

1980, March 12. 150th Anniversary of the Liverpool and Manchester Railway
Des: D. Gentleman. All multicoloured

12p (design 1)	0.30	0.30
12p (design 2)	0.30	0.30
12p (design 3)	0.30	0.30
12p (design 4)	0.30	0.30
12p (design 5)	0.30	0.30
Se-tenant strip of five	0.85	0.85
Gutter Pairs (*)	2.25	
First Day Cover		1.00
Stamp card	1.50	3.50

(* = the gutter pairs comprise two horizontal se-tenant strips of the stamps separated by a horizontal gutter)

INTERNATIONAL STAMP EXHIBITION

Montage of London buildings and monuments (50p)

1980, April 9. LONDON 1980, International Stamp Exhibition
Des: J. Matthews. Printed by line-engraving. No phosphor

50p deep brown	0.80	0.75
Gutter Pair	1.75 ✓	
First Day Cover		0.75
Stamp card	0.50 ✓	1.50
Miniature Sheet	1.00 ✓	1.25
First Day Cover		1.25

NB – The miniature sheet issued on May 7, 1980 was sold at 75p, the extra 25p being donated towards the finances of staging the International Stamp Exhibition, LONDON 1980. The stamp is known to exist in shades of green: the shades were caused by the speed of the ink-drying operation. Attempts have been made to create artificially the 'green' shades.

Buckingham Palace (10½pp)
Albert Memorial (12p)
Royal Opera House (13½p)
Hampton Court (25p)
Kensington Palace (17½p)

1980, May 7. London Landmarks
Des: Sir Hugh Casson

10½p multicoloured	0.20	0.20
12p multicoloured	0.25	0.30
13½p multicoloured	0.30	0.30
15p multicoloured	0.35	0.35
17½p multicoloured	0.40	0.30
Set	0.80 ✓	0.90
Gutter Pairs	2.00	
First Day Cover		1.00
Stamp card	1.50	3.50

Charlotte Bronte (12p)

George Eliot (13½p)
Emily Bronte (15p)
Mrs. Gaskell (17½p)

1980, July 9. Famous Women/Europa 1980
Des: Barbara Brown

12p multicoloured	0.20	0.20
13½p multicoloured	0.25	0.25
15p multicoloured	0.25	0.30
17½p multicoloured	0.30	0.25
Set	1.10	0.75
Gutter Pairs	2.50	
First Day Cover		0.90
Stamp card	1.75	3.00

Her Majesty Queen Elizabeth The Queen Mother (12p)

1980, August 4. The Queen Mother's 80th Birthday
Des: Jeffery Matthews

12p multicoloured	0.40	0.30
Gutter Pair	1.00	
First Day Cover		0.60
Stamp card	0.60	1.00

Sir Henry Wood (12p)
Sir Thomas Beecham (13½p)
Sir Malcolm Sargent (15p)
Sir John Barbirolli (17½p)

1980, September 10. Music – British Conductors
Des: Peter Gauld

12p multicoloured	0.20	0.20
13½p multicoloured	0.25	0.25
15p multicoloured	0.25	0.30

17½p multicoloured	0.35	0.30
Set	0.90	0.80
Gutter Pairs	2.00	
First Day Cover		0.90
Stamp card	1.50	2.50

NB – These stamps exist on paper which reveals differences in the degree of 'shine' on the surface.

Athletics (12p)
Rugby (13½p)
Boxing (15p)
Cricket (17½p)

1980, October 10. Sports
Des: Robert Goldsmith. Printed in litho by Questa
Pref: 14x14¾

12p multicoloured	0.25	0.25
13½p multicoloured	0.30	0.30
15p multicoloured	0.35	0.35
17½p multicoloured	0.40	0.40
Set	0.90	0.80
Gutter Pairs	2.25	
First Day Cover		0.90
Stamp card	1.50	2.50

Christmas tree (10p)
Candles, ivy and ribbon (12p)
Mistletoe and apples (13½p)
Paper chains with crown and bell (15p)
Holly wreath and ornaments (17½p)

1980, November 10. Christmas
Des: Jeffery Matthews

10p multicoloured (one phosphor band)	0.15	0.15
12p multicoloured	0.20	0.16
13½p multicoloured	0.25	0.25
15p multicoloured	0.30	0.30

5 x 3 stamp. cyl/block *(handwritten)*

17½p multicoloured	0.30	0.30
Set	1.00	0.90
Gutter Pairs	2.50	
First Day Cover		1.00
Stamp card	1.50	2.50

NB – These stamps exist on paper which reveals differences in the degree of 'shine' on the surface.

St. Valentine's Day (14p)
Morris Dancers (18p)
Lammastide (22p)
Medieval Mummers (25p)

1981, February 6. Folklore/Europa 1981
Des: Fritz Wegner

14p multicoloured	0.20	0.20
18p multicoloured	0.30	0.30
22p multicoloured	0.35	0.35
25p multicoloured	0.40	0.40
Set	1.50	1.00
Gutter Pairs	3.50	
First Day Cover		1.00
Stamp card	1.50	2.25

Blind Man and Guide Dog (14p)
Deaf and Dumb Alphabet (18p)
Person in Wheelchair (22p)
Foot Artist (25p)

1981, March 25. International Year of Disabled People
Des: John Gibbs

14p multicoloured	0.25	0.25
18p multicoloured	0.30	0.35
22p multicoloured	0.35	0.40
25p multicoloured	0.45	0.45
Set	1.10	1.00
Gutter Pairs	2.75	
First Day Cover		0.90
Stamp card	1.50	2.25

Small tortoiseshell (14p)
Large Blue (18p)
Peacock (22p)
Chequered Skipper (25p)

1981, May 13. Butterflies
Des: Gordon Beningfield

14p multicoloured	0.25	0.25
18p multicoloured	0.30	0.35
22p multicoloured	0.35	0.40
25p multicoloured	0.45	0.45
Set	1.10	1.00
Gutter Pairs	2.75	
First Day Cover		0.90
Stamp card	1.50	3.00

Glenfinnan, Scotland (14p)
Derwentwater, England (18p)
Stackpole Head, Wales (20p)
Giant's Causeway, Northern Ireland (22p)
St. Kilda, Scotland (25p)

1981, June 24. National Trusts
Des: Michael Fairclough

14p multicoloured	0.25	0.25
18p multicoloured	0.35	0.35
20p multicoloured	0.35	0.35
22p multicoloured	0.40	0.45
25p multicoloured	0.45	0.45
Set	1.20	1.15
Gutter Pairs	3.00	
First Day Cover		1.20
Stamp card	1.50	3.00

Cockle Dredging (14p)
Hauling Side Trawl (18p)
Lobster Potting (22p)
Hauling Seine Net (25p)

Prince Charles and Lady Diana Spencer from a portrait by Lord
Snowdon (14p and 25p)

1981, July 22. Wedding of Prince Charles and Lady Diana Spencer
Des: Jeffery Matthews

14p multicoloured	0.30 *(yb Bbr* 0.30	
25p multicoloured	0.60	0.50
Set	1.00	0.75
Gutter Pairs	2.50	
First Day Cover		1.50
Souvenir Pack	2.00 ✓	
Stamp card	1.75 ✓	3.00

7 *consols* v2

NB – a folder with text printed in Japanese and containing
these two stamps was put on sale at the international stamp
exhibition held in Tokyo in 1981. Later a modified version of
this folder was made available through the British Philatelic
Bureau. Price of original folder: £5,. Price of modified folder: £2.
A folder containing one of each of the stamps was prepared
for a promotion with Cadbury Typhoo.

1981, September 23. Fishing
Des: Brian Saunders.

14p multicoloured	*3 stamps*	0.25	0.25
18p multicoloured		0.35	0.40
22p multicoloured	*cyl block*	0.40	0.45
25p multicoloured		0.50	0.50
Set *Present*		1.10	1.00
Gutter Pairs		2.75	
First Day Cover			1.10
Stamp card	✓	1.50	2.25

Father Christmas with sacks of toys (11½p)
The head of Christ (14p)
Angel in flight (18p)
Joseph and Mary with Donkey (22p)
The Three Wise Man on their camels following the star (25p)

Expeditions (14p)
Skills (18p)
Service (22p)
Recreation (25p)

1981, August 12. Duke of Edinburgh's Award 25th Anniversary
Des: Philip Sharland. Printed in Litho by Waddingtons. Perf 14

14p multicoloured	0.25	0.25
18p multicoloured	0.35	0.35
22p multicoloured	0.40	0.40
25p multicoloured	0.50	0.45
Set	1.10	1.00
Gutter Pairs	2.75	
First Day Cover		1.00
Stamp card	1.50	2.25

1981, November 18. Christmas
Des: Samantha Brown 11½p, Tracy Jenkins 14p, Lucinda
Blackmore 18p, Stephen Moore 22p, Sophie Sharp 25p

11½p multicoloured (one phosphor band)		20	20
14p multicoloured	*3 stamps*	25	25
18p multicoloured	*cyl block*	35	40
22p multicoloured		45	40
25p multicoloured		50	50
Set *Present*		1.25	1.20
Gutter Pairs		3.00	
First Day Cover			1.10
Stamp card	✓	1.50	3.00

Darwin and Giant Tortoises (15½p)
Darwin and Iguanas (19½p)
Darwin and Darwin's Finches (26p)
Darwin and Prehistoric Skulls (29p)

1982, February 10. Centenary of the death of Charles Darwin.
Des: David Gentleman.

15½p, 19½p, 26p, 29p *Come blot with eyloos*		
Set	1.10	1.10
Gutter Pairs	2.75	
First Day Cover		1.20✔
Stamp cards	1.50 ✔	3.50

Boy's Brigade (15½p)
Girl's Brigade (19½p)
Scouts (26p)
Guides and Brownies (29p)

1982, March 24. Youth Organisations.
Des: Brian Sanders.

15½p, 19½p, 26p, 29p		
Set	1.20	1.30
Gutter Pairs	3.00	
First Day Cover		1.20 ✔
Stamp cards	1.50	3.50

Ballet (15½p)
Pantomime (19½p)
Shakespearean drama (26p)
Opera (29p)
All designs incorporate the CEPT symbol.

1982, April 28. British Theatre/Europa.
Des: Adrian George.

15½p, 19½p, 26p, 29p *4×3 stan corner block wit cy*		
Set	2.25	1.25
Gutter Pairs	5.00	
First Day Cover *1 Benham*		1.20 ✔
Stamp cards	1.50 ✔	3.50

HENRY VIII/MARY ROSE

Henry VIII and 'Mary Rose' (15½p)
Admiral Blake and 'Triumph' (19½p)
Lord Nelson and 'HMS Victory' (24p)
Lord Fisher and 'HMS Dreadnought' (26p)
Viscount Cunningham and 'HMS Warspite' (29p)

1982, June 16. Maritime Heritage.
Des: Marjorie Seynor. Printed in recess and photogravure by Harrison.

15½p, 19½p, 24p, 26p, 29p *5×3 damp vrt cyl block.*		
Set	2.25 ✱	1.25
Gutter Pairs	5.00	
First Day Cover		1.25✔
Stamp cards	1.75 ✔	4.00

British Textiles
William Morris: Strawberry Thief

'Strawberry Thief', 1883 by William Morris (15½p)
'Scarlet Tulips', 1906 by F. Steiner and Co (19½p)
'Cherry Orchard', 1930 by Paul Nash (26p)
'Chevrons', 1973 by Andrew Foster (29p)

1982, July 23. British Textiles.
Des: Peter Hatch Patnership.
15½p, 19½p, 26p, 29p *4 cyl Block3 /*

Set	1.25	1.25
Gutter Pairs	3.00	
First Day Cover		1.20✔
Stamp cards	1.75 ✓	3.50

'History of Communications (15½p)'
'Technology Today' (26p)
(These stamps measure 72.3mm by 20.3mm.)

1982, September 8. Information Technology Year.
Des: Brian Delaney and Darrell Ireland.
15½p, 26p   *2+2 c.w. block par*

Set	0.75	0.80
Gutter Pairs	2.00	
First Day Cover		0.90✔
Stamp cards	1.00 ✓	2.50

Austin Seven and Metro (15½p)
Ford Model T and Escort (19½p)
Jaguar SS1 and XJ6 (26p)
Rolls Royce Silver Ghost and Silver Spirit (29p)

1982, October 13. British Motor Cars.
Des: Stanley Paine. Printed in litho by Questa.
Perf: 14¾×14.
15½p, 19½p, 26p, 29p

Set	1.40	1.25
Gutter Pairs	3.25	
First Day Cover		1.25 ✓
Stamp cards	1.75	3.50

While Shepherds Watched (12½p)
The Holly and the Ivy (15½p)
I Saw Three Ships (19½p)
We Three Kings of Orient Are (26p)

Good King Wenceslas (29p)

1982, November 17. Christmas.
Des: Barbara Brown.
12½p (one phosphor band), 15½p, 19½p, 26p, 29p

Set	1.50 ^	1.40
Gutter Pairs	3.50	
First Day Cover		1.25 ✔
Stamp cards	1.75 ✓	4.00

Salmon (15½p)
Pike (19½p)
Trout (26p)
Perch (29p)

1983, January 26. British River Fishes.
Des: Alex Jardine.   *— 4×3 star cyl block b*
15½p, 19½p, 26p, 29p

Set	1.50	1.40
Gutter Pairs	3.50	
First Day Cover *ad 30 Benham*		1.20 ✔
Stamp cards	1.75✓	4.00

Tropical island (15½p)
Hot arid desert (19½p)
Lush arable land (26p)
Cold mountainous region (29p)

1983, March 9. Commonwealth Day.
Des: Donald Hamilton Fraser based on an original idea by
Stafford Cliff.
15½p, 19½p, 26p, 29p *~ 4 corner block with big s blks.*

Set	1.50	1.40
Gutter Pairs	3.50	
First Day Cover *Benhangelt*		1.20✔
Stamp cards	1.75 ✓	3.50

QEII SPECIALS

The Humber Bridge (16p)
Thames Flood Barrier (20½p)
'Iolair' Emergency Support Vessel (28p)

1983, May 25. Europa – Engineering Achievements.
Des: Michael Taylor.
16p, 20½p, 28p *Gold Black 28p 16p 20½p*

Set ✓	2.00	1.50
Gutter Pairs	4.50	
First Day Cover *Benham*		1.20✓
Stamp cards *2 sets*	1.50	3.00

Musketeer and pikeman of the Royal Scots (16p)
The Royal Welch Fusiliers (20½p)
Riflemen of the 95th Rifles – The Royal Green Jacket (26p)
Irish Guards (28p)
The Parachute Regiment (31p)

1983, July 6. The British Army.
Des: Eric Stemp.
16p, 20½p, 26p, 28p, 31p

Set	1.50	1.60
Gutter Pairs	3.50	
First Day Cover		1.50 ✓
Stamp cards	1.75 ✓	4.00

Sissinghurst (16p)
Biddulph Grange (20½p)
Blenheim (28p)
Pitmedden (31p)

1983, August 24. British Gardens.
Des: Liz Butler. Printed in litho by Waddingtons. Perf: 14 x 14¼.
16p, 20½p, 28p, 31p *7 x 7 stamp block*

Set	*1 Pro* 1.40	1.20
Gutter Pairs	3.25	
First Day Cover ✓		1.20✓
Stamp cards	1.75 ✓	3.50

Merry-go-round (16p)
Menagerie and fairground rides (20½p)
Side shows (28p)
Trading in farm produce (**31p**)

1983, October 5. Fairs and Shows.
Des: Andrew Restall.
16p, 20½p, 28p, 31p

Set	1.40	1.20
Gutter Pairs	3.25	
First Day Cover		1.20✓
Stamp cards	1.75	3.50

Flurry of birds posting Christmas greetings (12½p)
Chimney pots with a dove and cat (16p)
Dove and blackbird under an umbrella (20½p)
Dove and blackbird under a street lamp (28p)
Hedge sculpture in shape of dove (31p)

1983, November 16. Christmas.
Des: Tony Meeuwissen.
12½p (one phosphor band), 16p, 20½p, 28p, 31p *5 x 3 extra block*

Set	*1 Pro* 1.50	1.40
Gutter Pairs	3.50	
First Day Cover		1.30✓
Stamp cards	1.75 ✓	3.50

QEII SPECIALS

Arms of The College of Arms (16p)
Arms of Richard III (20½p)
Arms of The Earl Marshal (28p)
Arms of the City of London (31p)

1984, January 17. Quincentenary of The College of Arms.
Des: Jeffrey Matthews. Perf: 14½.
16p, 20½p, 28p, 31p

Set	1.40	1.25
Gutter Pairs	3.25	
First Day Cover		1.25
Stamp cards	1.75	4.00

Highland Cow (16p)
Chillingham Wild Bull (20½p)
Hereford Bull (26p)
Welch Black Bull (28p)
Irish Moiled Cow (31p)

1984, March 6. Cattle.
Des: Barry Driscoll.
16p, 20½p, 26p, 28p, 31p

Set	1.60	1.40
Gutter Pairs	4.00	
First Day Cover		1.40
Stamp cards	1.75	4.00

Liverpool – International Garden Festival (16p)
Durham – Milburngate Shopping Centre (20½p)

Bristol – Bush House, City Docks Area (28p)
Perth – Commercial Street Housing Scheme (31p)

1984, April 19. Urban Renewal.
Des: Trickett and Webb and Ronald Maddox.
16p, 20½p, 28p, 31p

Set	1.50	1.25
Gutter Pairs	3.50	
First Day Cover		1.25
Stamp cards	1.75	3.50

Europa 'bridge' and CEPT emblem (both values – design 1)
Europa abducted by Zeus in the shape of a bull and the
emblem of the European Parliament (both values – design 2)

**1984, May 15. 25th Anniversary of CEPT and Second
Direct Elections to the European Parliament.**
Des: J. Larriviere (design 1), Fritz Wegner (design 2). The two
designs were printed in se-tenant pairs throughout the sheet.
16p, 16p (se-tenant pair), 20½p, 20½p (se-tenant pair)

Set	2.10	2.00
Gutter Pairs	4.75	
First Day Cover		1.40
Stamp cards	1.75	4.00

Lancaster House and flags of participating nations (31p)

1984, June 5. London Economic Summit.
Des: Paul Hogarth.
31p

	0.60	0.70
Gutter Pairs	1.75	
First Day Cover		1.00
Stamp cards	0.50	2.00

The earth from space (16p)
Navigational chart of the English Channel (20½p)
Aerial photograph of the Greenwich Observatory (28p)
Airy's transit telescope (31p)

1984, June 21. Centenary of the Greenwich Meridian.
Des: Jerry Barney and Howard Walker. Printed in litho by
Questa. Perf: 14 x 14½.
16p, 20½p, 28p, 31p

Set	1.50	1.40
Gutter Pairs	3.50	
First Day Cover		1.25 ✓
Stamp cards	1.75	3.50

'Education for development' (17p)
'Promoting the arts' (22p)
'Technical training' (31p)
'Language and libraries' (34p)

1984, September 25. 50th Anniversary of the British Council.
Des: Francis Newell, John Sorrell and Brian Sanders.
17p, 22p, 31p, 34p   + Corner blocks with gg blocks.

Set	1.50	1.30
Gutter Pairs	3.50	
First Day Cover		1.25 ✓
Stamp cards	1.75 ✓	3.50

NB – sheets of these stamps sold at the international stamp
exhibition held in Melbourne, Australia, in September 1984 had
the gutter margins overprinted with the exhibition logo.

Original Bath Mail Coach of 1784 (16p)
Attack on the Exeter Mail in 1816 (16p)
The Norwich Mail in a thunderstorm 1827 (16p)
The Holyhead and Liverpool Mails 1828 (16p)
The Edinburgh Mail snowbound in 1831 (16p)

Corner blk with 3 rows of 5 + half plate Value

1984, July 31. 200th Anniversary of the first Mail Coach run from Bristol and Bath to London.
Des: Keith Bassford and Stanley Paine. Printed in recess and
photogravure by Harrison.
16p, 16p, 16p, 16p, 16p (se-tenant)

Set	1.50	1.40
Gutter Pairs	3.50	
First Day Cover		1.25 ✓
Stamp cards	1.75 ✓	4.00

(Gutter pairs comprise two horizontal se-tenant strips of the
five stamps separated by a gutter.)

Holy Family (13p)
Arrival in Bethlehem (17p)
Shepherd and Lamb (22p)
Virgin and Child (31p)
Offering of Frankincense (34p)

1984, November 20. Christmas.
Des: Yvonne Gilbert.
13p, (one centre band), 17p, 22p, 31p, 34p
13p (stars printerd on back)

13p (stars printerd on back)	0.60	
Set	1.60	1.60
Gutter Pairs	3.75	
First Day Cover		1.25 ✓
Stamp cards	1.75 *	3.00
Booklet (*)	5.50	

(* - booklet with a Manger Scene cover containing 20 3p
stamps, sold at £2.30 – a discount of 30p – the stamps having
an all-over five-pointed star pattern printed on the back.)

Flying Scotsman (17p)
Golden Arrow (22p)
Cheltenham Flyer (29p)
Royal Scot (31p)
Cornish Riviera (34p)

1985, January 22. Famous Trains.
Des: Terence Cuneo.
17p, 22p, 29p, 31p, 34p   *5×3 stamps with cyl blocks*

Set	2.25	2.10
Gutter Pairs	5.00	
First Day Cover		2.25 ✓
Stamp cards	3.25 ✓	9.00

Buff-tailed Bumble Bee (17p)
Seven-Spotted Ladybird (22p)
Wart-biter Bush-cricket (29p)
Stag Beetle (31p)
Emperor Butterfly (34p)

1985, March 12. Insects.
Des: Gordon Beningfield.
17p, 22p, 29p, 31p, 34p   *– cyl block*

Set	1.75	1.60
Gutter Pairs	4.00	
First Day Cover		1.60 ✓
Stamp cards	1.75 ✓	4.50

'Water Music' by Handel (17p)
'The Planet Suite' by Holst (22p)
'The First Cuckoo' by Delius (31p)
'Sea Picture' by Elgar (34p)

1985, May 14. European Music Year. British Composers.
Des: Wilson McLean. Perf 14 x 14½.
17p, 22p, 31p, 34p

Set	2.50	1.75
Gutter Pairs	6.00	
First Day Cover		1.75
Stamp cards	1.75	3.50

RNLI Lifeboat and dinghy in distress (17p)
Beachy Head Lighthouse (22p)
Marecs A Satellite (31p)
Trinity House Buoy (34p)

1985, June 18. Safety at Sea.
Des: Newell and Sorell. Printed in litho by Waddingtons. Perf
14½ x 14.
17p, 22p, 31p, 34p

Set	1.60	1.50
Gutter Pairs	3.75	
First Day Cover		1.40
Stamp cards	1.75	3.50

Datapost motorcyclist and plane (17p)
Postbus in country side (22p)
Parcel delivery (13p)
Postman delivering letters (34p)

1985, July 30. 350th Anniversary of Royal Mail service to the public.
Des: Paul Hogarth.
17p, 22p, 31p, 34p
17p 'D' pattern printed

on gummed side	0.60	
Set	1.60	1.50
Gutter Pairs	3.75	
First Day Cover		1.40
Stamp cards	1.75	3.50
Booklet (*)	3.00	

(* - booklet containing 10 of the **17p** stamp, sold at £1.53, each stamp having a 'D' pattern printed on the gummed side. The cover of the booklet shows a Datapost van and plane, and Concorde).

King Arthur and Merlin (17p)
The Lady of the Lake (22p)
Guinevere and Lancelot of the Lake (31p)
Sir Galahad (34p)

1985, September 3. Arthurian Legend.
Des: Yvonne Gilbert.
17p, 22p, 31p, 34p

Set	1.60	1.50
Gutter Pairs	3.75	
First Day Cover		1.40
Stamp cards	1.75	4.00

Peter Sellers from photograph by Bill Brandt (17p)
David Niven by Cornel Lucas (22p)
Charles Chaplin by Snowdon (29p)
Vivien Leigh by Angus McBean (31p)
Alfred Hitchcock by Howard Coster (34p)

1985, October 8. British Film Year.
Des: Keith Bassford.
17p, 22p, 29p, 31p, 34p

Set	2.25	2.10
Gutter Pairs	5.00	
First Day Cover		2.25
Stamp cards	1.75	5.00

Principal Boy (12p)
Genie (17p)
Pantomime Dame (22p)
Good Fairy (31p)
Pantomime Cat (34p)

1985, November 19. Christmas – Pantomime.
Des: Adrian George.
12p (one phosphor band), 17p, 22p, 31p, 34p

12p ('stars' on gummed side)	0.55	
Set	1.60	1.50
Gutter Pairs	3.75	
First Day Cover		1.50
Stamp cards	1.75	4.50
Christmas Card Pack		
containing 50 of **12p** value	30.00	
Booklet (*)	5.00	

(* - booklet containing 20 of the **12p** stamps, sold at £2.40. Cover shows Cinderella's slipper on a cushion).

North Sea Drilling Rig and light bulb (17p)
Thermometer and laboratory (22p)
Garden hoe and steelworks (31p)
Loaf of bread and cornfield (34p)

1986, January 14. Industry Year.
Des: Keith Bassford. Printed in litho by Questa. Perf: 14½ x 14.
17p, 22p, 31p, 34p

Set	1.50	1.40
Gutter Pairs	3.50	
First Day Cover		1.40
Stamp cards	1.75	3.50

Edmond Halley as the Comet (17p)
The Giotto space probe (22p)
'Maybe twice in a lifetime' (31p)
The Comet's Orbit (34p)

1986, February 18. Halley's Comet.
Des: Ralph Steadman.
17p, 22p, 31p, 34p

Set	1.50	1.40
Gutter Pairs	3.50	
First Day Cover		1.40
Stamp cards	2.25	3.50

The Queen at the age of 2, 16 and 26 (17p)
The Queen at the age of 32, 47 and 56 (17p)

1986, April 21.The Queen's 60th Birthday.
Des: Jeffrey Matthews.
17p, 17p (se-tenant pair), **34p, 34p** (se-tenant pair)

Set	2.25	2.25
Gutter Pairs	5.00	
First Day Cover		2.20
Stamp cards	1.75	4.00

Barn Owl (17p)
Pine Marten (22p)
Wild Cat (31p)
Natterjack Toad (34p)

1986, May 20. Nature Conservation – Europa.
Des: Ken Lilly.
17p, 22p, 31p, 34p

Set	2.50	1.80
Gutter Pairs	5.50	
First Day Cover		1.75
Stamp cards	1.75	4.00

The peasant working on his land (17p)
The freeman and his craft (22p)
The knight and his retinue (31p)
The lord at head of table (**34p**)

1986, June 17. Medieval Life. 900th Anniversary of the Domesday Book.
Des:Tayburn.
17p, 22p, 31p, 34p

Set	1.60	1.50
Gutter Pairs	3.75	
First Day Cover		1.50
Stamp cards	1.75	3.50

Sprinter's feet on starting blocks (17p)
Oarsman (22p)
Weightlifter with bar (29p)
Man looking through the sights of a rifle (31p)
Hockey player (34p)

1986, July 15. Sport.
Des: Nick Cudworth.
17p, 22p, 29p, 31p, 34p

Set	1.90	1.75
Gutter Pairs	4.50	
First Day Cover		1.75
Stamp cards	2.25	4.50

The 34p value commemorates the centenary of the Hockey
Association and the Sixth World Hockey Cup for Men; the
other values commemorate the Commonwealth Games held
in Edinburgh.

Prince Andrew and Miss Sarah Ferguson (both values)

1986, July 22. Royal Wedding.
Des: Jeffery Matthews.
12p (one phosphor band), **17p**

Set	0.75	0.75
Gutter Pairs	2.00	
First Day Cover		1.00
Stamp cards	1.25	3.00

Ballot-paper cross (34p)

1986, August 19. Commonwealth Parliamentary Association Conference.
Des: John Gibbs. Printed in litho by Questa. Perf: 14 x 14½.

34p	0.75	0.80
Gutter Pairs	2.00	
First Day Cover		0.80
Stamp cards	0.50	1.50

Lord Dowding and the Hurricane (17p)
Lord Tedder and the Typhoon (22p)
Lord Trenchard and the DH 9A (29p)

Sir Arthur Harris and the Lancaster (31p)
Lord Portal and the Mosquito (34p)

1986, September 16. Royal Air Force.
Des: Brian Sanders.
17p, 22p, 29p, 31p, 34p

Set	2.25	2.25
Gutter Pairs	5.00	
First Day Cover		2.25
Stamp cards	2.25	5.50

The Glastonbury Thorn (12p), (13p)
The Tanad Valley Plygain (18p)
The Hebrides Tribute (22p)
The Dewsbury Church Knell (31p)
The Hereford Boy Bishop (34p)

1986, November 18. Christmas Traditions.
Des: Lynda Gray.
12p (one phosphor band – issued December 2, 1986), **13p** (one phosphor band), **18p, 22p, 31p, 34p**
13p ('stars' printed on gummerd side) 0.50

Set	2.00	2.25
Gutter Pairs	4.50	
First Day Cover		2.25
Stamp cards	1.75	5.00
Christmas Card Pack		
(36 at 13p with stars on gummed side)	7.50	

Gaillardia (18p)
Echinops (22p)
Echeveria (31p)
Colchicum (34p)

1987, January 6. Flowers.
Des: Jeffery Matthews from photographs by Alfred Lammer.
18p, 22p, 31p, 34p

Set	1.50	1.60

QEII SPECIALS

Gutter Pairs	3.50	
First Day Cover		1.75
Stamp cards	1.75	4.00

An apple (18p)
Planets moving around the sun (22p)
Flask of water and refraction of light (31p)
The earth and an artificial satellite (34p)

1987, March 24. Sir Isaac Newton.
Des: Sarah Goodwin.
18p, 22p, 31p, 34p

Set	1.50	1.60
Gutter Pairs	3.50	
First Day Cover		1.75
Stamp cards	1.75	4.00

Willis Faber Dumas Building, Ipswich (18p)
Pompidou Centre, Paris (22p)
Staatgalerie, Stuttgart (31p)
European Investment Bank, Luxembourg (34p)

1987, May 12. British Architects in Europe. CEPT.
Des: Minale Tattersfield Studio.
18p, 22p, 31p, 34p

Set	2.50	1.75
Gutter Pairs	5.50	
First Day Cover		1.70
Stamp cards	1.75	3.50

First aid duties in 1887 (18p)
First aid in wartime (22p)
First aid at events (31p)
Transplant organs flights (34p)

1987, June 16. St John Ambulance Centenary.
Des: Debbie Cook. Printed in litho by Questa. Perf:
14 x 14½
18p, 22p, 31p, 34p

Set	1.50	1.60
Gutter Pairs	3.50	
First Day Cover		1.70
Stamp cards	1.75	3.50

Arms of the Lord Lyon, King of Arms (18p)
Arms of His Royal Highness The Duke of Rothesay (22p)
Arms of the Royal Scottish Academy of Painting, Sculpture and
Architecture (31p)
Arms of The Royal Society of Edinburgh (34p)

1987, July 21. Scottish Heraldry.
Des: Jeffery Matthews.
18p, 22p, 31p, 34p

Set	1.50	1.60
Gutter Pairs	3.50	
First Day Cover		1.70
Stamp cards	1.75	4.00

Landseer's painting 'Monarch of the Glen', the Great Exhibition, Grace Darling's Rescue (18p)
Launching of Brunel's 'Great Eastern', Mrs Beeton's Book of Household Management, Prince Albert (22p)
The Albert Memorial, Disraeli, the first ballot box (31p)
Marconi's broadcast to Paris, Queen Victoria's diamond jubilee, the Boer War (34p)

1987, September 8. Victorian Britain.
Des: Carroll and Dempsey Studio. Printed in recess and photogravure by Harrison.
18p, 22p, 31p, 34p

Set	1.75	1.60
Gutter Pairs	4.00	
First Day Cover		1.70
Stamp cards	1.75	4.00

Pottery by Bernard Leach (18p)
Pottery by Elizabeth Fritsch (26p)
Pottery by Lucie Rie (31p)
Pottery by Hans Coper (34p)

1987, October 13. Studio Pottery.
Des: Tony Evans.
18p, 26p, 31p, 34p

Set	1.50	1.60
Gutter Pairs	3.50	
First Day Cover		1.70
Stamp cards	1.75	3.50

Decorating the Christmas tree (13p)
Child looking out of a window (18p)
Father Christmas in sleigh and child asleep (26p)
A child reading a book surrounded by toys (31p)
Child playing a recorder and a snowman (34p)

1987, November 17. Christmas.
Des: M. Foreman.
13p (one phosphor band), 18p, 26p, 31p, 34p

13p with double lined star on gummed side		0.50
Set	1.50	1.50
Gutter pairs	3.50	
First day cover	1.50	
Stamp cards	1.75	3.25
Folder		
(containing 36 of 13p with star on gummed side)		5.50

Short-spined seascorpion (18p)
Yellow waterlily (26p)
Bewick's Swan (31p)
Morchella esculenta (34p)

1988, January 19. Bicentenary of Linnean Society.
Des: E. Hughes.
18p, 26p, 31p, 34p

Set	1.50	1.50
Gutter pairs	3.50	
First day cover	1.50	
Stamp cards	1.75	3.25

Revd William Morgan (18p)
William Salesbury (26p)
Bishop Richard Davies (31p)
Bishop Richard Parry (34p)

1988, March 1. 400th Anniversary of the Welsh Bible.
Des: K. Bowen.
18p, 26p, 31p, 34p

136

QEII SPECIALS

Set	1.50	1.50
Gutter pairs	3.50	
First day cover	1.50	
Stamp cards	1.75	3.25

Gymnastics (**18p**)
Downhill skiing (**26p**)
Tennis (**31p**)
Football (**34p**)

1988, March 22. Sports Organisations.
Des: J. Sutton.
18p, 26p, 31p, 34p

Set	1.50	1.50
Gutter pairs	3.50	
First day cover	1.50	
Stamp cards	1.50	3.25

'Mallard' (**18p**)

'Queen Elizabeth' (**26p**)
Glasgow tram (**31p**)
Handley Page H.P.45 'Horatius' (**34p**)

1988, May 10. Transport and Mail Services. Europa.
Des: M. Dempsey.
18p, 26p, 31p, 34p

Set	2.50	1.75
Gutter pairs	5.50	
First day cover	1.50	
Stamp cards	1.25	3.00

Settler and clipper (**18p**)
British and Australian Parliament Buildings
and Queen Elizabeth II (**18p**)
W. G. Grace and tennis racquet (**34p**)
Shakespeare, John Lennon and Sydney Opera House (**34p**)

1988, June 21. Australian Bicentenary.
Des: G. Emery. Printed in litho by Questa.
18p, 34p in se-tenant pairs

Set of four in two se-tenant pairs	1.50	1.50
Gutter pairs	3.50	
First day cover	1.50	
Stamp cards	1.25	3.50

Spanish off The Lizard (**18p**)
English Fleet leaving Plymouth (**18p**)
Fighting off the Isle of Wight (**18p**)
English attacking at Calais (**16p**)
Armada in the North Sea (**18p**)

1988, July 19. Spanish Armada.
Des: G. Evernden.
18p in se-tenant strip of five

Set of five in se-tenant strip	1.50	1.50
Gutter pairs	3.50	
First day cover	1.75	
Stamp cards	1.50	4.50

The Owl and the Pussy cat (**19p**)
Edward Lear as a bird (**27p**)
'Cat' (**32p**)
There was a Young Lady whose bonnet (35p)

1988, September 6. Centenary of death of Edward Lear.
Des: M. Swatridge and S. Dew.
19p, 27p, 32p, 35p

Set	1.75	1.75
Gutter pairs	4.00	
First day cover	1.75	
Stamp cards	1.25	3.50

QEII SPECIALS

Miniature sheet (containing one of each value, with a surcharge to help fund the international stamp exhibition, Stamp World London 90).
Issued on September 27, 1988.   2.50   3.00
First day cover   3.75

1988, October 18. Castle high value definitives.
See under Machin decimal high value definitives.

Journeying to Bethlehem (14p)
Shepherds following the Star (19p)
Three Wise Men (27p)
The Nativity (32p)
The Annunciation (35p)

1988, November 15. Christmas.
Des: L. Trickett.
14p (one phosphor band), 19p, 27p, 32p, 35p
Set   1.75   1.75
Gutter pairs   4.00
First day cover 1.75
Stamp cards   1.50   3.50
NB: examples exist of the 14p design with the denomination 13p, printed before the decision about an increase in postage rates, and released in error.

Atlantic Puffin (19p)
Avocet (27p)
Oystercatcher (32p)
Northern Gannet (35p)

1989, January 17.
Centenary of the Royal Society for the Protection of Birds.
Des: D. Cordery.
19p, 27p, 32p, 35p
Set   1.75   1.75
Gutter pairs   4.00

First day cover   1.75
Stamp cards   1.50   4.25

Rose (19p)
Cupid (19p)
Yachts (19p)
Fruit (19p)
Teddy Bear (19p)

1989, January 31. Greetings stamps.
Des: P. Sutton.
19p se-tenant strip of five
Issued in booklets in panes of ten
containing two of each design
Se-tenant strip   10.00   9.00
Booklet pane of 10 15.00
Booklet   15.00
First day cover   8.00
Stamp cards

Fruit and vegetables (19p)
Meat (27p)
Dairy products (32p)
Cereals (35p)

1989, March 7. Food and Farming Year.
Des: Sedley Place Ltd.
19p, 27p, 32p, 35p
Set   1.50   1.50
Gutter pairs   3.50
First day cover 1.50
Stamp cards   1.25   3.25

QEII SPECIALS

1 38

Mortar board (**19p**)
Cross on ballot paper (**19p**)
Posthorn (**35p**)
Globe (**35p**)
Designs are of firework displays

1989, April 11. Anniversaries and Events.
Des: Lewis Moberly.
19p, 35p in se-tenant pairs

Set of two se-tenant pairs	1.50	1.50
Gutter pairs	3.50	
First day cover	1.50	
Stamp cards	1.25	4.00

Anniversaries and events commemorated are the 150th anniversary of Public Education in England, the Direct Elections to the European Parliament, the Postal, Telegraph and Telephone International Congress and the Inter-Parliamentary Centenary Conference.

Toy aeroplane and locomotive (**19p**)
Building bricks (**27p**)
Board games and dice (**32p**)
Robot, boat and doll's house (**35p**)

1989, May 16. Toys and Games. Europa.
Des: D. Fern.
19p, 27p, 32p, 35p

Set	2.50	1.75
Gutter pairs	5.50	
First day cover	1.50	
Stamp cards	1.25	3.25

Ironbridge, Shropshire (**19p**)
Tin mine, St Agnes Head, Cornwall (**27p**)
Cotton Mills, New Lanark, Strathclyde (**32p**)
Pontcysylite Aqueduct, Clwyd (**35p**)

1989, July 4. Industrial Archaeology.
Des: R. Maddox.
19p, 27p, 32p, 35p

Set	1.50	1.50
Gutter pairs	3.50	
First day cover	1.50	
Stamp cards	1.25	3.25

Miniature sheet (containing one of each value, but with the designs in a horizontal format, with a surcharge to help fund the international stamp exhibition, Stamp World London 90). Issued on July 25, 1989.

	2.00	2.25
First day cover	3.5	

Snowflake (**19p**)
Fly (**27p**)
Blood cells (**32p**)
Microchip (**35p**)

1989, September 5.
150th Anniversary of the Microscopical Society.
Des: K. Bassford. Printed in litho by Questa.
19p, 27p, 32p, 35p

Set	1.50	1.50
Gutter pairs	3.50	
First day cover	1.50	
Stamp cards	1.25	3.25

Royal Mail coach (**20p**)
The Blues and Royals (**20p**)
Lord Mayor's coach (**20p**)
St Paul's Cathedral (**20p**)
Blues and Royals Drum Horse (**20p**)

1989, October 17.
Lord Mayor's Show. Des: P. Cox.
20p in se-tenant strip of five

Set in se-tenant strip	1.50	1.50
Gutter pairs	3.50	
First day cover	1.50	
Stamp cards	1.50	4.00

Peasants – from stained glass window (**15p**)
Arches and Roundels, West Front (**15p + 1p**)
Octagon Tower (**20p + 1p**)
Arcade from West Transept (**34p + 1p**)
Triple Arch from West Front (**37p + 1p**)

1989, November 14.
Christmas. 800th Anniversary of Ely Cathedral.
Des: D. Gentleman.
15p (one phosphor band), **15p + 1p** (one phosphor band),
20p + 1p, 34p + 1p, 37p + 1p

Set	1.75	1.75
Gutter pairs	4.00	
First day cover	1.75	
Stamp cards	1.50	4.00

NB: four of the stamps carried a surcharge for charity.

1990, January 10. 150th Anniversary of the Penny Black.
See under the Machin decimal definitives, and Stamp World
London 1990 miniature sheet of May 3, 1990.

Kitten (**20p**)
Rabbit (**29p**)
Duckling (**34p**)
Puppy (**37p**)

**1990, January 23. 150th Anniversary of the Royal Society
for the Prevention of Cruelty to Animals.**
Des: T. Evans. Printed in litho by Questa.
20p, 29p, 34p, 37p

Set	1.75	1.75
Gutter pairs	3.50	
First day cover	1.75	
Stamp cards	1.50	4.50

Teddy Bear (**20p**)
Dennis the Menace (**20p**)
Punch (**20p**)
Cheshire Cat (**20p**)
The Man in the Moon (**20p**)
The Laughing Policeman (**20p**)
Clown (**20p**)
Mona Lisa (**20p**)
Queen of Hearts (**20p**)
Stan Laurel (**20p**)

1990, February 6. Greetings stamps: Smiles.
Des: Michael Peters and Partners Ltd.
20p se-tenant in a booklet pane of ten
Issued in booklets in panes of ten containing one of each
design

Booklet pane of 10	11.00	10.00
Booklet	12.00	
First day cover	10.00	

Alexandra Palace (**20p**)
Glasgow School of Art (**20p**)
British Philatelic Bureau, Edinburgh (29p)
Templeton Carpet Factory, Glasgow (37p)

1990, March 6.
Europa and Glasgow 1990 European City of Culture.
Des: P. Hogarth.
20p, 20p, 29p, 37p

Set	2.25	1.75
Gutter pairs	5.00	
First day cover	1.75	
Stamp cards	1.50	3.50

NB: the two 20p designs were issued in separate sheets, not as se-tenant pairs. The 20p Alexandra Palace design also appears as a pane of four in the £5 'London Life' prestige stamp booklet issued on March 20, 1990.

Export Achievement Award (20p and 37p)
Technological Achievement Award (20p and 37p)

1990, April 10. 25th Anniversary of The Queen's Awards for Export and Technology.
Des: S. Broom. Printed in litho by Questa.
20p in se-tenant pairs, **37p** in se-tenant pairs

Set of four in two se-tenant pairs	1.60	1.60
Gutter pairs	3.50	
First day cover	1.60	
Stamp cards	1.50	3.50

Portraits of Queen Victoria and Queen Elizabeth II (20p)

1990, May 3.
Stamp World London 90 international stamp exhibition.
Des: Sedley Place Design Ltd; engraved by C. Matthews. Printed in recess and photogravure by Harrison. Issued only as a miniature sheet.
20p Miniature Sheet
NB: the border of the sheet includes the Penny Black and Britannia from the 1913-1934 'Seahorse' design. The sheets were sold at £1 each, the surcharge being used to help fund the exhibition.

Miniature sheet	1.75	2.25
First day cover	2.50	

Cycad and Sir Joseph Banks Building (**20p**)
Stone Pine and Princess of Wales Conservatory (**29p**)
Willow Tree and Palm House (**34p**)
Cedar Tree and Pagoda (**37p**)

1990, June 5. 150th Anniversary of Kew Gardens.
Des: P. Leith.
20p, 29p, 34p, 37p

Set	1.50	1.50
Gutter pairs	3.50	
First day cover	1.50	
Stamp cards	1.50	3.50

Thomas Hardy and Clyffe Clump, Dorset (20p)

1990, July 10.
150th Anniversary of the birth of Thomas Hardy.
Des: J. Gibbs.
20p

Single stamp	0.40	0.40
Gutter pair	1.00	
First day cover	0.60	
Stamp card	0.50	2.50

Queen Elizabeth The Queen Mother (20p)
Queen Elizabeth (29p)
Elizabeth, Duchess of York (34p)
Lady Elizabeth Bowes-Lyon (37p)

1990, August 2.
90th birthday of Queen Elizabeth The Queen Mother.
Des: J. Gorham from photographs by Norman Parkinson,
Dorothy Wilding, B. Park and Rita Martin.
20p, 29p, 34p, 37p

Set	3.00	2.25
Gutter pairs	6.50	
First day cover	2.25	
Stamp cards	2.75	6.00

NB: the same designs were used in 2002 in memory of The
Queen Mother although the borders were changed to black in
memory of the Queen Mother.

Victoria Cross (20p)
George Cross (20p)
Distinguished Service Cross and Distinguished Service Medal
(20p)
Military Cross and Military Medal (20p)
Distinguished Flying Cross and Distinguished Flying Medal (20p)

1990, September 11. Gallantry Awards.
Des: J. Gibbs and J. Harwood.
20p, 20p, 20p, 20p, 20p, issued in separate sheets, and not as a
se-tenant strip

Set	2.00	1.50
Gutter pairs	4.50	
First day cover	1.50	
Stamp cards	1.75	4.00

Armagh Observatory, Jodrell Bank Telescope and La Palma
Telescope (22p)
Early telescope and diagram of Moon and Tides by Newton
(26p)
Greenwich Old Observatory and astronomical equipment
(31p)
Stonehenge, Gyroscope and Navigation by the stars (37p)

1990, October 16. Astronomy.
Des: J. Fisher. Printed in litho by Questa.
22p, 26p, 31p, 37p

Set	1.75	1.75
Gutter pairs	4.00	
First day cover	1.75	
Stamp cards	1.50	4.00

Building a snowman (17p)
Fetching a Christmas tree (22p)
Carol singers (26p)
Tobogganing (31p)
Ice-skating (37p)

1990, November 13. Christmas.
Des: J. Gorham and A. Davidson.
17p (one phosphor band), 22p, 26p, 31p, 37p

Set	1.75	1.75
Gutter pairs	4.00	
First day cover	1.75	
Booklet (pane of 20 of the 17p stamp)	7.00	
Stamp cards	1.75	4.00

(NB: the 17p was also sold in £3.40 booklets containing a pane
of 20 stamps.)

King Charles Spaniel (22p)
Pointer (26p)
Two Hounds in a landscape (31p)
A Rough Dog (33p)
Fino and Tiny (37p)

1991, January 8. Dogs: paintings by George Stubbs.
Des: Carroll, Dempsey and Thirkell Ltd.
22p, 26p, 31p, 33p, 37p

Set	2.00	2.00
Gutter pairs	4.50	
First day cover	2.00	
Stamp cards	2.25	4.00

Thrush's Nest (1st)
Shooting Star and Rainbow (1st)

Magpies and Charm Bracelet (1st)
Black cat (1st)
Kingfisher and key (1st)
Mallard and frog (1st)
Four-leaf clover, boot and matchbox (1st)
Pot of Gold at the end of the Rainbow (1st)
Butterflies (1st)
Wishing Well and sixpence (1st)

1991, February 5. Greetings stamps: Good luck.
Des: J. Meeuwissen.
1st se-tenant in a booklet pane of ten
Issued in booklets in panes of ten containing one of each
design

Booklet pane of 10	6.00	6.00
Booklet	7.00	
First day cover	6.00	

Michael Faraday (22p)
Charles Babbage (22p)
Sweep of radar of East Anglia (31p)
Gloster Whittle E28/39 airplane over East Anglia (37p)

1991, March 5. Scientific Achievements.
Des: P. Till (22p values), J. Harwood (31p, 37p).
22p, 22p, 31p, 37p

Set	1.75	1.75
Gutter pairs	4.00	
First day cover	1.75	
Stamp cards	1.75	3.50

NB: the 22p values were issued in separate sheets, and not se-
tenant.

Designs as for the Greetings stamps of February 6, 1990, but
the values in each case changed to 1st

1991, March 26. Greetings stamps: Smiles.
Des: Michael Peters and Partners Ltd.
1st se-tenant in a booklet pane of ten
Issued in booklets in panes of ten containing one of each
design

Booklet pane of 10	5.00	5.50
Booklet	6.00	
First day cover	5.50	

NB: these designs were also used for Smilers sheets in 2000
and 2001 – see separate listing of such sheets.

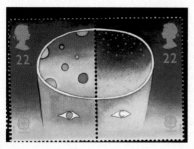

Man looking at Space (design over two se-tenant **22p** values)
Space looking at Man (design over two se-tenant **37p** values)

1991, April 23. Europe in Space. Europa.
Des: J-M. Folon.
22p, 22p in se-tenant pair, **37p, 37p** in se-tenant pairs

Set of two se-tenant pairs	2.25	2.00
Gutter pairs	5.00	
First day cover	1.80	
Stamp cards	1.50	3.50

Fencing (22p)
Hurdling (26p)
Diving (31p)
Rugby (37p)

1991, June 11. World Student Games, Sheffield and World Cup Rugby Championships, London.
Des: Huntley Muir Partners.
22p, 26p, 31p, 37p

Set	1.75	1.75
Gutter pairs	4.00	
First day cover	1.75	
Stamp cards	1.50	3.50

Silver Jubilee (22p)

Mme Alfred Carrière (26p)
Rosa moyesii (31p)
Harvest Fayre (33p)
Mutabilis (37p)

1991, July 16. Ninth World Conference of Roses, Belfast.
Des: Yvonne Skargon. Printed in litho by Questa.
22p, 26p, 31p, 33p, 37p

Set	2.00	2.00
Gutter pairs	4.50	
First day cover	2.00	
Stamp cards	1.75	4.50

Iguanodon (22p)
Stegosaurus (26p)
Tyrannosaurus (31p)
Protoceratops (33p)
Triceratops (37p)

1991, August 20. 150th Anniversary of the identification of Dinosaurs by Owen.
Des: B. Kneale.
22p, 26p, 31p, 33p, 37p

Set	2.25	2.25
Gutter pairs	5.00	
First day cover	2.25	
Stamp cards	1.75	4.50

Maps of Hamstreet, in
1816 (24p)
1906 (28p)
1959 (33p)
1991 (39p)

1991, September 17. Bicentenary of Ordnance Survey.
Des: H. Brown. Printed in recess and litho by Harrison (24p), in

litho by Harrison (28p) and in litho by Questa (33p, 39p).

24p, 28p, 33p, 39p

Set	2.00	2.00
Gutter pairs	4.50	
First day cover	2.00	
Stamp cards	1.75	3.25

NB: the 28p design is known with the denomination of 26p, from supplies printed before an increase in postage rates affected the denominations of this set.

Adoration of the Magi (18p)
Mary with Jesus in stable (24p)
The Holy Family and angel (28p)
The Annunciation (33p)
The Flight into Egypt (39p)

1991, November 12. Christmas.
Des: D. Driver.
18p (one phosphor band), **24p, 28p, 33p, 39p**

Set	2.00	2.00
Gutter pairs	4.50	
First day cover	2.00	
Booklet (pane of 20 of the 18p stamp)	6.25	
Stamp cards	1.75	4.00

NB: the 18p was also sold in £3.60 booklets containing a pane of 20 stamps.

Fallow deer (18p)
Hare (24p)
Fox (28p)
Redwing (33p)
Welsh Mountain sheep (39p)

1992, January 14. Wintertime (The Four Seasons).
Des: J. Gorham and K. Bowen.
18p (one phosphor band), **24p, 28p, 33p, 39p**

Set	1.95	1.75
Gutter pairs	4.50	
First day cover	1.75	
Stamp cards	2.75	4.50

The **39p** design also appears as a pane of four in the £6 'Cymru Wales' prestige stamp booklet issued on February 25, 1992.

Spray of flowers (1st)
Double locket (1st)
Key (1st)
Toy car and cigarette cards (1st)
Compass and map (1st)
Pocket watch (1st)
Penny red stamp and pen (1st)
Pearl necklace (1st)
Marbles (1st)
Starfish and a bucket and spade (1st)

1992, January 28. Greetings stamps: Memories.
Des: Trickett and Webb Limited.
1st se-tenant in a booklet pane of ten
Issued in booklets in panes of ten containing one of each design

Booklet pane of 10	5.50	5.50
Booklet	6.00	
First day cover	5.50	

Queen Elizabeth II,
In Coronation robes (24p)
In Garter robes (24p)
With Prince Andrew as a baby (24p)
At Trooping the Colour (24p)
With emblem of the Commonwealth (24p)

1992, February 6. 40th Anniversary of the Accession.
Des: Why Not Associates. Printed in litho by Questa.
24p, 24p, 24p, 24p, 24p in a se-tenant strip of five

Set in se-tenant strip	3.00	3.25
Gutter pairs	6.50	
First day cover	2.75	
Stamp cards	2.75	5.50

Tennyson,
In 1888 (24p)
In 1856 (28p)

In 1864 (33p)
As a young man (39p)

1992, March 10. Centenary of the death of Alfred, Lord Tennyson.
Des: Irene von Treskow.
24p, 28p, 33p, 39p

Set	2.00	1.75
Gutter pairs		4.50
First day cover	1.75	
Stamp cards	2.50	3.50

British Olympic Association logo – designed by K. Bassford (24p)
British Paralympic Association symbol – designed by K. Bassford (24p)
The above two designs were issued as se-tenant pairs in the sheet, printed in litho by Questa
'Santa Maria' – Christopher Columbus – designed by K. Bassford and S. Paine, printed in recess and litho by Harrison (24p)
'Kaisei' – Operation Raleigh – designed by K. Bassford and S. Paine, printed in recess and litho by Harrison (39p)
British Pavilion at Expo '92 in Seville – designed by K. Bassford, printed in litho by Questa (39p)
The above three designs were issued in separate sheets

1992, April 7. International Events.
Designers and printers given with descriptions of designs.
24p, 24p issued as se-tenant pairs, **24p, 39p, 39p**

Set	2.75	2.00
Gutter pairs	6.00	
First day cover	2.00	
Stamp cards	2.75	5.00

Events commemorated are the Olympic Games, Paralympics '92, 500th anniversary of the discovery of America by Columbus, Operation Raleigh, and EXPO '92.

Pikeman (24p)
Drummer (28p)
Musketeer (33p)
Standard bearer (39p)

1992, June 16. 350th Anniversary of the Civil War.
Des: J. Sancha.
24p, 28p, 33p, 39p

Set	1.85	1.75
Gutter pairs	4.50	
First day cover	1.75	
Stamp cards	2.50	3.25

Gilbert and Sullivan operas:
The Yeoman of the Guard (18p)
The Gondoliers (24p)
The Mikado (28p)
The Pirates of Penzance (33p)
Iolanthe (39p)

1992, July 21. 150th Anniversary of the birth of Sir Arthur Sullivan.
Des: Lynda Gray.
18p (one phosphor band), **24p, 28p, 33p, 39p**

Set	2.00	1.75
Gutter pairs	4.50	
First day cover	1.75	
Stamp cards	2.75	3.25

Acid rain kills – by Christopher Hall (24p)
Ozone layer – by Lewis Fowler (28p)
Greenhouse effect – by Sarah Warren (33p)
Bird of hope – by Alice Newton-Mold (39p)

1992, September 15. Protection of the Environment.
Paintings by children, in conjunction with the BBC Television programme 'Blue Peter'.

24p, 28p, 33p, 39p

Set	1.75	1.75
Gutter pairs	4.00	
First day cover	1.75	
Stamp cards	2.75	3.00

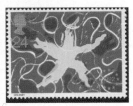

European Star (24p)

1992, October 13. Single European Market.
Des: D. Hockney.

24p

Single stamp	0.50	0.40
Gutter pair	1.50	
First day cover	0.60	
Stamp card	0.50	2.00

Angel Gabriel (18p)
Madonna and Child (24p)
King carrying Gold (28p)
Shepherds (33p)
Kings with Frankincense and Myrrh (**39p**)

1992, November 10. Christmas.
Des: Carroll, Dempsey and Thirkell Ltd.

18p (one phosphor band), 24p, 28p, 33p, 39p

Set	2.25	1.75
Gutter pairs	5.00	
First day cover	1.75	
Booklet (pane of 20 of the 18p stamp)	6.25	
Stamp cards	2.75	4.00

NB: the 18p was also sold in £3.60 booklets containing a pane of 20 stamps.

Mute Swan Cob (18p)
Cygnet and Decoy (24p)
Swans and Cygnet (28p)
Eggs in nest (33p)
Young swan (39p)

1993, January 19.
600th Anniversary of Abbotsbury Swannery.
Des: David Gentleman.

18p (one phosphor band), 24p, 28p, 33p, 39p

Set	3.00	3.00
Gutter pairs	6.50	
First day cover	3.00	
Stamp cards	4.25	5.50

Long John Silver (1st)
Tweedledum and Tweedledee (1st)
William (1st)
Mole and Toad (1st)
Teacher and Wilfred (1st)
Peter Rabbit and Mrs Rabbit (1st)
Snowman and Father Christmas (1st)
The Big Friendly Giant and Sophie (1st)
Bill Badger and Rupert Bear (1st)
Aladdin and the Genie (1st)

1993, January 28. Greetings stamps: Gift Giving.
Des: Newell and Sorell.
1st se-tenant in a booklet pane of ten
Issued in booklets in panes of ten containing one of each design

Booklet pane of 10	6.00	5.50
Booklet	6.50	
First day cover	5.50	
Stamp cards	10.00	15.50

NB: the Peter Rabbit and Mrs Rabbit design also appears as a pane of four in the £5.64 'The Story of Beatrix Potter' prestige stamp booklet issued on August 10, 1993.

QEII SPECIALS

Decorated dial (24p)
Escapement, Remontoire and Eusée (28p)
Balance, Spring and Temperature compensator (33p)
Movement seen from back (39p)

1993, February 16.
300th Anniversary of the birth of John Harrison.
Des: H. Brown and D. Penny. Printed in litho by Questa.
24p, 28p, 33p, 39p

Set	1.75	1.75
Gutter pairs	4.00	
First day cover	1.75	
Stamp cards	3.25	4.50

1993, March 2. £10 definitive.
See under Machin decimal high value definitives.

Dendrobium hellwigianum (18p)
Paphiopedilum Maudiae 'Magnificum' (24p)
Cymbidium lowianum (28p)
Vanda Rothschildiana (33p)
Dendrobium vexillarius var albiviride (39p)

1993, March 16.
14th World Orchid Conference, Glasgow.
Des: Pandora Sellars.
18p (one phosphor band), 24p, 28p, 33p, 39p

Set	1.75	1.75
Gutter pairs	4.00	
First day cover	1.75	
Stamp cards	4.25	5.50

'Family Group' by Henry Moore (24p)
'Kew Gardens' by Edward Bawden (28p)
'St Francis and the Birds' by Stanley Spencer (33p)
'Still Life: Odyssey I' by Ben Nicholson (39p)

1993, May 11. Contemporary Art. Europa.
Des: A. Dastor.
24p, 28p, 33p, 39p

Set	2.50	2.00
Gutter pairs	5.50	
First day cover	2.00	
Stamp cards	3.25	4.50

Emperor Claudius (24p)
Emperor Hadrian (28p)
Goddess Roma (33p)
Christ (39p)

1993, June 15. Roman Britain.
Des: J. Gibbs.
24p, 28p, 33p, 39p

Set	1.85	1.75
Gutter pairs	4.50	
First day cover	1.75	
Stamp cards	3.25	4.50

Grand Union Canal (24p)
Stainforth and Keadby Canal (28p)
Brecknock and Abergavenny Canal (33p)

Crinan Canal (39p)

1993, July 20. Inland Waterways.
Des: T. Lewery. Printed in litho by Questa.
24p, 28p, 33p, 39p

Set	1.75	1.75
Gutter pairs	4.00	
First day cover	1.75	
Stamp cards	3.25	4.50

Horse Chestnut (18p)
Blackberry (24p)
Hazel (28p)
Rowan (33p)
Pear (39p)

1993, September 14. Autumn (The Four Seasons).
Des: Charlotte Knox.
18p (one phosphor band), **24p, 28p, 33p, 39p**

Set	2.00	1.75
Gutter pairs	4.50	
First day cover	1.75	
Stamp cards	4.25	5.50

The Reigate Squire (24p)
The Hound of the Baskervilles (24p)
The Six Napoleons (24p)
The Greek Interpreter (24p)
The Final Problem (24p)

1993, October 12. Sherlock Holmes.
Des: A. Davidson. Printed in litho by Questa.
24p, 24p, 24p, 24p, 24p in se-tenant strip

Set in se-tenant strip of five	2.00	2.00
Gutter pairs	4.50	
First day cover	2.50	
Stamp cards	4.25	5.50

Bob Cratchit and Tiny Tim (19p)
Mr and Mrs Fezziwig (25p)
Scrooge (30p)
The Prize Turkey (35p)
Scrooge's nephew (41p)

1993, November 9. Christmas:
'A Christmas Carol' by Charles Dickens.
Des: Q. Blake.
19p (one phosphor band), **25p, 30p, 35p, 41p**

Set	2.25	2.00
Gutter pairs	5.00	
First day cover	2.00	
Booklet (20 at 19p)	7.00	
Booklet (10 at 25p)	5.75	
Stamp cards	4.25	5.50

Photographs of locomotives by Colin Gifford:
Class 5 and Class B1 on the West Highland Line (19p)
Class A1 at Kings Cross (25p)
Class 4 at Blythe North (30p)
Class 4 near Wigan Central (35p)
Castle Class crossing Worcester and Birmingham Canal (41p)

1994, January 18. The Age of Steam.
Des: B. Delaney One phosphor band (**19p**); two phosphor
bands (others).
19p, 25p, 30p, 35p, 41p

Set	2.50	2.25
Gutter pairs	5.50	
First day cover	2.25	
Stamp cards	4.25	5.50

Dan Dare (1st)
The Three Bears (1st)
Rupert Bear (1st)
Alice (1st)
Noggin and the Ice Dragon (1st)
Peter Rabbit (1st)
Little Red Riding Hood (1st)
Orlando the Marmalade Cat (1st)
Biggles (1st)
Paddington Bear (1st)

1994, February 1. Greetings stamps: Messages.
Des: Newell and Sorell.
1st se-tenant in a booklet pane of ten
Issued in booklets in panes of ten containing one of each design

Booklet pane of 10	6.50	5.50
Booklet	7.00	
First day cover	5.50	
Stamp cards	10.00	15.50

Paintings by The Prince of Wales:
Castell Y Waun/Chirk Castle, Clwyd, Wales (19p)
Ben Arkle, Sutherland, Scotland (25p)
Mourne Mountains, County Down, Northern Ireland (30p)
Dersingham, Norfolk, England (35p)
Dolwyddelan, Gwynedd, Wales (41p)

1994, March 1.
25th Anniversary of the Investiture of The Prince of Wales.
19p (one phosphor band), 25p, 30p, 35p, 41p

Set	2.00	2.00
Gutter pairs	4.50	
First day cover	2.00	
Stamp cards	4.25	5.50

NB: The 30p also appears as a pane of four in the £6.04
'Northern Ireland' prestige stamp book issued on July 26, 1994.

Bathing at Blackpool (19p)
Where's My Little Lad (25p)
Wish You Were Here (30p)
Punch and Judy Show (35p)
'The Tower Crane' machine (41p)

1994, April 12. Centenary of Picture Postcards.
Des: M. Dempsey and B. Dare. Printed in litho by Questa. One
phosphor band (19p), two phosphor bands (others).
19p, 25p, 30p, 35p, 41p

Set	2.00	1.75
Gutter pairs	4.50	
First day cover	2.00	
Stamp cards	4.25	5.50

British Lion and French Cockerel – designed by G. Hardie (25p
and 41p)
Hands over a train – designed by J.-P. Cousin (25p and 41p)
1994, May 3. Opening of Channel Tunnel.
25p, 25p in se-tenant pair, 41p, 41p in se-tenant pair

Set of two se-tenant pairs	2.00	2.25
Gutter pairs	4.50	
First day cover	2.00	
Stamp cards	3.25	4.50

Douglas Boston and groundcrew (25p)
HMS Warspite (25p)
Commandos on Gold Beach (25p)
Infantry on Sword Beach (25p)
Tank and infantry (25p)

1994, June 6. 50th Anniversary of D-Day.

QEII SPECIALS

Des: K. Bassford. Printed in litho by Questa.
25p, 25p, 25p, 25p, 25p in se-tenant strip

Set of five in se-tenant strip	2.50	2.25
Gutter pairs	5.50	
First day cover	2.00	
Stamp Cards	4.25	5.50

St Andrew's (19p)
Muirfield (25p)
Carnoustie (30p)
Royal Troon (35p)
Turnberry (41p)

1994, July 5. British Golf Courses.
Des: P. Hogarth.
19p (one phosphor band), **25p, 30p, 35p, 41p**

Set	2.25	2.25
Gutter pairs	5.00	
First day cover	2.00	
Stamp cards	4.25	5.50

Royal Welsh Show, Llanelwedd (19p)
Wimbledon Tennis Championships (25p)
Cowes Week (30p)
Test Match at Lord's (35p)
Braemar Gathering (41p)

1994, August 2. Summertime (The Four Seasons).
Des: M. Cook.
19p (one phosphor band), **25p, 30p, 35p, 41p**

Set	2.00	2.00
Gutter pairs	4.50	
First day cover	2.00	
Stamp cards	4.25	5.50

Ultrasonic imaging (25p)
Scanning electron microscopy (30p)
Magnetic resonance imaging (35p)
Computed tomography (41p)

1994, September 27. Medical Discoveries. Europa.
Des: P. Vermier and J.-P. Tibbles. Printed in photogravure by Enschedé.
25p, 30p, 35p, 41p

Set	2.50	2.25
Gutter pairs	5.50	
First day cover	2.00	
Stamp cards	3.25	4.50

Mary and Joseph (19p)
Three Wise Men (25p)
Mary with doll (30p)
Shepherds (35p)
Angels (41p)

1994, November 1. Christmas: Children's Nativity Plays.
Des: Yvonne Gilbert.
19p (one phosphor band), **25p, 30p, 35p, 41p**

Set	2.00	2.00
Gutter pairs	4.50	
First day cover	2.00	
Booklet (20 at 19p)	6.75	
Booklet (10 at 25p)	4.25	
Stamp cards	4.25	5.50

Black cat (19p)

Siamese and tabby cat (25p)
Ginger cat (30p)
Tortoiseshell and Abyssinian cat (35p)
Black and white cat (41p)

1995, January 17. Cats.
Des: Elizabeth Blackadder. Printed in litho by Questa. One
phosphor band (19p), two phosphor bands (others).
19p, 25p, 30p, 35p, 41p

Set	2.25	2.00
Gutter pairs	5.00	
First day cover	2.25	
Stamp cards	5.25	7.50

Plant sculptures by Andy Goldsworthy:
Dandelion (19p)
Chestnut leaves (25p)
Garlic leaves (30p)
Hazel leaves (35p)
Spring grass (41p)

1995, March 14. Springtime (The Four Seasons).
One phosphor band (**19p**), two phosphor bands (others).
19p, 25p, 30p, 35p, 41p

Set	2.25	2.00
Gutter pairs	5.00	
First day cover	2.25	
Stamp cards	5.25	6.50

'La Danse à la Campagne' by Renoir (1st)
'Troilus and Criseyde' by Peter Brookes (1st)
'The Kiss' by Rodin (1st)
'Girls on the Town' by Beryl Cook (1st)
'Jazz' by Andrew Mockett (1st)
'Girls performing a Kathak Dance' (1st)
'Alice Keppel with her daughter' by Alice Hughes (1st)
'Children Playing' by L. S. Lowry (1st)
'Circus Clowns' by Emily Firmin and Justin Mitchell (1st)
'All the Love Poems of Shakespeare' (detail) by Eric Gill (1st)

1995, March 21. Greetings stamps: Art.

Des: Newell and Sorell. Printed in litho by Walsall.
1st se-tenant in a booklet pane of ten
Issued in booklets in panes of ten containing one of each
design

Booklet pane of 10	5.00	5.50
Booklet	6.00	
First day cover	5.50	
Stamp cards	10.00	15.50

Fireplace decoration (19p)
Oak seedling (25p)
Carved table leg (30p)
St David's Head, Dyfed, Wales (35p)
Elizabethan window (41p)

1995, April 11. Centenary of The National Trust.
Des: T. Evans. One phosphor band (19p), two phosphor bands
(**25p, 35p**), phosphor paper (**30p, 41p**).
19p, 25p, 30p, 35p, 41p

Set	2.00	2.00
Gutter pairs	4.50	
First day cover	2.00	
Stamp cards	5.25	6.50

NB: The 25p also appeared in a pane of six in the £6 'The
National Trust' prestige stamp book issued on April 25, 1995.

British troops and French civilians –
designed by J. Gorham (19p)
Hands and Red Cross – designed by J.-M. Folon (19p)
Searchlights in a 'V' over St Paul's Cathedral – designed by J.
Gorham (25p)
Hand releasing Dove of Peace – designed by J.-M. Folon (25p)
Symbolic hands – designed by J.-M. Folon (30p)

1995, May 2. Peace and Freedom. Europa.

One phosphor band (**19p**), two phosphor bands (others). All issued in separate sheets.

19p, 19p, 25p, 25p, 30p

Set	2.25	2.00
Gutter pairs	5.00	
First day cover	2.00	
Stamp cards	5.25	6.50

NB: The design with St Paul's Cathedral was also used as a 1st class stamp in a miniature sheet in 2005.

The Time Machine (25p)
The First Men in the Moon (30p)
The War of the Worlds (35p)
The Shape of Things to Come (41p)

1995, June 6. Novels of H. G. Wells.
Des: Siobhan Keaney. Printed in litho by Questa.

25p, 30p, 35p, 41p

Set	1.85	1.85
Gutter pairs	4.50	
First day cover	2.00	
Stamp cards	4.25	5.50

The Swan, 1595 (25p)
The Rose, 1592 (25p)
The Globe, 1599 (25p)
The Hope, 1613 (25p)
The Globe, 1614 (25p)

1995, August 8.
Reconstruction of Shakespeare's Globe Theatre.
Des: C. Hodges. Printed in litho by Walsall.

25p, 25p, 25p, 25p, 25p in se-tenant strip

Set of five in se-tenant strip	2.00	2.00
Gutter pairs	4.50	
First day cover	2.00	
Stamp cards	5.25	6.50

Sir Rowland Hill and Uniform Penny Postage Petition (19p)
Sir Rowland Hill and Penny Black (25p)
Marconi and early wireless (41p)
Marconi and 'Titanic' (60p)

1995, September 5. Pioneers of Communications.
Des: The Four Hundred; engraved by C. Slania. Printed in recess and litho by Harrison.

19p (one phosphor band), **25p, 41p, 60p**

Set	2.00	2.00
Gutter pairs	4.50	
First day cover	2.00	
Stamp cards	4.25	5.50

Harold Wagstaff (19p)
Gus Risman (25p)
Jim Sullivan (30p)
Billy Batten (35p)
Brian Bevan (41p)

1995, October 3. Centenary of Rugby League.
Des: C. Birmingham. One phosphor band (**19p**), two phosphor bands (others).

19p, 25p, 30p, 35p, 41p

Set	2.00	2.00
Gutter pairs	4.50	
First day cover	2.00	
Stamp cards	5.25	7.50

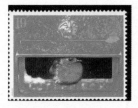

Robin in letter box (19p)
Robin on railings (25p)
Robin on milk bottles (30p)
Robin on road sign (35p)
Robin on front door handle (41p)

1995, October 30. Christmas: Christmas Robins.
Des: K. Lilly. One phosphor band (**19p**), two phosphor bands (others).
19p, 25p, 30p, 41p, 60p

Set	2.25	2.25
Gutter pairs	5.00	
First day cover	2.25	
Booklet (20 at 19p)	7.00	
Booklet (10 at 25p)	4.25	
Booklet (4 at 60p)	4.25	
Stamp cards	5.25	6.50

NB: The 19p design was used for Smilers sheets in 2000 and 2001.

Wee, fleeket, cowran, tim'rous beastie (19p)
O, my Love's like a red, red rose (25p)
Scots, Wha hae wi Wallace bled (41p)
Should auld acquaintance be forgot (60p)

1996, January 25. Bicentenary of death of Robert Burns.
Des: Tayburn Design Consultancy. Printed in litho by Questa.
One phosphor band (**19p**), two phosphor bands (others).
19p, 25p, 41p, 60p

Set	2.00	2.00
Gutter pairs	4.50	
First day cover	2.25	
Stamp cards	4.25	5.50

MORE! LOVE (1st)
Sincerely (1st)
Do you have something for the HUMAN CONDITION? (1st)
MENTAL FLOSS (1st)
4:55P.M. DON'T RING (1st)
Dear lottery prize winner (1st)
I'm writing to you because you don't listen to a word I say .. (1st)
FETCH THIS, FETCH THAT. LET THE CAT DO IT. (1st)
My day starts before I'm ready for it (1st)
THE CHEQUE IN THE POST (1st)

1996, February 26. Greetings stamps: Cartoons.
Des: M. Wolff. Printed in litho by Walsall. All-over phosphor.
1st se-tenant in a booklet pane of ten
Issued in booklets in panes of ten containing one of each design

Booklet pane of 10	5.00	5.50
Booklet	6.00	
First day cover	5.00	
Stamp cards	10.00	15.50

1996, November 11.
As above, but with two phosphor bands.
1st se-tenant in a booklet pane of ten
Issued in booklets in panes of ten containing one of each design

Booklet pane of 10	16.00	16.00
Booklet	17.50	

NB: The above designs were used for Smilers sheets in 2001 and 2002.

Paintings by C. F. Tunnicliffe:
Muscovy Duck (19p)
Lapwing (25p)
White-front Goose (30p)
Bittern (35p)
Whooper Swan (41p)

1996, March 12. 50th Anniversary of the Wildfowl and Wetlands Trust.
Des: Moseley Webb.
19p (one phosphor band), **25p, 41p, 60p**

Set	2.00	2.25
Gutter pairs	4.50	
First day cover	2.50	
Stamp cards	5.25	6.50

Odeon (**19p**)
Laurence Olivier and Vivien Leigh (25p)
Cinema ticket (30p)
Pathé News (35p)
'Big Screen Showing' (41p)

1996, April 16. Centenary of Cinema.
Des: The Chase. One phosphor band (**19p**), two phosphor bands (others).
19p, 25p, 41p, 60p

Set	2.00	2.25
Gutter pairs	4.50	
First day cover	2.50	
Stamp cards	5.25	6.50

Dixie Dean (19p)
Bobby Moore (25p)
Duncan Edwards (30p)
Billy Wright (35p)
Danny Blanchflower (41p)

1996, May 14. European Football Championships.
Des: H. Brown. Printed in litho by Questa. One phosphor band (**19p**), two phosphor bands (others).
19p, 25p, 41p, 60p

Set	2.50	2.25
Gutter pairs	5.50	
First day cover	2.25	
Stamp cards	5.25	6.50

NB: All of the stamps in this set also appeared as panes in the

£6.48 'European Football Championships' prestige stamp booklet, issued on May 14, 1996.

Athlete (26p)
Throwing the Javelin (26p)
Basketball (26p)
Swimming (26p)
Athlete and Olympic rings (26p)

1996, July 9. Olympic Games and Paralympic Games.
Des: N. Knight. Printed in litho by Questa.
26p, 26p, 26p, 26p, 26p in se-tenant strip

Set of five in se-tenant strip	2.00	2.00
Gutter pairs	4.50	
First day cover	2.25	
Stamp cards	3.75	6.50

Dorothy Hodgkin (20p)
Margot Fonteyn (26p)
Elizabeth Frink (31p)
Daphne du Maurier (37p)
Marea Hartman (43p)

1996, August 6. Famous Women. Europa.
Des: Stephanie Nash. One phosphor band (**20p**), two phosphor bands (others).
20p, 26p, 31p, 37p, 43p

Set	2.50	2.50
Gutter pairs	5.50	
First day cover	2.50	
Stamp cards	3.75	6.50

Muffin the Mule (20p)
Sooty (26p)
Stingray (31p)
The Clangers (37p)
Dangermouse (43p)

1996, September 3.
50th Anniversary of Children's Television.
Des: Tutssels. Printed in photogravure by Enschedé. One phosphor band (**20p**), two phosphor bands (others). Perf: 14? x 14.

20p, 26p, 31p, 37p, 43p

Set	2.25	2.25
Gutter pairs	5.00	
First day cover	2.50	
Stamp cards	5.25	6.50

NB: The 20p also appeared in the £6.15 '75th Anniversary of the BBC' prestige stamp booklet issued on September 23, 1997, but printed in photogravure by Harrison, and with perf: 15 x 14. Price: 60p mint.

Triumph TR3 (20p)
MG TD (26p)
Austin Healey 100 (37p)
Jaguar XK120 (43p)
Morgan Plus 4 (63p)

1996, October 1. Classic Sports Cars.
Des: S. Clay. One phosphor band (**20p**), two phosphor bands (others).

20p, 26p, 37p, 43p, 63p

Set	2.50	2.25
Gutter pairs	5.00	
First day cover	2.25	
Stamp cards	3.75	6.50

The Three Kings (2nd)
The Annunciation (1st)
The Journey to Bethlehem (31p)
The Nativity (43p)
The Shepherds (63p)

1996, October 28. Christmas.
Des: Laura Stoddart. One phosphor band (**2nd**), two phosphor bands (others).

2nd, 1st, 31p, 43p, 63p

Set	2.50	2.25
Gutter pairs	5.00	
First day cover	2.75	
Booklet (20 at 2nd)	7.00	
Booklet (10 at 1st)	4.25	
Stamp cards	5.25	6.50

Gentiana acaulis (1st)
Magnolia grandiflora (1st)
Camellia japonica (1st)
Tulipa (1st)
Fuchsia 'Princess of Wales' (1st)
Tulipa gesneriana (1st)
Guzmania splendens (1st)
Iris latifolia (1st)
Hippeastrum rutilum (1st)
Passiflora coerulea (1st)

1997, January 6. Greetings stamps: Flower paintings.
Des: Tutssls. Printed in litho by Walsall. Two phosphor bands. Perf: 14?.
1st se-tenant in a booklet pane of ten
Issued in booklets in panes of ten containing one of each design

Booklet pane of 10	5.00	5.50
Booklet	6.00	
First day cover	5.50	
Stamp cards	10.00	15.50

NB: The Gentiana acaulis, Tulipa and Iris latifolia designs also appear in the £7.23 'The Glory of the Garden prestige stamp

book issued on May 25, 2004. Perf: 15 × 14. Price: £4.50 mint, £4.50 used.
The above designs were also used for a Smilers sheet in 2003.

King Henry VIII (26p)
Catherine of Aragon (26p)
Anne Boleyn (26p)
Jane Seymour (26p)
Anne of Cleves (26p)
Catherine Howard (26p)
Catherine Parr (26p)

1997, 450th Anniversary of the Death of King Henry VIII.
Des: Kate Stephens. Two phosphor bands.
26p (King Henry VIII) issued as a separate stamp in sheets
26p, 26p, 26p, 26p, 26p, 26p (wives of King Henry VIII) issued in a se-tenant strip

Set comprising single		
and a se-tenant strip of six	3.00	3.25
Gutter pairs	6.50	
First day cover	3.75	
Stamp cards	5.25	8.50

St Columba in boat (26p)
St Columba on Iona (37p)
St Augustine with King Ethelbert (43p)
St Augustine with a model of a cathedral (63p)

1997, March 11. Religious Anniversaries.
Des: Claire Melinsky. Printed in photogravure by Enschedé.
Two phosphor bands.
26p, 37p, 43p, 63p

Set	2.25	2.25
Gutter pairs	5.00	
First day cover	2.50	
Stamp cards	4.25	5.50

1997, March 18. Self-adhesive definitives.
The Machin design but in a horizontal format – the self-adhesive definitives are listed under the Machin Decimal Definitives.

1997, April 21. Royal Golden Wedding.
The Machin definitive to pay the 1st class rate was issued in gold – listed under Machin Decimal Definitives.

Dracula (26p)
Frankenstein (31p)
Dr Jekyll and Mr Hyde (37p)
The Hound of the Baskervilles (43p)

1997, May 13. Tales of Horror. Europa.
Des: J. Pollock. Printed in photogravure by Walsall. Two phosphor bands.
26p, 31p, 37p, 43p

Set	2.50	2.25
Gutter pairs	5.00	
First day cover	2.50	
Stamp cards	4.25	5.50

Supermarine Spitfire MkIIA and Reginald Mitchell (20p)
Avro Lancaster MkI and Roy Chadwick (26p)
De Havilland Mosquito B MkXVI and Ronald Bishop (37p)
Gloster Meteor T Mk7 and George Carter (43p)
Hawker Hunter FGA Mk9 and Sir Sydney Camm (63p)
The faces of the aircraft designers feature in the cloud formations

1997, June 10. British Aircraft Designers.
Des: Turner Duckworth. One phosphor band (**20p**), two phosphor bands (others).

20p, 26p, 37p, 43p, 63p

Set	3.00	2.25
Gutter pairs	6.50	
First day cover	2.75	
Stamp cards	3.75	6.50

Carriage horse (20p)
Lifeguards horse (26p)
Blues and Royals drum horse (43p)
Duke of Edinburgh's horse (63p)

1997, July 8.
'All The Queen's Horses'. 50th Anniversary of the British Horse Society.
Des: J.-L. Benard. Printed in litho by Walsall. One phosphor band (**20p**), two phosphor bands (others).

20p, 26p, 43p, 63p

Set	2.25	2.25
Gutter pairs	5.00	
First day cover	2.50	
Stamp cards	4.25	5.50

Haroldswick, Shetland (20p)
Painswick, Gloucestershire (26p)
Beddgelert, Gwynedd (43p)
Ballyroney, County Down (63p)

1997, August 12. Sub Post Offices.
Des: T. Millington. Printed in photogravure by Enschedé. One phosphor band (**20p**), two phosphor bands (others).

20p, 26p, 43p, 63p

Set	2.25	2.25
Gutter pairs	5.00	
First day cover	2.50	
Stamp cards	4.25	5.50

Noddy (20p)
Famous Five (26p)
Secret Seven (37p)
Faraway Tree (43p)
Malory Towers (63p)

1997, September 9.
Centenary of the birth of Enid Blyton.
Des: C. Birmingham. Printed in photogravure by Enschedé. One phosphor band (20p), two phosphor bands (others).

20p, 26p, 37p, 43p, 63p

Set	2.50	2.50
Gutter pairs	5.50	
First day cover	2.50	
Stamp cards	5.25	6.50

Children and Father Christmas pulling Christmas cracker (2nd)
Father Christmas with Christmas cracker (1st)
Father Christmas riding on a Christmas cracker (31p)
Father Christmas with a snowball (43p)
Father Christmas on a chimney (63p)

1997, October 27. Christmas. 150th Anniversary of the Christmas cracker.
Des: M. Thomas (1st) and J. Gorham (others). One phosphor band (**2nd**), two phosphor bands (others).

2nd, 1st, 31p, 43p, 63p

Set	2.50	2.50
Gutter pairs	5.50	
First day cover	2.50	
Booklet (20 at 2nd)	6.75	
Booklet (10 at 1st)	5.00	
Stamp cards	5.25	6.50

NB: The 1st class design was used for Smilers sheets in 2000 and 2001.

QEII SPECIALS

Queen Elizabeth II and Prince Philip Wedding photograph of 1947 (20p and 43p)
Queen Elizabeth II and Prince Philip photographed in 1997 (26p and 63p)

1997, November 13. Royal Golden Wedding.
Des: D. Driver (158), Lord Snowdon (158). One phosphor band (158), two phosphor bands (others).

20p, 26p, 43p, 63p

Set	2.25	2.25
Gutter pairs	5.00	
First day cover	2.50	
Stamp cards	5.25	5.50

Common Dormouse (20p)
Lady's Slipper Orchid (26p)
Song Thrush (31p)
Shining Ram's-horn Snail (37p)
Mole Cricket (43p)
Devil's Bolette (63p)

1998, January 20. Endangered Species.
Des: R. Maude. Printed in litho by Questa. One phosphor band (**20p**), two phosphor bands (others).

20p, 26p, 31p, 37p, 43p, 63p

Set	3.00	3.00
Gutter pairs	6.50	
First day cover	3.00	
Stamp cards	6.25	7.50

Portraits of Diana, Princess of Wales:
By Lord Snowdon (**26p**)
At British Lung Foundation function (26p)
Wearing tiara (26p)
During visit to Birmingham (26p)
In evening dress (26p)

1998, February 3. Diana, Princess of Wales Memorial.
Des: B. Robinson. Two phosphor bands.

26p, 26p, 26p, 26p, 26p in se-tenant strip

Set of five in se-tenant strip	2.00	2.25
Gutter pairs	4.50	
First day cover	2.25	

Lion of England and Griffin of Edward III (26p)
Flacon of Plantagenet and Bull of Clarence (26p)
Lion of Mortimer and Yale of Beaufort (26p)
Greyhound of Richmond and Dragon of Wales (26p)
Unicorn of Scotland and Horse of Hanover (26p)

1998, February 24. The Queen's Beasts. 650th Anniversary of the Order of the Garter.
Des: Jeffery Matthews. Printed in recess and litho by Harrison. Two phosphor bands.

26p, 26p, 26p, 26p, 26p in se-tenant strip

Set of five in se-tenant strip	2.00	2.25
Gutter pairs	4.50	
First day cover	2.50	
Stamp cards	5.25	6.50

1998, March 10. Wilding definitives.
For definitives in the Wilding designs, but with decimal currency, see under Decimal Definitives. Adapted from G. Knipe design (Wilding definitives of 1952-54) by Dew Gibbons Design Group. Issued in 20p, 26p and 37p values. Only issued in the 1998 £7.49 Wilding definitives stamp booklet.

St John's Point Lighthouse (20p)
Smalls Lighthouse (26p)
Needles Rock Lighthouse (37p)
Bell Rock Lighthouse (43p)
Eddystone Lighthouse (63p)

1998, March 24. Lighthouses.
Des: D. Davis and J. Boon. Printed in litho by Questa. One phosphor band (**20p**), two phosphor bands (others).
20p, 26p, 37p, 43p, 63p

Set	2.75	2.50
Gutter pairs	6.00	
First day cover	2.60	
Stamp cards	5.25	6.50

Tommy Cooper (20p)
Eric Morecambe (26p)
Joyce Grenfell (37p)
Les Dawson (43p)
Peter Cook (63p)

1998, April 23. Comedians.
Des: Gerald Scarfe. Printed in litho by Questa. One phosphor band (**20p**), two phosphor bands (others).
20p, 26p, 37p, 43p, 63p

Set	2.60	2.50
Gutter pairs	5.75	
First day cover	2.60	
Stamp cards	5.25	6.50

NB: Examples exist of the 37p design but with the denomination 30p, printed before an increase in postal rates, and issued in error.

Hands forming the shape of a heart (20p)
Adult holding the hand of a child (26p)
Hands forming a cradle (43p)
Hand taking a pulse (63p)

1998, June 23.
50th Anniversary of the National Health Service.
Des: V. Frost, using photographs by A. Wilson. Printed in litho by Questa. One phosphor band (**20p**), two phosphor bands (others).
20p, 26p, 43p, 63p

Set	2.25	2.50
Gutter pairs	5.00	
First day cover	2.60	
Stamp cards	4.25	5.50

The Hobbit (20p)
The Lion, The Witch and the Wardrobe (26p)
The Phoenix and the Carpet (37p)
The Borrowers (43p)
Through The Looking Glass (63p)

1998, July 21. Children's Fantasy Novels.
Des: P. Malone. Printed in photogravure by De La Rue. One phosphor band (**20p**), two phosphor bands (others).
20p, 26p, 37p, 43p, 63p

Set	2.75	2.75
Gutter pairs	6.00	
First day cover	2.75	
Stamp cards	5.25	6.50

Woman in costume of yellow feathers (20p)
Woman in blue costume (26p)
Children in white and gold robes (43p)
Child dressed as a tree (63p)

1998, August 25. Notting Hill Carnival. Europa.
Des: T. Hazael. Printed in photogravure by Walsall. One phosphor band (**20p**), two phosphor bands (others).
20p, 26p, 43p, 63p

Set	2.50	2.50
Gutter pairs	5.50	
First day cover	2.60	
Stamp cards	4.25	5.50

Bluebird of Sir Malcolm Campbell (20p)
Sunbeam of Sir Henry Segrave (26p)
Babs of John G. Parry Thomas (30p)
Railton Mobil Special of John R. Cobb (43p)
Bluebird CN7 of Donald Campbell (63p)

1998, September 29. British Land Speed Records.
Des: Roundel Design Group. Printed in photogravure by De La Rue. One centre phosphor band (**20p**), two phosphor bands (others). Perf: 15 x 14.
20p, 26p, 30p, 43p, 63p

Set	2.50	2.75
Gutter pairs	5.50	
First day cover	2.75	
Stamp cards	5.25	6.50

NB: The 26p also appears in the £6.16 'Breaking Barriers' prestige stamp book issued on October 13, 1988, but printed in photogravure by Walsall, with perf: 14? x 13?, and with the one phosphor band printed on the left or right of the stamp. Price: 75p mint (either left or right band).

Angel with hands in blessing (20p)
Angel praying (26p)
Angel playing lute (30p)
Angel playing flute (43p)
Angel praying (63p)

1998, November 2. Christmas. Angels.
Des: Irene von Treskow. Printed in photogravure by De La Rue. One phosphor band (20p), two phosphor bands (others).
20p, 26p, 30p, 43p, 63p

Set	2.50	2.75
Gutter pairs	5.50	
First day cover	2.70	
Booklet (20 at 20p)	6.50	
Booklet (10 at 26p)	4.50	
Stamp cards	5.25	6.50

From January 1999 Royal Mail embarked on a 25 month programme of special stamp issues to mark the new Millennium. During 1999 and 2000 each design includes the inscription 'Millennium' and the year, and is numbered. The designs for 1999 looked back over the previous Millennium, by exploring twelve different 'tales'.

Greenwich Meridian and clock – designed by David Gentleman (20p)
Worker and blast furnace – designed by P. Howson (26p)
Photograph of leaves – designed by Z. and Barbara Baran (43p)
Computer inside head – designed by E. Paolozzi (63p)

1999, January 12. The Inventors' Tale.
Printed in photogravure by Enschedé (**26p**), or De La Rue (others). One phosphor band (**20p**), two phosphor bands (others). Perf: 14 x 14?.
20p, 26p, 43p, 63p

Set	2.50	2.50
Gutter pairs	5.50	
First day cover	3.00	
Stamp cards	4.25	6.50

NB: The 63p also appears in the £6.99 'World Changers' prestige stamp book issued on September 21, 1999, but printed in photogravure by Questa, perf: 13½ x 14. Price: £1.75 mint.

Globe surrounded by aircraft – designed by G. Hardie (20p)
Woman on bicycle – designed by Sara Fanelli (26p)
Railway Station – designed by J. Lawrence (43p)
Captain Cook and man – designed by A. Klimowski (63p)

1999, February 2. The Travellers' Tale.
Printed in photogravure by Enschedé (**20p** and **63p**), by De La Rue (**26p**), or litho by Enschedé (**43p**). One phosphor band (**20p**), two phosphor bands (others).
20p, 26p, 43p, 63p

Set	2.50	2.50
Gutter pairs	5.50	
First day cover	3.00	
Stamp cards	4.25	6.50

Cow with markings of child being vaccinated – designed by P. Brookes (20p)
Patient on trolley – designed by Susan Macfarlane (26p)
Penicillin mould – designed by M. Dempsey (43p)
Test tube baby – designed by A. Gormley (63p)

1999, March 2. The Patients' Tale.
Printed in photogravure by Questa. One phosphor band (**20p**), two phosphor bands (others).
20p, 26p, 43p, 63p

Set	2.50	2.50
Gutter pairs	5.50	
First day cover	3.00	
Stamp cards	4.25	6.50

NB: The 20p also appears in the £6.99 'World Changers' prestige stamp book issued on September 21, 1999.

Norman and dove – designed by J. Byrne (20p)
Pilgrim Fathers and Red Indian – designed by W. McLean (26p)
Sailing ship and emigration to Australia – designed by J. Fisher (43p)
Face superimposed on hummingbird – designed by G. Powell (63p)

1999, April 6. The Settlers' Tale.
Printed in litho (**20p**) or photogravure (others) by Walsall. One phosphor band (**20p**), two phosphor bands (others).
20p, 26p, 43p, 63p

Set	2.50	2.50
Gutter pairs	5.50	
First day cover	3.00	
Stamp cards	4.25	6.50

NB: The 26p also appears in a £2.60 booklet issued on May 12, 1999.

Woven threads – designed by P. Collingwood (19p)
Salts Mill, Saltaire – designed by D. Hockney (26p)
Hull of ship on slipway – designed by R. Sanderson (44p)
Lloyd's Building – designed by B. Neiland (64p)

1999, May 4. The Workers' Tale.
Printed in litho (**19p**) or photogravure (others) by De La Rue. One phosphor band (**19p**), two phosphor bands (others).
19p, 26p, 44p, 64p

Set	2.50	2.50
Gutter pairs	5.50	
First day cover	3.00	
Stamp cards	4.25	6.50

NB: The 26p from this set also appears in a £2.60 booklet issued on May 12, 1999, printed in photogravure by Walsall. Price: £1.50 mint.

Freddie Mercury – designed by P. Blake (19p)
Bobby Moore holding the World Cup – designed by M. White (26p)
Dalek– designed by Lord Snowdon (44p)
Charlie Chaplin – designed by R. Steadman (64p)

1999, June 1. The Entertainers' Tale.
Printed in photogravure by Enschedé. One phosphor band (19p), two phosphor bands (others).
19p, 26p, 44p, 64p

Set	2.50	2.50
Gutter pairs	5.50	
First day cover	3.00	
Stamp cards	4.25	6.50

Photographs of Prince Edward and Miss Sophie Rhys-Jones by John Swannell:
Facing front (**26p**)
Facing sideways (**64p**)

1999, June 15. Royal Wedding.
Des: J. Gibbs. Printed in photogravure by De La Rue.
26p, 64p

Set	1.50	1.50
Gutter pairs	3.50	
First day cover	2.25	
Stamp cards	3.25	3.50

Suffragette behind bars – designed by Natasha Kerr (19p)
Tap – designed by M. Craig-Martin (26p)

Children – designed by A. Drummond (44p)
'MAGNA CARTA' – designed by A. Kitching (64p)

1999, July 6. The Citizens' Tale.
Printed in photogravure by De La Rue. One phosphor band (19p), two phosphor bands (others).
19p, 26p, 44p, 64p

Set	2.50	2.50
Gutter pairs	5.50	
First day cover	3.00	
Stamp cards	4.25	6.50

DNA – designed by M. Curtis (19p)
Galapagos Finch and skeleton – designed by R. Harris Ching (26p)
Light polarised by magnetism – designed by C. Gray (44p)
Saturn – from Hubble Space Telescope photograph (64p)

1999, August 3. The Scientists' Tale.
Printed in photogravure (**19p, 64p**) or litho (others) by Questa. One phosphor band (**19p**), two phosphor bands (others). Perf: 13½ x 14 (**19p, 64p**), 14 x 14½ (**26p, 44p**).
19p, 26p, 44p, 64p

Set	2.50	2.50
Gutter pairs	5.50	
First day cover	3.00	
Stamp cards	4.25	6.50

NB: The 26p and 44p also appear in the £6.99 'World Changers' prestige stamp book issued on September 21, 1999, but perf: 14½ x 14. Price: £3 pair mint.

Saturn – from Hubble Space Telescope photograph (64p) – same design as used for The Scientists' Tale of August 3.

1999, August 11. Solar Eclipse.
Printed in photogravure by De La Rue. Perf: 14 x 14½.
Miniature sheet, comprising four **64p**

Miniature sheet	10.00	10.00
First day cover	10.00	

NB: The Solar Eclipse miniature sheet was issued to commemorate the solar eclipse that happened over Great Britain in August 1999.

Upland landscape – designed by D. Tress (**19p**)
Horse-drawn seed drill – designed by C. Wormell (**26p**)
Peeling potato – designed by Tessa Traeger (**44p**)
Combine harvester in field – designed by R. Cooke (64p)

1999, September 7. The Farmers' Tale.
Printed in photogravure by De La Rue. One phosphor band
(**19p**), two phosphor bands (others).
19p, 26p, 44p, 64p

Set	2.50	2.50
Gutter pairs	5.50	
First day cover	3.00	
Stamp cards	4.25	6.50

NB: The 26p also appears in a £2.60 booklet issued on
September 21, 1999, printed in photogravure by Walsall. Price:
£1.50 mint.

'Hark the Herald Angels Sing – designed by B.
Neuenschwander (19p)
King James I and Bible – designed by Claire Melinsky (26p)
St Andrews Cathedral, Fife – designed by Catherine Yass (44p)
Nativity – designed by C. Aitchison (64p)

1999, November 2. The Christians' Tale.
Printed in photogravure by De La Rue. One phosphor band
(**19p**), two phosphor bands (others).
19p, 26p, 44p, 64p

Set	2.50	2.50
Gutter pairs	5.50	
First day cover	3.00	
Booklet (20 at **19p**)	6.75	
Booklet (10 at **26p**)	4.75	
Stamp cards	4.25	6.50

Robert the Bruce – designed by A. Davidson (19p)
Cavalier and horse – designed by R. Kelly (26p)
War Graves Cemetery – designed by D. McCullin (44p)
Soldiers with boy – designed by C. Corr (64p)

1999, October 5. The Soldiers' Tale.
Printed in litho (**19p**) or photogravure (others) by Walsall. One
phosphor band (**19p**), two phosphor bands (others).
19p, 26p, 44p, 64p

Set	2.50	2.50
Gutter pairs	5.50	
First day cover	3.00	
Stamp cards	4.25	6.50

'World of the Stage' – by Allen Jones (19p)
'World of Music' – by Bridget Riley (26p)
'World of Literature' – by Lisa Milroy (44p)
'New Worlds' – by Sir Howard Hodgkin (64p)

1999, December 7. The Artists' Tale.
Printed in photogravure by Walsall. One phosphor band (**19p**),
two phosphor bands (others).
19p, 26p, 44p, 64p

Set	2.50	2.50
Gutter pairs	5.50	
First day cover	3.00	
Stamp cards	4.25	6.50

Globe showing North America (64p)
Globe showing Asia (64p)
Globe showing Middle East (64p)
Globe showing Europe (64p)

1999, December 14. Millennium Timekeeper.
Des: David Gentleman. Printed in gravure by De La Rue.

Miniature sheet containing **64p, 64p, 64p, 64p**

Miniature sheet	11.00	11.00
First day cover	10.00	
Stamp cards	9.50	18.50

NB: The miniature sheet exists with the margin overprinted 'EARL'S COURT, LONDON 22 – 28 MAY 2000 THE STAMP SHOW 2000' sold with tickets to The Stamp Show 2000 at £10: first put on sale on March 1, 2000. Price: £15.00 mint.

2000, January 6. Millennium definitive.
A revised version of the Machin definitive design – listed under Machin decimal definitives.

NB: The designs for the Millennium series in 2000 are of photographs of projects undertaken to celebrate the Millennium.

Barn owl (19p)
Night sky (26p and 1st)
River Goyt and textile mills (44p)
Cape Gannets (64p)

2000, January 18. Above and Beyond.
Printed in litho (**44p**) or gravure (others) by Questa. One phosphor band (**19p**), two phosphor bands (others).

19p, 26p, 44p, 64p

Set	2.50	2.50
Gutter pairs	5.50	
First day cover	3.00	
Stamp cards	4.25	6.50

Printed in gravure by Walsall. Only from £2.70 stamp booklet issued on May 26, 2000.

1st (design as 26p)	1.50	1.50

Millennium beacon (19p)
Garratt locomotive and train (26p)
Lightning (44p)
Floodlighting (64p)

2000, February 1. Fire and Light.
Printed in gravure by De La Rue. One phosphor band (**19p**), two phosphor bands (others).

19p, 26p, 44p, 64p

Set	2.50	2.50
Gutter pairs	5.50	
First day cover	3.00	
Stamp cards	4.25	6.50

Pebbles (19p)
Frog's legs and water lilies (26p)
Cliff Broadwalk (44p)
Reflections in water (64p)

2000, March 7. Water and Coast.
Printed in litho (**44p**) or gravure (others) by Walsall. One phosphor band (**19p**), two phosphor bands (others).

19p, 26p, 44p, 64p

Set	2.50	2.50
Gutter pairs	5.50	
First day cover	3.00	
Stamp cards	4.25	6.50

River Braid (2nd)
South American leaf-cutter ants (1st)
Solar sensors (44p)
Hydroponic leaves (64p)

2000, April 4. Life and Earth.
Printed in gravure by De La Rue. One phosphor band (**2nd**),
two phosphor bands (others).
2nd, 1st, 44p, 64p

Set	2.50	2.50
Gutter pairs	5.50	
First day cover	3.00	
Stamp cards	4.25	6.50

NB: the 1st also appears in the £2.70 stamp booklet issued on
May 26, 2000.

Pottery glaze (2nd)
Tate Modern (1st)
Road marking for bicycle (45p)
People in Salford (65p)

2000, May 2. Art and Craft.
Printed in gravure by Enschedé. One phosphor band (**2nd**),
two phosphor bands (others).
2nd, 1st, 45p, 65p

Set	2.50	2.50
Gutter pairs	5.50	
First day cover	3.00	
Stamp cards	4.25	6.50

2000, May 22/23. The Stamp Show 2000.
Two miniature sheets were issued - one on May 22, the other
on May 23 - including Machin definitives. These are listed under
the Machin decimal definitives.

Children playing (2nd)
Millennium Bridge, Gateshead (1st)
Daisies (45p)
African hut and thatched cottage (65p)

2000, June 6. People and Places.
Printed in gravure (**2nd, 45p**) or litho (others) by Walsall. One
phosphor band (2nd), two phosphor bands (others).
2nd, 1st, 45p, 65p

Set	2.50	2.50
Gutter pairs	5.50	
First day cover	3.00	
Stamp cards	4.25	6.50

Raising the Stone (2nd)
Horse's hooves (1st)
Cyclist and reflection (45p)
Bluebell wood (65p)

2000, July 4. Stone and Soil.
Printed in gravure in Enschedé. One phosphor band (**2nd**), two
phosphor bands (others).
2nd, 1st, 45p, 65p

Set	2.50	2.50
Gutter pairs	5.50	
First day cover	3.00	
Stamp cards	4.25	6.50

NB: The 1st also appears in a £2.70 stamp booklet issued on
September 5, 2000, printed in gravure by Walsall. Price: 75p
mint.
The 65p also appears in the £7 'Treasury of Trees' prestige
stamp book issued on September 18, 2000, printed in gravure
by Walsall. Price: £1.50 mint.

Roots of trees (2nd)
Sunflower (1st)
Sycamore seeds (45p)
Doire Dach Forest (65p)

2000, August 1. Tree and Leaf.
Printed in gravure in De La Rue. One phosphor band (**2nd**), two phosphor bands (others).
2nd, 1st, 45p, 65p

Set	2.50	2.50
Gutter pairs	5.50	
First day cover	3.00	
Stamp cards	4.25	6.50

NB: The 2nd, 45p and 65p also appear in the £7 'Treasury of Trees' prestige stamp book issued on September 18, 2000, printed in gravure by Walsall. Price: £3 mint.

Royal Family group photograph by J. Swannell taken on The Queen Mother's 99th birthday:
Queen Elizabeth II (27p)
Prince William (27p)
The Queen Mother (27p)
Prince Charles (27p)

2000, August 4.
The 100th birthday of The Queen Mother.
Des: J. Gibbs. Printed in gravure by De La Rue.
Miniature sheet containing the four **27p** designs as part of the entire photograph

Miniature sheet	4.00	4.00
First day cover	5.00	
Stamp cards	9.50	10.50

NB: the **27p** design showing The Queen Mother, and the entire

miniature sheet but in a slightly larger size, also appeared in the £7.03 'The Life of the Century' prestige stamp book issued on August 4, 2000, printed in gravure by Questa. Price: single 27p stamp: £1.25 mint.

Head of Gigantiops (2nd)
Gathering water lilies on Norfolk Broads (1st)
X-Ray of hand with computer mouse (45p)
Tartan wool holder (65p)

2000, September 5. Mind and Matter.
Printed in litho by Walsall. One phosphor band (**2nd**), two phosphor bands (others).
2nd, 1st, 45p, 65p

Set	2.50	2.50
Gutter pairs	5.50	
First day cover	3.00	
Stamp cards	4.25	6.50

Acrobats (2nd)
Footballers (1st)
Bather (45p)
Hen's egg (magnified) (65p)

2000, October 3. Body and Bone.
Printed in litho (**2nd**) or gravure by Questa. One phosphor band (2nd), two phosphor bands (others).
2nd, 1st, 45p, 65p

Set	2.50	2.50
Gutter pairs	5.50	
First day cover	3.00	
Stamp cards	4.25	6.50

Virgin and Child stained glass window (2nd)
Floodlit church (1st)
Latin gradual (45p)
Chapter House ceiling of York Minster (65p)

2000, November 7. Spirit and Faith.
Printed in gravure by De La Rue. One phosphor band (**2nd**),
two phosphor bands (others).
2nd, 1st, 45p, 65p

Set	2.50	2.50
Gutter pairs	5.50	
First day cover	3.00	
Booklet (20 at **2nd**)	6.25	
Booklet (10 at **1st**)	4.75	
Stamp cards	4.25	6.50

Church bells (2nd)
Eye (1st)
Top of a harp (45p)
Figure in latticework (65p)

2000, December 5. Sound and Vision.
Printed in gravure by De La Rue. One phosphor band (**2nd**),
two phosphor bands (others).
2nd, 1st, 45p, 65p

Set	2.50	2.50
Gutter pairs	5.50	
First day cover	3.00	
Stamp cards	4.25	6.50

Children's face paintings, representing:
Flower (2nd)
Tiger (1st)
Owl (45p)
Butterfly (65p)

2001, January 16. Looking to The Future.
Des; Why Not Associates. Printed in gravure by De La Rue.
One phosphor band (**2nd**), two phosphor bands (others).
2nd, 1st, 45p, 65p

Set	2.50	2.50
Gutter pairs	5.50	
First day cover	3.00	
Stamp cards	5.00	6.50

Hallmarks, representing:
Love (1st)
THANKS (1st)
abc (1st)
WELCOME (1st)
Cheers (1st)

2001, February 6. Occasions stamps.
Des: Springpoint Design. Printed in gravure by Enschedé. Issued
in separate sheets.
1st, 1st, 1st, 1st, 1st

Set	2.75	3.00
Gutter pairs	6.00	
First day cover	3.00	
Stamp cards	8.00	7.50

NB: These designs were also used for Smilers sheets in 2001.

Dog and man sitting on bench (1st)
Dog in bath (1st)
Boxer (1st)
Cat handbag (1st)
Cat on gate (1st)
Dog in car (1st)
Cat at window (1st)

QEII SPECIALS

Dog looking over fence (1st)
Cat watching bird (1st)
Cat in wash basin (1st)

2001, February 13. Cats and Dogs.
Des: Johnson Banks. Printed in gravure by Walsall. Issued as a self-adhesive sheetlet which could be folded to form a booklet containing one of each of the ten designs.

1st, 1st, 1st, 1st, 1st, 1st, 1st, 1st, 1st, 1st

Sheetlet	7.50	7.50
First day cover	6.50	
Stamp Cards	10.00	15.50

NB: the ten designs, together with two 1st class definitives, were also issued in a £3.24 'Cats and Dogs' stamp book on February 13, 2001.

Sections of a barometer:
Rain (19p)
Fair (27p)
Stormy (45p)
Very dry (65p)

2001, March 13. The Weather.
Des: H. Brown and T. Meeuwissen. Printed in gravure by De La Rue. One phosphor band (**19p**), two phosphor bands (others).

19p, 27p, 45p, 65p

Set	2.75	3.00
Gutter pairs	6.00	
First day cover	3.50	
Stamp cards	5.25	8.50
Miniature sheet		
(containing one of each value)	7.00	7.00
First day cover	7.00	

Vanguard Class submarine (2nd)
Swiftsure Class submarine (1st)
Utility Class submarine (45p)
Holland type submarine (65p)

2001, April 10.
Centenary of Royal Navy Submarine Service.
Des: D. Davis. Printed in gravure by Questa. One phosphor band (**2nd**), two phosphor bands (others). Perf: 15 x 14. PVA gum.

2nd, 1st, 45p, 65p

Set	2.75	2.50
Gutter pairs	6.00	
First day cover	3.50	
Stamp cards	4.75	6.50

NB: The four stamps are also in the £6.76 'Unseen and Unheard' prestige stamp book issued on October 22, 2001. Perf: 15? x 15. Price: £5.50 mint or used.
The 1st class design also appears twice in self-adhesive form, together with four 1st class definitives, in a £1.62 stamp booklet issued on April 17, 2001. Price: £35 mint, £15 used.

White Ensign (1st)
Union Jack (1st)
Jolly Roger (1st)
Flag of Chief of Defence Staff (1st)

2001, April 10.
Centenary of Royal Navy Submarine Service. Flags.
Issued as a miniature sheet. Printed in gravure by Questa. PVA gum.

Miniature sheet		
(containing one of each value)	3.50	3.75
First day cover	3.75	
Stamp cards	10.00	14.00

NB: The White Ensign and Jolly Roger designs also appear in self adhesive form with four 1st class definitives in a £1.62 stamp booklet issued on October 22, 2001. Price per pair: £10 mint, £9 used.
The Union Jack design was used for a Smilers sheet in 2005.

QEII SPECIALS

Front views of double deck buses. The illustrations extend into the sheet margins, and across the sheet, so that some of the illustrations span two stamps.
Leyland X2 open top, B Type, Leyland Titan TD1, AEC Regent I (1st)
AEC Regent I, Daimler COG5, Guy Arab II Utility, AEC Regent III RT (1st)
AEC Regent III RT, Bristol K open top, AEC Routemaster, Bristol Lodekka FSF (1st)
Bristol Lodekka FSF, Leyland PD3 'Queen Mary', Leyland Atlantean, Daimler Fleetline (1st)
Daimler Fleetline, MCW Metrobus, Leyland Olympian, Dennis Trident (1st)

2001, May 15. Double-deck buses.
Des: M. English. Printed in gravure by Questa.
1st, 1st, 1st, 1st, 1st in se-tenant strip

Set of five in **se-tenant strip**	2.50	2.50
Gutter pairs	5.50	
First day cover	3.00	
Miniature sheet		
(containing one of each value – arranged as two pairs and a single)	2.50	2.50
First day cover	3.00	
Stamp cards	8.50	15.50

Toque hat (1st)
Butterfly hat (E)
Top hat (45p)
Spiral hat (65p)

2001, June 19. Hats.
Des: Rose Design, from photographs by N. Knight.
Printed in litho by Enschedé.
1st, E, 45p, 65p

Set	2.75	2.75
Gutter pairs	6.00	
First day cover	3.00	
Stamp cards	4.75	6.50

Common frog (1st)
Great diving beetle (E)
Three-spined stickleback (45p)
Southern Hawker Dragonfly (65p)

2001, July 10. Pond Life. Europa.
Des: J. Gibbs. Printed in gravure by De La Rue.
1st, E, 45p, 65p

Set	3.00	3.00
Gutter pairs	6.50	
First day cover	3.50	
Stamp cards	4.75	6.50

Policeman (1st)
Clown (1st)
Mr Punch (1st)
Judy (1st)
Beadle (1st)
Crocodile (1st)

2001, September 4. Punch and Judy.
Des: K. Bernstein, from puppets made by Bryan Clarke.
Printed in gravure by Walsall. PVA gum. Perf: 14 x 15.
1st, 1st, 1st, 1st, 1st, 1st in a se-tenant strip

Set of six in **se-tenant strip**	2.75	2.75
Gutter pairs	6.00	
First day cover	3.25	
Stamp cards	6.25	8.50

NB: The Mr Punch and Judy designs also appear in self-adhesive form with four 1st class definitives in a £1.62 stamp booklet issued on September 4, 2001, printed in gravure by Questa. Perf: 14 x 15½. Price per pair: £10 mint, £9 used.

Carbon molecule – printed in litho and silk screen (2nd)
Globe – printed in litho and recess (1st)
Dove – printed in litho and embossing (E)
Crosses – printed in litho (40p)
'The Ad-dressing of Cats' by T. S. Eliot printed on open book – printed in litho (45p)
Boron molecule – printed in litho with hologram (65p)

2001, October 2. Nobel Prizes.
Des: P. Vermier; engraved by Inge Madle (1st). Printed by Enschedé. One phosphor band (2nd), phosphor band around stamp (others).
2nd, 1st, E, 40p, 45p, 65p

Set	4.00	3.75
Gutter pairs	9.00	
First day cover	5.00	
Stamp cards	6.25	8.50

How the Whale got his Throat (1st)
How the Camel got his Hump (1st)
How the Rhinoceros got his Skin (1st)
How the Leopard got his Spots (1st)
The Elephant's Child (1st)
The Sing Song of Old Man Kangaroo (1st)
The Beginning of the Armadillos (1st)
The Crab that played with the Sea (1st)
The Cat that walked by Himself (1st)
The Butterfly that stamped (1st)

2002, January 15. The Just So Stories by Rudyard Kipling.
Des: I. Cohen. Printed in gravure by Walsall. Issued as a self-adhesive sheetlet containing one of each of the ten designs.
1st, 1st, 1st, 1st, 1st, 1st, 1st, 1st, 1st, 1st

Sheetlet	5.25	5.50
First day cover	5.50	
Stamp Cards	6.00	21.00

Robins with snowman (2nd)
Robins on bird table (1st)
Robins skating on bird bath (E)
Robins with Christmas pudding handing from branch of tree (45p)
Robins in nest made of paper chains (65p)

2001, November 6. Christmas. Robins.
Des: A. Robins and H. Brown. Printed in gravure by De La Rue. Self-adhesive.
2nd, 1st, E, 45p, 65p

Set	3.00	3.00
First day cover	5.00	
Booklet (20 at **2nd**)	7.50	
Booklet (10 at **1st**)	5.50	
Stamp cards	5.25	7.50

NB: The 2nd and 1st class values were also issued in separate stamp books, in the form of folders.
The 2nd and 1st class designs were used for Smilers stamps in 2004.

Portraits of Queen Elizabeth II:
In 1952, by Dorothy Wilding (2nd)
In 1968, by Cecil Beaton (1st)
In 1978, by Lord Snowden (E)
In 1984, by Yousef Karsh (45p)
In 1996, by Tim Graham (65p)

2002, February 6. Golden Jubilee.
Des: Kate Stephens. Printed in gravure by De La Rue. One phosphor band (2nd), two phosphor bands (others). Wmk: 50 (sideways).
2nd, 1st, E, 45p, 65p

Set	3.50	3.00
Gutter pairs	7.50	
First day cover	3.75	
Stamp cards	4.00	7.00

NB: The five stamps are also available in a £7.29 'A Gracious Accession' prestige stamp book, but with the watermark upright. Price: £5,25 mint, £5.50 used.

Rabbits, inscribed 'a new baby' – designed by I. Bilbey (1st)
'LOVE' – designed by A. Kitching (1st)
'hello' written in sky – designed by Hoop Associates (1st)
Bear pulling topiary tree in shape of house in pot – designed by
G. Percy (1st)
|Flowers inscribed 'best wishes' – designed by I. Bilbey (1st)

2002, March 5. Occasions.
Printed in litho by Questa. Issued in separate sheets.
1st, 1st, 1st, 1st, 1st

Set	2.50	2.50
Gutter pairs	5.50	
First day cover	3.25	
Stamp cards	4.00	7.00

NB: The 'hello' design also appears in a self-adhesive booklet,
together with four 1st gold definitives, issued on March 4, 2003.
Price: £2.75 mint or used.
These designs were also used for Smilers sheets in 2002.

Studland Bay (27p)
Luskentyre (27p)
Cliffs of Dover (27p)
Padstow Harbour (27p)
Broadstairs (27p)
St Abb's Head (27p)
Dunster Beach (27p)
Newquay (27p)
Portrush (27p)
Sand-spit (27p)

2002, March 19. British Coastlines.
Des: R. Cooke. Printed in litho by Walsall.
27p, 27p, 27p, 27p, 27p, 27p, 27p, 27p, 27p, 27p
in a se-tenant block of ten

Set of ten in **se-tenant block**	4.00	4.00
Gutter pairs	8.50	
First day cover	5.25	
Stamp cards	6.00	13.50

Slack wire act (2nd)
Lion tamer (1st)
Trick tri-cyclists (E)
Krazy kar (45p)
Equestrienne (65p)

2002, April 10. Circus. Europa.
Des: R. Fuller. Printed in gravure by Questa. One phosphor
band (2nd), two phosphor bands (others).
2nd, 1st, E, 45p, 65p

Set	3.25	3.00
Gutter pairs	6.50	
First day cover	3.75	
Stamp cards	4.00	7.00

Designs as for
The Queen Mother 90th birthday issue of 1990:
20p design (1st)
29p design (E)
34p design (45p)
37p design (65p)

2002, April 25. The Queen Mother Memorial Issue.
Des: J. Gorham. Printed in gravure by De La Rue.
1st, E, 45p, 65p

Set	2.75	2.75
Gutter pairs	6.00	
First day cover	3.75	

Airbus A340-600 (2nd)
Concorde (1st)
Trident (E)
VC 10 (45p)
Comet (65p)

2002, May 2. Airliners.
Des: Roundel. Printed in gravure by De La Rue. One phosphor band (2nd), two phosphor bands (others).
2nd, 1st, E, 45p, 65p

Set	3.25	3.25
Gutter pairs	7.00	
First day cover	3.75	
Stamp cards	4.00	7.50

NB: The 1st class design also appears twice in self-adhesive form with four 1st class definitives in a £1.62 stamp booklet issued on May 2, 2002, printed in gravure by Questa. Price: £1.75 mint or used.

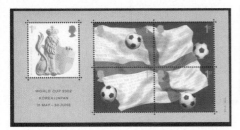

Lion with shield of St George – designed by Sedley Place (1st)
Football with quarters of the English flag – designed by H. Brown:
Top left (1st)
Top right (1st)
Bottom left (1st)
Bottom right (1st)

2002, May 21. World Cup Football Championships.
Printed in gravure by Walsall.
1st (St George design)

Single stamp	0.75	0.75
Gutter pair	1.75	
First day cover	2.25	

Miniature sheet, containing the Lion and the four English flag designs

Miniature sheet	2.50	2.75

First day cover	2.75	
Stamp cards	4.00	7.50

NB: The 1st class designs showing the top left and top right of the English flag also appear twice in self-adhesive form with four 1st class definitives in a £1.62 stamp booklet issued on May 21, 2002. Price per pair: £4 mint or used.
The 1st class design showing the bottom right of he English flag also appeared on Smilers sheets.

Swimming (2nd)
Running (1st)
Cycling (E)
Long jump (47p)
Wheelchair racing (68p)

2002, July 16. 17th Commonwealth Games, Manchester.
Des: Madeleine Bennett. Printed in gravure by Enschedé. One phosphor band (**2nd**), two phosphor bands (others).
2nd, 1st, E, 47p, 68p

Set	3.00	3.00
Gutter pairs	6.50	
First day cover	3.75	
Stamp cards	4.00	7.50

Tinkerbell (2nd)
Wendy, John and Michael Darling flying by Big Ben (1st)
Crocodile and the alarm clock (E)
Captain Hook (47p)
Peter Pan (68p)

2002, August 20. Peter Pan.
Des: Tutsells. Printed in gravure by De La Rue. One phosphor band (2nd), two phosphor bands (others).
2nd, 1st, E, 47p, 68p

Set	3.00	3.00
Gutter pairs	6.50	
First day cover	3.75	
Stamp cards	5.00	8.00

Millennium Bridge (2nd)
Tower Bridge (1st)
Westminster Bridge (E)
Blackfriars Bridge (47p)
London Bridge (68p)

2002, September 10. Bridges of London.
Des: Sarah Davies and Robert Maude. Printed in litho by Questa. One phosphor band (**2nd**), two phosphor bands (others).

2nd, 1st, E, 47p, 68p		
Set	3.00	3.00
Gutter pairs	6.50	
First day cover	3.75	
Stamp cards	4.00	7.50

NB: the 1st class design also appears twice in self-adhesive form with four 1st class definitives in a £1.62 booklet issued on September 10, 2002. Printed in gravure by Questa. Price: £1.75 mint, £1.75 used.

Planetary nebula in Aquila (1st)
Seyfert 2 galaxy in Pegasus (1st)
Planetary nebula in Norma (1st)
Seyfert 2 galaxy in Circinus (1st)

2002, September 24. Astronomy.
Des: Rose Design. Printed in gravure by Questa. Miniature sheet, containing the four designs

Miniature sheet	2.50	2.50
First day cover	2.50	
Stamp cards	4.00	7.50

NB: the design of the miniature sheet also appears in a larger size in the £6.83 'Across the Universe' prestige stamp book issued on September 21, 2002.

Pillar box of 1857 in green (2nd)
Pillar box of 1874 (1st)
Air mail box of 1934 (E)
Pillar box of 1939 (47p)
Pillar box of 1980 (68p)

2002, October 8.
150th Anniversary of the first Pillar Box.
Des: Silk Pearce; engraved by C. Slania. Printed in recess and litho by Enschedé. One phosphor band (**2nd**), two phosphor bands (others).

2nd, 1st, E, 47p, 68p		
Set	3.00	3.00
Gutter pairs	6.50	
First day cover	3.75	
Stamp cards	3.25	7.50

Blue spruce (2nd)
Holly (1st)
Ivy (E)
Mistletoe (47p)
Pine cone (68p)

2002, November 5. Christmas. Christmas Flowers.
Des: Rose Design. Printed in gravure by De La Rue. One phosphor band (**2nd**), two phosphor bands (others). Self-adhesive.

2nd, 1st, E, 47p, 68p		
Set	3.00	3.00
First day cover	3.75	
Booklet (24 at **2nd**)	7.50	
Booklet (12 at **1st**)	5.25	
Stamp cards	3.25	7.50

NB: the 2nd and 1st class stamps also appear in stamp booklets (folders).

Photographs by S. Dalton of
Barn Owl about to land – five different views (1st)
Kestrel in flight – five different views (1st)

2003, January 14. Birds of Prey.
Des: J. Gibbs. Printed in litho by Walsall.
1st, 1st, 1st, 1st, 1st, 1st, 1st, 1st, 1st, 1st, issued in se-tenant blocks of ten, comprising the five Barn Owl designs above the five Kestrel designs

Set in **se-tenant block** of ten	4.50	5.50
Gutter pairs	15.00	
First day cover	5.50	
Stamp cards	5.00	15.00

Gold star, See me, Playtime (1st)
I 'love' U (1st)
Angel, Poppet, Little terror (1st)
Yes, No, Maybe (1st)
Oops! Sorry, Will try harder (1st)
I did it! You did it! We did it! (1st)

2003, February 4. Occasions stamps.
Des: UNA, Sarah Wiegand and M. Exon. Printed in litho by Questa.
1st, 1st, 1st, 1st, 1st, 1st, in se-tenant block of six

Set in **se-tenant block** of six	2.50	2.50
Gutter pairs	5.50	
First day cover	3.75	
Stamp Cards	3.25	8.75

NB: these designs also appeared as Smilers sheets.

The genetic jigsaw (2nd)
Ape looking at scientist behind bars (1st)
DNA snakes and ladders (E)
Animals dressed as scientists (47p)
Looking into a DNA crystal ball (68p)

2003, February 25.
50th Anniversary of the Discovery of DNA.
Des: William Murray Hamm and P. Brookes. Printed in litho by Enschedé. One phosphor band (2nd), two phosphor bands (others).
2nd, 1st, E, 47p, 68p

Set	3.00	3.00
Gutter pairs		6.50
First day cover	4.25	
Stamp cards	3.00	8.50

NB: the 2nd and E designs also appear in the £6.99 'Microcosmos' prestige stamp book issued on February 25, 2003.

Strawberry (1st)
Potato (1st)
Apple (1st)
Red Pepper (1st)
Pear (1st)
Orange (1st)
Tomato (1st)
Lemon (1st)
Brussels sprout (1st)
Aubergine (1st)

2003, March 25. Fruit and Veg.
Des: Johnson Banks. Printed in gravure by Walsall. Self-adhesive.
1st, 1st, 1st, 1st, 1st, 1st, 1st, 1st, 1st, 1st in se-tenant block of six

Set in **se-tenant block** of six	4.00	4.25
Gutter pairs	8.50	
First day cover	5.00	
Stamp Cards	5.25	15.00

NB: These stamps were issued with various self-adhesive stickers, such as of eyes, ears and mouths, so that the fruit and vegetables could be made to resemble faces.

Amy Johnson with bi-plane (2nd)
1953 Everest team (1st)
Freya Stark in the desert (E)
Ernest Shackleton (42p)
Francis Chichester with Gipsy Moth IV (47p)
Robert Falcon Scott at the South Pole (68p)

2003, April 29. Extreme Endeavours.
Des: H. Brown. Printed in gravure by Questa. One phosphor
band (**2nd**), two phosphor bands (others). Perf: 15 x 14?.
2nd, 1st, E, 42p, 47p, 68p

Set	3.50	3.50
Gutter pairs	7.50	
First day cover	5.00	
Stamp cards	3.25	9.50

NB: The 1st class design also appears twice, in self adhesive
form, with four 1st class definitives in a £1.62 stamp booklet
issued on April 29, 2003. Printed in gravure by De La Rue. Perf:
14 ?. Price: £2 mint, £2 used.

Coronation procession (1st)
Children reading poster (1st)
The Queen seated in the Coronation Chair (1st)
Children producing Royal montage (1st)
The Queen in Coronation robes – by Cecil Beaton (1st)
Children racing during street party (1st)
Coronation Coach passing through Admiralty Arch (1st)
Children in fancy dress (1st)
Coronation Coach outside Buckingham Palace (1st)
Children at street party (1st)
The scenes of the Coronation are in colour; the scenes of the
celebrations are in black and white.

2003, June 2. 50th Anniversary of the Coronation.
Des: Kate Stephens. Printed in gravure by De La Rue.
1st, 1st, 1st, 1st, 1st, 1st, 1st, 1st, 1st, 1st in se-tenant block

Set of ten in **se-tenant block**	4.00	4.25
Gutter pairs	8.50	
First day cover	5.00	
Stamp cards	5.25	15.00

NB: Eight of these designs also appear in the £7.46 'A Perfect
Coronation' prestige stamp book issued on June 2, 2003.

Photographs of Prince William:
By Brendan Beirne (28p)
By Tim Graham (2000) (E)
By Camera Press (47p)
By Tim Graham (2001) (68p)

2003, June 17. 21st birthday of Prince William.
Des: Madeleine Bennett. Printed in gravure by Walsall.
28p, E, 47p, 68p

Set	2.75	2.75
Gutter pairs	6.00	
First day cover	4.00	
Stamp cards	2.25	15.00

Loch Assynt, Sutherland (2nd)
Ben More, Isle of Mull (1st)
Rothiemurchus, Cairngorms (E)
Dalveen Pass, Lowther Hills (42p)
Glenfinnan Viaduct, Lochaber (47p)
Papa Little, Shetland Islands (68p)

2003, July 15. A British Journey: Scotland.
Des: Phelan Barker. Printed in gravure by De La Rue. One
phosphor band (**2nd**), two phosphor bands (others).
2nd, 1st, E, 42p, 47p, 68p

Set	3.50	3.75
Gutter pairs	7.50	
First day cover	5.00	
Stamp cards	3.25	9.00

NB: The 1st class design also appears twice, in self adhesive
form, with four 1st class definitives in a £1.68 stamp booklet
issued on July 15, 2003. Price: £2 mint, £2 used.

'The Station' (1st)
'Black Swan' (E)
'The Cross Keys' (42p)
'The Mayflower' (47p)
'The Barley Sheaf' (68p)

2003, August 12. Pub Signs. Europa.
Des: Elmwood. Printed in gravure by De La Rue.
1st, E, 42p, 47p, 68p

Set	3.50	3.50
Gutter pairs	7.50	
First day cover	4.50	
Stamp cards	2.75	7.50

NB: The 1st class design also appears in a £7.44 'Letters by Night' prestige stamp book issued on March 16, 2004.

Meccano Constructor Biplane (1st)
Wells-Brimtoy bus (E)
Hornby M1 locomotive (42p)
Dinky Toys Ford Zephyr (47p)
Mettoy Space Ship Eagle (68p)

2003, September 18. Toys.
Des: Trickett and Webb. Printed in gravure by Enschedé.
1st, E, 42p, 47p, 68p

Set	3.50	3.50
Gutter pairs	7.50	
First day cover	4.50	
Stamp cards	2.25	13.50
Miniature sheet,		
containing one of each value	3.50	3.50
First day cover	4.50	

NB: The 1st class design also appears twice, in self adhesive form, with four 1st class definitives in a £1.68 stamp booklet issued on September 18, 2003. Printed in gravure by De La Rue. Price: £2.75 mint, £2.75 used.

Coffin of Denytenamun (2nd)
Alexander the Great (1st)
Sutton Hoo helmet (E)
Sculpture of Parvati (42p)
Mask of Xiuhtecuhtli (47p)
Hoa Hakananai'a (68p)

2003, October 7. Treasures from the British Museum.
Des: Rose Design. Printed in gravure by Walsall. One phosphor band (2nd), band at right (42p, 68p), two phosphor bands (others).
2nd, 1st, E, 42p, 47p, 68p

Set	3.50	3.75
Gutter pairs	7.50	
First day cover	5.00	
Stamp cards	3.25	9.00

Ice Sculptures by Andy Goldsworthy:
Spiral (2nd)
Star (1st)
Wall (E)
Ball (42p)
Hole (47p)
Pyramids (68p)

2003, November 4. Christmas. Ice Sculptures.
Des: D. Davis. Printed in gravure byDe La Rue. One phosphor band (2nd), two phosphor bands (others). Self-adhesive.
2nd, 1st, E, 42p, 47p, 68p

Set	5.00	5.00
First day cover	5.50	
Booklet (24 at 2nd)	8.00	
Booklet (12 at 1st)	5.50	
Stamp cards	3.25	12.00

NB: The 1st class and 2nd class design also appear in stamp booklets (folders).
These stamps were normally issued with the backing paper

QEII SPECIALS

stripped away. However, the 1st class stamps exist with the backing paper still in place, from stamps given each year to Post Office employees.
The 2nd and 1st class designs appear as Smilers sheets.

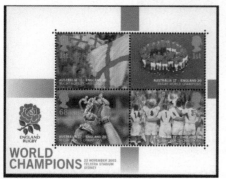

England fans and England flag (1st)
England team standing in a circle (1st)
The Rugby World Cup (1st)
The England team after winning the Rugby World Cup (1st)

2003, December 19.
England winning the Rugby World Cup.
Des: Why Not Associates. Printed in litho by Walsall.
Miniature sheet, containing one of each design

Miniature sheet	3.00	3.00
First day cover	3.75	

'Dolgoch' on the Rheilffordd Tayllyn Railway (20p)
CR 439 on the Bo'ness and Kinneil Railway (28p)
GCR 8K on the Grand Central Railway (E)
GWR Manor on the Severn Valley Railway (42p)
SR West Country on the Bluebell Railway (47p)
BR Standard on the Keighley and Worth Valley Railway (68p)

2004, January 13. Classic Locomotives.
Des: Roundel. Printed in litho by De La Rue. One phosphor band (**2nd**), two phosphor bands (others).
20p, 28p, E, 42p, 47p, 68p

Set	3.75	3.75
Gutter pairs	8.00	
First day cover	5.00	
Stamp cards	3.25	15.50
Miniature sheet,		
containing one of each value	20.00	15.00
First day cover	15.00	

NB: The 28p, E and 42p designs also appears in the £7.44

'Letters by Night' prestige stamp book issued on March 16, 2004.

Envelopes within a design of:
A postman (1st)
A face (1st)
A duck (1st)
A baby (1st)
An aircraft (1st)

2004, February 3. Occasions.
Des: S. Kambayashi. Printed in litho by De La Rue.
1st, 1st, 1st, 1st, 1st in a se-tenant strip

Set of five in **se-tenant strip**	2.25	2.25
Gutter pairs	5.00	
First day cover	3.50	
Stamp cards	2.25	7.50

NB: These designs also appear as a Smilers sheet.

Middle Earth (1st)
Forest of Lothlórien (1st)
The Fellowship of the Ring (1st)
Rivendell (1st)
The Hall at Bag End (1st)
Orthanc (1st)
Doors of Durin (1st)
Barad-dûr (1st)
Minas Tirth (1st)
Fangorn Forest (1st)

2004, February 26.
The Lord of The Rings by J. R. R. Tolkien.
Des: HGV Design. Printed in litho by Walsall.
1st, 1st, 1st, 1st, 1st, 1st, 1st, 1st, 1st, 1st in se-tenant block

Set of ten in se-tenant block	4.50	4.50
Gutter pairs	9.50	
First day cover	5.00	
Stamp cards	4.25	15.00

Ely Island, Lower Lough Erne (2nd)
Giant's Causeway, Antrim coast (1st)
Slemish, Antrim Mountains (E)
Banns Road, Mourne Mountains (42p)
Glenelly Valley, Sperrins (47p)
Islandmore, Strangford Lough (68p)

2004, March 16. A British Journey: Northern Ireland.
Des: Phelan Barker. Printed in gravure by Enschedé. One
phosphor band (**2nd**), two phosphor bands (others).
2nd, 1st, E, 42p, 47p, 68p

Set	3.75	3.75
Gutter pairs	8.00	
First day cover	5.00	
Stamp cards	2.75	9.50

NB: The 28p design also appears twice in self-adhesive form
with four 1st class definitives in a £1.68 stamp booklet issued
on March 16, 2004. Price: £1.75 mint, £1.75 used.

'Lace 1 (trial proof) 1968' by Sir Terry Frost (28p)
'Coccinelle' by Sonia Delaunay (57p)

2004, April 6. Entente Cordiale.
Des: Rose Design. Printed in gravure by Walsall.
28p, 57p

Set	1.50	1.50
Gutter pairs	3.50	
Traffic light gutter pairs	6.00	
First day cover	3.25	
Stamp cards	1.25	4.00

NB: Stamps in the same designs were issued by France.

RMS Queen Mary 2 (1st)
SS Canberra (E)
RMS Queen Mary (42p)
RMS Mauretania (47p)
SS City of New York (57p)
PS Great Western (68p)

2004, April 13. Ocean Liners.
Des: J. Gibbs. Printed in gravure by De La Rue.
1st, E, 42p, 47p, 57p, 68p

Set	4.00	4.25
Gutter pairs	8.50	
First day cover	5.00	
Stamp cards	3.25	15.50
Miniature sheet,		
containing one of each value	7.00	7.00
First day cover	7.00	

NB: The 1st class design also appears in self-adhesive form with
four 1st class definitives in a £1.68 stamp booklet issued on
April 13, 2004. Price: £1.75 mint, £1.75 used.

Dianthus Allwoodii group (2nd)
Dahlia Garden Princess (1st)
Clematis Arabella (E)
Miltonia French Lake (42p)
Lilium Lemon Pride (47p)
Delphinium Clifford Sky (68p)

2004, May 25.
Bicentenary of the Royal Horticultural Society.
Des: Rose Design. Printed in gravure by Enschedé. One
phosphor band (**2nd**), two phosphor bands (others).
2nd, 1st, E, 42p, 47p, 68p

Set	3.75	3.75
Gutter pairs	8.00	
First day cover	5.00	
Stamp cards	3.25	15.50
Miniature sheet,		
containing one of each value	6.00	6.00
First day cover	6.00	

NB: All values also appear in the £7.23 'The Glory of the Garden prestige stamp book issued on May 25, 2004. These booklets also contain three values from the Flowers Greetings stamps issued on January 6, 1997, but with perf: 15 x 14, and are listed as a footnote to that issue.
The 1st class design appears on Smilers sheets.

Barmouth Bridge (2nd)
Hyddgen, Plynlimon (1st)
Brecon Beacons (40p)
Pen-pych, Rhondda Valley (43p)
Rhewl, Dee Valley (47p)
Marloes Sands (68p)

2004, June 15. A British Journey: Wales. Europa.
Des: Phelan Barker. Printed in gravure by De La Rue. One phosphor band (2nd), two phosphor bands (others).
2nd, 1st, 40p, 43p 47p, 68p

Set	3.75	3.75
Gutter pairs	8.00	
First day cover	5.00	
Stamp cards	2.75	9.00

NB: The 1st class design also appears in self-adhesive form with four 1st class definitives in a £1.68 stamp booklet issued on June 15, 2004. Price: £2.50 mint, £2.50 used.

Penny Black with citation to Sir Rowland Hill (1st)
William Shipley (40p)
R, S and A as typewriter keys (43p)
Brush for sweeping chimneys (47p)
Typeface by Eric Gill (57p)
Zero Waste (68p)

2004, August 10.
250th Anniversary of the Royal Society of Arts.
Des: D. Birdsall. Printed in litho by Walsall.
1st, 40p, 43p, 47p, 57p, 68p

Set	4.75	4.75
Gutter pairs	10.00	

First day cover	6.00	
Stamp cards	2.75	9.50

Pine Marten (1st)
Roe Deer (1st)
Badger (1st)
Yellow-necked mouse (1st)
Wild Cat (1st)
Red Squirrel (1st)
Stoat (1st)
Natterer's Bat (1st)
Mole (1st)
Fox (1st)

2004, September 16. Woodland Animals.
Des: Kate Stephens. Printed in gravure by Enschedé.
1st, 1st, 1st, 1st, 1st, 1st, 1st, 1st, 1st,
1st in se-tenant block

Set of ten in se-tenant block	4.50	4.50
Gutter pairs	9.50	
First day cover	5.75	
Stamp cards	4.25	15.00

2004, October 5.
Opening of the Scottish Parliament Building.
Des: H. Brown. Printed in gravure by De La Rue.
Miniature sheet, comprising one **2nd**, two **1st** and two **40p** Scotland definitives

Miniature sheet	3.50	3.50
First day cover	5.50	

Photographs taken during The Crimean War of:
Pte McNamara (2nd)
Piper Muir (1st)
Sgt Major Edwards (40p)
Sgt Powell (57p)

Sgt Major Poole (68p)
Sgt Glasgow (£1.12)

2004, October 12. The Crimean War.
Des: Atelier Works. Printed in litho by Walsall. One phosphor band (**2nd**), two phosphor bands (others).
2nd, 1st, 40p, 57p, 68p, £1.12

Set	5.00	5.00
Gutter pairs	10.50	
Traffic light gutter pairs	12.00	
First day cover	7.50	
Stamp cards	2.75	9.00

Father Christmas on roof (2nd)
Father Christmas welcoming the sunrise (1st)
Father Christmas battling against the wind (40p)
Father Christmas holding umbrella (57p)
Father Christmas holding torch (68p)
Father Christmas sheltering by a chimney (£1.12)

2004, November 2. Christmas.
Des: R. Briggs. Printed in gravure by De La Rue. One phosphor band (**2nd**), two phosphor bands (others).
2nd, 1st, 40p, 57p, 68p, £1.12

Set	5.00	5.00
First day cover	7.50	
Booklet (24 at **2nd**)	7.00	
Booklet (12 at **1st**)	4.75	
Stamp cards	3.25	15.00
Miniature sheet, comprising one of each value, but conventionally gummed	5.00	5.00
First day cover	7.50	

NB: The 1st class and 2nd class designs also appear in stamp booklets (folders).
These stamps were normally issued with the backing paper stripped away. However, the 1st class stamps exist with the backing paper still in place, both with and without the rouletting to separate individual stamps, from stamps given each year to Post Office employees.
The 2nd and 1st class designs appear as Smilers sheets.

British Saddleback pigs (1st)
Khaki Campbell ducks (1st)

Clydeside mare with foal (1st)
Dairy Shorthorn cattle (1st)
Border Collie (1st)
Light Sussex chickens (1st)
Suffolk sheep (1st)
Bagot goat (1st)
Norfolk Black turkeys (1st)
Embden geese (1st)

2005, January 11. Farm Animals.
Des: C. Wormell. Printed in gravure by Enschedé.
1st, 1st, 1st, 1st, 1st, 1st, 1st, 1st, 1st, 1st in se-tenant block

Set of ten in **se-tenant block**	4.00	4.00
Gutter pairs	8.50	
First day cover	5.00	
Stamp cards	4.25	15.50

Old Harry Rocks, Studland Bay (2nd)
Wheal Coates, St Agnes (1st)
Start Point, start Bay (40p)
Horton Down, Wiltshire (43p)
Chiselcombe, Exmoor (57p)
St James's Stone, Lundy (68p)

2005, February 8. A British Journey: South-west England.
Des: J. Phelan and Lissa Barker. Printed in gravure by De La Rue. One phosphor band (2nd), two phosphor bands (others).
2nd, 1st, 40p, 43p, 57p, 68p

Set	4.00	4.00
Gutter pairs	8.50	
First day cover	5.00	
Stamp cards	2.75	9.00

Scenes from 'Jane Eyre' by Paula Rego:
Mr Rochester (2nd)
Come to me (1st)

In the comfort of her bonnet (40p)
La Ligne des Rats (57p)
Refectory (68p)
Inspection (£1.12)

2005, February 24.
150th Anniversary of the death of Charlotte Brontë.
Des: P. Willberg. Printed in litho by Walsall. One phosphor band
(**2nd**), two phosphor bands (others).
2nd, 1st, 40p, 57p, 68p, £1.12

Set	4.50	4.50
Gutter pairs	9.50	
First day cover	5.50	
Stamp cards	3.25	15.00
Miniature sheet,		
containing one of each design	4.50	4.50
First day cover	5.50	

NB: All designs also appear in the £7.43 'The Brontë Sisters'
prestige stamp book issued on February 24, 2005. issued on
June 15, 2004.

Heads or Tails (1st)
Rabbit and Top Hat (40p)
Coloured scarves and tube (47p)
Ace of Hearts (68p)
Three fezzes and pyramids (£1.12)
The designs include 'magical' features. Rubbing the 1st class
stamp with a coin reveals either the head or tail of a coin.

2005, March 15. Magic!
Des: Tathem Design; illustration by George Hardie. Printed in
gravure by Walsall.
1st, 40p, 47p, 68p, £1.12

Set	4.25	4.25
Gutter pairs	9.00	
First day cover	5.50	
Stamp cards	2.25	7.50

NB: The 1st class design is also found in a Smilers sheet issued
on March 15, 2005.

2005, March 22. The Castle Definitives of 1955.
The miniature sheet is listed under 'Wilding definitives with
decimal values'. The sheet contains new value versions of the
four original Castle GB definitives of 1955 using adaptations of
the original plates used in 1955.

Hadrian's Wall (2nd)
Uluru Kata Tjuta National Park (2nd)
Stonehenge (1st)
Wet Tropics of Queensland (1st)
Blenheim Palace (47p)
Greater Blue Mountains Area (47p)
Heart of Neolithic Orkney (68p)
Pumululu National Park (68p)

2005, April 21. World Heritage Sites.
Des: Jason Godfrey from photographs by Peter Marlow. Litho
printed by Enschedé. One phosphor band (**2nd**), two phosphor
bands (others).
**2nd, 2nd se-tenant, 1st, 1st se-tenant, 47p, 47p se-tenant,
68p, 68p se-tenant**

Set of four se-tenant pairs	4.50	4.50
Gutter pairs	9.50	
First day cover	5.50	
Stamp cards	3.00	8.00

NB: This is a joint issue with Australia Post.

Photographs of Prince Charles with Mrs Camilla Parker Bowles:
At the Mey Games in the Scottish Highlands – by Christopher Furlong (30p)
At Birkhall - by Carolyn Robb (68p)

2005, April 8 (*). The Wedding of Prince Charles and Mrs Camilla Parker Bowles.
Des: Rose Design, Printed in litho by Enschedé.
Miniature sheet,
containing two of the 30p and two of the 68p design

Miniature sheet	2.50	2.50
First day cover	4.00	

(* - while the first day handstamps and the miniature sheet are dated April 8, 2005, the wedding took place on April 9)

Ensign of the Scots Guards (2nd)
The Queen taking the salute (1st)
Trumpeter of the Household Cavalry (42p)
Welsh Guardsman (60p)
The Queen on horseback (68p)
The Queen with Duke of Edinburgh in an open carriage (£1.12)

2005, June 7. Trooping the Colour.
Des: Why Not Associates. Printed in litho by Walsall. One phosphor band (**2nd**), two phosphor bands (others).
2nd, 1st, 42p, 60p, 68p, £1.12

Set	4.50	4.50
Gutter pairs	9.50	
First day cover	5.50	
Stamp cards	2.75	7.50
Miniature sheet,		
containing one of each value	4.50	4.50
First day cover	5.50	

Searchlights in a 'V' over St Paul's Cathedral – designed by J. Gorham (1st)
(originally issued on May 2, 1995)

2005, July 5. End of the War.
Des: Jeffery Matthews. Printed in gravure by Enschedé.
Miniature sheet containing St Paul's Cathedral design plus five 1st class definitives

Miniature sheet	2.25	2.25
First day cover	3.00	

Norton F.1 (1st)
BSA Rocket 3 (40p)
Vincent Black Shadow (42p)
Triumph Speed Twin (47p)
Brough Superior (60p)
Royal Enfield (68p)

2005, July 19. Motorcycles.
Des: Atelier works, with illustrations by Michael English. Printed in litho by Walsall.
1st, 40p, 42p, 47p, 60p, 68p

Set	4.00	4.00
Gutter pairs	8.50	
First day cover	5.00	
Stamp cards	2.75	7.50

Designs as for the Olympic and Paralympic Games stamps of 1996, but inscribed '1st'

2005, August 12. London declared 2012 Olympic Games Host City
Printed in litho by Walsall. Miniature sheet (containg one of each of the five designs, plus a second of the Athlete with Olympic rings design.

Miniature sheet	2.50	2.50
First day cover	4.00	

Eating rice (2nd)
Drinking tea (1st)
Eating sushi (42p)
Eating pasta (47p)
Eating chips (60p)
Eating an apple (68p)

2005, August 23. Changing Tastes in Britain. Europa.
Des: Rose Design, with illustrations by Catell Ronca. Printed in gravure by Enschedé. One phosphor band (**2nd**), two phosphor bands (others).
2nd, 1st, 42p, 47p, 60p, 68p

Set	4.00	4.00
Gutter pairs	8.50	
First day cover	5.00	
Stamp cards	2.75	7.50

Inspector Morse (2nd)
Emmerdale (1st)
Rising Damp (42p)
The Avengers (47p)
The South Bank Show (60p)
Who Wants To Be A Millionaire? (68p)

2005, September 15. Classic ITV.

Des: Kate Stephens.. Printed in litho by De La Rue. One phosphor band (**2nd**), two phosphor bands (others).

2nd, 1st, 42p, 47p, 60p, 68p

Set	4.00	4.00
Gutter pairs	8.50	
First day cover	5.00	
Stamp cards	2.75	7.50

NB: the 1st class design is also found on a Smilers sheet.

Images from a painting by William Heath:
The Entrepreante with British Belle Isle (1st)
Nelson wounded (1st)
Entrepreante and the French Achille (42p)
The schooner Pickle (42p)
Nelson attacking in two columns (68p)
Putting to sea from Cadiz (68p)

2005, October 18. Trafalgar.

Des: Dick Davis. Printed in litho by Walsall.

1st, 1st se-tenant, 42p, 42p se-tenant, 68p, 68p se-tenant

Set of **three se-tenant pairs**	4.00	4.00
Gutter pairs	8.50	
First day cover	5.00	
Stamp cards	2.75	7.50
Miniature sheet		
containing the six stamps	4.00	4.00
First day cover	5.00	

NB: the stamps also appear in a 'Battle of Trafalgar' prestige stamp book issued on October 18, 2005.

The Madonna and Child as seen through the eyes of different cultures:
Haiti (2nd)
European (1st)
European (42p)
North American Indian (60p)
India (68p)
Australian Aborigine (£1.12)

2005, November 1. Christmas. Madonna and Child.

Des: Irene von Treskow. Printed in gravure by De La Rue. One phosphor band (**2nd**), two phoshor bands (others). Self-adhesive.

2nd, 1st, 42p, 60p, 68p, £1.12

Set	4.50	4.50
First day cover	5.50	
Booklet (24 at **2nd**)	7.00	
Booklet (12 at **1st**)	4.75	
Stamp cards	2.75	7.50
Miniature sheet,		
containing the six stamps –		
normal gumming	4.50	4.50
First day cover	5.50	

NB: the 2nd and 1st class stamps also appear in stamp books.

Exhibition cards
A card with a 'Flowers' design, stamped and cancelled with the 31p and 34p Flowers stamps of 1987 was made available at several stamp exhibitions, starting with Capex 87 in Toronto which opened on June 13, 1987.

Booklets containing 'Special Issues'

1984, November 20. Christmas.

£2.30 (containing 20 of the 13p 1984 Christmas stamp, the stamps having an all-over five-pointed star printed on the back). Cover shows a Manger Scene 5.50

1985, July 30. 350th Anniversary of Royal Mail service to the public.

£1.53 (containing 10 of the 17p '350th Anniversary' stamp, with an all-over 'D' pattern and printed on the back). Cover shows a Datapost van and plane, and Concorde 3.00

1985, November 19. Christmas.

£2.40 (containing 20 of the 12p 1985 Christmas stamp). Cover shows Cinderella's slipper on a cushion 5.00

VENDING MACHINE LABELS

On May 1, 1984 machines were installed at four locations which automatically 'print' labels in values of the basic first-class inland rate, the basic second class rate, or any denomination from ½p to 16p inclusive, values available extended to 16½p and 17p on August 28. 1984. The experiment ceased on April 30, 1985.

The labels are designed by Martin Newton and involve a red value and frame with Queen's portrait printed on phosphor-coated white security paper with a grey-green background design.

Packs are available containing either:

3½p, 12½p and **16p** labels	1.25
16½p and **17p** labels	1.50
or	
all combinations from ½p to 16p	11.00

First day covers were available from The Post Office bearing the **3½p, 12½p** and **16p** labels. 2.50

SMILERS SHEETS

At The Stamp Show 2000 Royal Mail introduced customised stamps by which a personal photograph could be printed on a label alongside a conventional stamp: these are known as Smilers sheets. In addition to such customised stamps, Royal Mail also made available sheets of the stamps on which decorative labels replace the photographs: these have been termed Generic sheets. Finally, bulk orders for sheets with customers own labels may be ordered: these are termed Business Smilers.
Below are listed the Generic sheets.

2000, May 22. The Stamp Show 2000.

Sheet of ten Smiles   20.00

2000, October 3. Christmas.
Sheet of 20 Robin looking through slit in pillar box. Copyright **'Post Office 2000'**   150.00
Sheet of **10** Father Christmas with Cracker.
Copyright 'Post Office 2000'   100.00

2001, June 5. Occasions: Hallmarks.
Sheets of **20** comprising four of each of the five designs
                                            70.00

2001, July 3. Smiles.
Sheet of **ten** Smiles stamps as May 22, 2000,
but with revised labels and border   90.00

2001, October 9. Christmas.
Sheet of **20** Robin looking through slit in pillar box.
Copyright 'Consignia 2001'   350.00
Sheet of **10** Father Christmas with Cracker.
Copyright 'Consignia 2001'   350.00

2001, December 18. Cartoons.
Sheet of **10** with labels of humorous quotes
                                            35.00

2002, April 23. Occasions: Pictorial messages.
Sheet of **20** comprising four of each of the five designs
                                            25.00

2002, May 21. Football World Cup.
Sheet of **20** of the lower right hand corner flag design
                                            20.00

2002, October 1. Smiles.
Sheet of **10** of the Teddy Bear design and ten of the Dennis
the Menace design   17.50

2002, October 1. Christmas.
Sheet of **20** of the Father Christmas with Cracker design
                                            15.00

2003, January 21. Flower paintings.
Sheet of **20** comprising two of each of the ten designs
                                            15.00

2003, February 4. Occasions.
Sheet of **20** comprising a multiple of the six designs
                                            14.00

2003, July 29. Cartoons Crossword.
Sheet of **20** comprising two of each of the ten designs, with
the labels forming a crossword   15.00

2003, September 30. Christmas: Winter Robins.
Sheet of **20** of the 1st class Winter Robins design.
Self-adhesive   12.50

2003, November 4. Christmas: Ice Sculptures.
Sheet of **20** of the 2nd class Ice Sculptures design. Self-adhs
Sheet of **20** of the 1st class Ice Sculptures design. Self-adhs
                                            17.50

2004, January 30. Hong Kong stamp exhibition.
Sheet of **20** of the Hello greetings stamp design
                                            10.00

2004, February 3. Occasions: Envelopes
Sheet of **20** comprising four of each of the five designs
                                            10.00

2004, May 25. Royal Horticultural Society.
Sheet of **20** of the 1st class design
                                            10.00

2004, July 27. Rule Britannia.
Sheet of **20** of the 1st class Union Flag design
                                            10.00

2004, November 2. Christmas: Father Christmas.
Sheet of **20** comprising 10 of the 2nd class and ten of the 1st
class designs   9.00

2005, January 11. Farm Animals.
Sheet of **20** comprising two of each of the ten designs
                                            10.50

2005, March 1. Magic!
Sheet of **20** of the 1st class design   9.50

2005, April 21. Pacific Explorer (Australia) stamp exhbt.
Sheet of **20** of the 1st class Hello design
                                            9.50

2005, June 21. White Ensign.
Sheet of **20** of the 1st class White Ensign design
                                            9.50

2005, September 15. ITV.
Sheet of **20** of the 1st class Emmerdale design
                                            9.50

2005, November 1. Christmas.
Sheet of **20** comprising 10 of the 1st class and ten of the 2nd
class Winter Robins designs   9.00

www.royalmint.com

ORDERING WITH THE ROYAL MINT HAS NEVER BEEN EASIER!

Consider the advantages of placing your order online:

- You can order online 24 hours a day, 7 days a week.

- Secure transactions using the very latest encryption technology guarantees your peace of mind.

- FREE Postage and Packing.

- Your order will be acknowledged by e-mail.

- You can track the status of your order.

- You can keep up to date with the latest coin, jewellery and giftware products.

FREEPOST SWC4207,
PO BOX 500, Pontyclun
CF72 8WP

OFFICIAL STAMPS

1d 'VR' official

In 1840 the **1d** black was prepared for issue with the Stars in the top corners replaced by the letters 'V' and 'R', but this stamp was never officially issued.

	£14,000	£20,000

The following comprise the stamps of the reigns of Queen Victoria and King Edward VII overprinted for use by Government Departments. Beware of fakes.
(Dates in brackets refer to the stamps overprinted – see main listing.)

A) Overprinted 'I.R OFFICIAL' for use by the Inland Revenue.

i) Stamps of Queen Victoria

½d green (1880 issue)	40.00	10.00
½d blue (1884 issue)	40.00	12.00
½d orange (1887 issue)	6.00	1.00
½d green (1900 issue)	8.00	3.50
1d lilac (1881 issue)	2.75	1.40
2½d lilac (1884 issue)	£250	45.00
2½d purple (blue paper) (1887 issue)	80.00	6.00
6d grey (1881 issue)	£225	35.00
6d purple (red paper) (1887 issue)	£250	40.00
1/- green (1884 issue)	£2900	£650
1/- green (1887 issue)	£350	65.00
1/- green, red (1900 issue)	£1,800	£500
5/- red (1884 issue)	£2800	£850
10/- blue (1884 issue)	£3800	£1000
£1 brown (1884 issue		
- Wmk: Imperial Crowns)	£30,000	£12,500
£1 brown (1888 issue		
- Wmk: Orbs)	£40,000	£18,000
£1 green (1891 issue)	£5500	£1300

£1 green

ii) Stamps of King Edward VII – De La Rue printing.

½d blue-green	20.00	2.00
1d red	15.00	1.25
2½d blue	£600	£140
6d purple	£100,000	£60,000
1/- green, red	£1700	350.00
5/- red	£7500	£4000
10/- blue	£38,000	£18,000
£1 green	£30,000	£14,000

B) Overprinted 'O.W OFFICIAL' for use by the Office of Works.

i) Stamps of Queen Victoria.

½d orange (1887 issue)	£150	65.00
½d green (1900 issue)	£250	£100
1d lilac (1881 issue)	£250	65.00
5d purple, blue (1887 issue)	£1500	£450
10d purple, red (1887 issue)	£2500	£700

ii) Stamps of King Edward VII – De La Rue printing.

½d blue-green	£400	£110
1d red	£380	£100
2d green, red	£1100	£160
2½d blue	£1400	£350
10d purple, red	£15,000	£3,000

C) Overprinted 'ARMY OFFICIAL' for use by the Army.

i) Stamps of Queen Victoria.

½d orange (1887 issue)	2.75	1.25
½d green (1900 issue)	3.00	5.00
1d lilac (1881 issue)	2.50	2.00
2½d purple (blue paper) (1887 issue)	20.00	10.00
6d purple (red paper) (1887 issue)	50.00	28.00

ii) Stamps of King Edward VII – De La Rue printing.

½d blue-green	4.00	1.25
1d red	4.00	1.25
6d purple	£125	45.00

D) Overprinted 'GOVT PARCELS' for use by the Government.

i) Stamps of Queen Victoria.

1d lilac (1881 issue)	50.00	10.00
1½d lilac (1884 issue)	£250	40.00
1½d purple, green (1887 issue)	55.00	4.00
2d green, red (1887 issue)	£110	12.00

4½d green, red (1887 issue)	£180	90.00
6d green (1884 issue)	£1300	£300
6d purple (red paper) (1887 issue)	£100	15.00
9d green (1884 issue)	£1100	£275
9d purple, blue (1887 issue)	£150	25.00
1/- brown (1881 issue – plate 13 or 14)	£600	£165
1/- green (1887 issue)	£250	80.00
1/- green, red (1887 issue)	£325	£125

ii) Stamps of King Edward VII – De La Rue printing.

1d red	25.00	10.00
2d green, red	£105	25.00
6d purple	£175	18.00
9d purple, blue	£180	65.00
1/- green, red	£325	£125

E) Overprinted 'BOARD OF EDUCATION'.

i) Stamps of Queen Victoria.

5d purple, blue (1887 issue)	£1250	£300
1/- green, red (1887 issue)	£4000	£2000

ii) Stamps of King Edward VII – De La Rue printing.

½d blue-green	£110	18.00
1d red	£110	18.00
2½d blue	£2200	£100
5d purple, blue	£10,000	£2500
1/- green, red	£50,000	-

F) Overprinted 'R.H. HOUSEHOLD' for use by Royal Household.

Stamps of King Edward VII – De La Rue printing.

½d blue-green	£250	£150
1d red	£210	£120

G) Overprinted 'ADMIRALTY OFFICIAL':
Stamps of King Edward VII – De La Rue printing.

½d blue-green	20.00	10.00
1d red	12.00	8.00
1½d purple, green	£150	60.00
2d green, red	£200	75.00
2½d blue	£225	65.00
3d purple (yellow paper)	£230	60.00

Did you miss the boat or did you take our advice?

In 1973, we recommended and sold the British definitive 1/2p (SG X842) with one phosphor band on side. We told our customers to buy them at 25p each. **WE WERE RIGHT!!!** Today this stamp is catalogued at £45.00 each. If you had taken our advice, for an outlay of only £50.00 in 1973, the current S.G catalogue value of your investment would be a staggering total of £9,000.00.

In 1999, we recommended our customers to buy the Princess Diana Welsh Language Presentation Packs. The catalogue value was only £2.50 each, but we were telling our customers to buy them for up to double catalogue value at £5.00 each. Within only 5 years, they had increased in catalogue value by 5,900%.

In 2003, we recommended our customers to buy the Coronation £1 green (SG 2378A). It was catalogued by Stanley Gibbons at £1.50 per stamp. Within one year, the S.G catalogue value had increased to £45 per stamp, an increase of 1,200%.

As recently as 2004, we told our customers to buy the Fruit and Veg presentation pack - it was catalogued at £4.50. We said ignore the catalogue value, it's cheap even at treble catalogue value - this pack increased in Stanley Gibbons Catalogue by over a 1000% in one year.

As everyone knows, investments can go down as well as up and the past is not necessarily a guide to the future. However, being selective and taking sound advice is the best way to make your hobby pay for itself.

PLEASE, PLEASE, PLEASE LISTEN TO US. Now we most strongly advise all of our customers to buy the GB 2004 Classic Locomotive Miniature Sheet (SG MS2423). The Catalogue value in Stanley Gibbons C.B.S catalogue 2005 edition is £3.75 each. We recommend you to buy it at the cheapest possible price from any dealer willing to sell...**BUY IT NOW!!!**

REGIONAL ISSUES

All stamps in this section are printed in photogravure by Harrisons and have perf 15 x 14 unless otherwise stated

England

Three Lions (*2nd)
Crowned Lion and shield of St George (1st)
Oak tree (E, 40p, 42p)
Tudor Rose (65p, 68p)

2001, April 23
Des: Sedley Place, from sculptures by D. Dathan. Printed in gravure by De La Rue. One phosphor band (2nd), two phosphor bands (others).

2nd	slate blue and silver	0.45	0.40
1st	red-brown and silver	0.55	0.50
E	olive-green and silver	0.75	0.65
65p	deep lilac and silver	1.75	1.80
68p	deep lilac and silver (July 4, 2002)	1.75	
1.75			
First day cover (2nd to 65p)		3.00	
First day cover (68p)		3.00	
Stamp cards		3.00	15.00

NB: the 2nd and 1st also appear printed in gravure by Questa in the £6.83 'Across the Universe' prestige stamp book of September 24, 2002.

2003, October 14. Designs with white borders
Designs as for April 23, 2001 but with a white margin around the stamp design. Printed in gravure by De La Rue (except where stated). One phosphor band (2nd), two phosphor bands (others).

2nd slate blue and silver	0.45	0.40
1st red-brown and silver	0.55	0.50
E olive-green and silver	0.75	0.65
40p olive-green and silver (May 11, 2004)		
	0.80	0.75
42p olive-green and silver (April 5, 2005		
– printed by Walsall)	0.85	0.85
42p olive-green and silver (May 10, 2005)		
	0.80	0.75
68p deep lilac and silver	1.20	1.00
First day cover (2nd, 1st, E, 68p)	2.50	
First day cover (40p)	2.50	
First day cover (42p)	2.50	
Stamp cards	2.00	10.00

NB: the 2nd, 1st and 40p also appear in prestige stamp books, printed by Walsall.

Northern Ireland

1958-1968
Des: W.Hollywood (3d, 4d, 5d), L.Philton (6d, 9d);
T. Collins (1/3, 1/6)

A) Wmk: Multiple St Edward's Crown. Non phosphor except where stated.

3d lilac (August 18, 1958)	0.15	0.15
a) one centre band	0.15	0.20
4d blue (February 7, 1966)	0.15	0.15
a) two phosphor band	0.15	0.15
6d purple (September 29, 1958)	0.20	0.20
9d green (two phosphor bands)		
(March 1, 1967)	0.35	0.40
1/3 green (August 29, 1958)	0.35	0.40
1/6 grey-blue (two phosphor bands)		
(March 1, 1967)	0.40	0.40
First Day Covers		
3d		25.00
6d, 1/3		30.00
4d		7.50
9d, 1/6		2.75

B) No wmk. Two phosphor bands and PVA gum except where stated.

4d blue (gum Arabic)	0.15	0.15
4d sepia (one centre band)		
(September 4, 1968)	0.15	0.25
4d red (February 26, 1969)	0.20	0.30
5d blue (September 4, 1968)	0.20	0.20
1/6 grey-blue	1.50	1.40

(NB – the 4d blue exists with either gum arabic or PVA gum: the PVA gum version was not placed on sale in Northern Ireland – price £8.50 mint).

First Day Covers	
4d sepia, **5d**	2.50
4d red	1.00

3p (same design, all values)

1971, July 7. Decimal Currency
Des: J. Matthews.

REGIONAL ISSUES

A) Two phosphor bands except where stated.
i) PVA gum. Original coated paper.

2½p pink (one centre band)	0.85	0.40
3p blue	0.40	0.40
5d violet	1.75	1.25
7½p brown	1.75	1.25

ii) PVA gum. Fluorescent coated paper.

2½p pink (one centre band)	5.25	2.00
3p blue	7.50	2.00
3p blue (one centre band)	0.40	0.20

iii) PVAD gum (blue tinged).

3p blue (one centre band)	0.95	0.40
3½p green (January 23, 1974)	0.30	0.25
a) one centre band	0.30	0.25
4½p grey-blue (November 6, 1974)	0.30	0.25
5½p deep violet (January 23, 1974)	0.30	0.25
a) one centre band	0.35	0.25
6½p green-blue (one centre band) (January 14, 1976)	0.30	0.20
7p red-brown (one centre band) (January 18, 1978)	0.35	0.25
8p red (January 23, 1974)	0.35	0.25
8½p green (January 14, 1976)	0.35	0.30
9d violet-blue (January 18, 1978)	0.35	0.30
10d orange (October 20, 1976)	0.35	0.40
a) one centre band	0.35	0.40
10½p grey-blue (January 18, 1978)	0.40	0.40
11p red (October 20, 1976)	0.40	0.40

B) Phosphor coated paper. PVAD gum (blue tinged).
Issued on July 23, 1980.

12p yellow-green	0.40	0.40
13½p red-brown	0.60	0.60
15p blue	0.50	0.45

C) Printed in litho by Questa. Perf: 13½ x 14. Phosphor coated paper, except 11½p and 12½p (left side band). PVAD gum (11½p, 14p, 18p, 22p), PVAD gum (others).

11½p mushroom (April 8, 1981)	0.70	0.75
12½p light green (February 24, 1982)	0.40	0.40
14p steel-blue (April 8, 1981)	0.50	0.50
15½p pale violet (February 24, 1982)	0.60	0.60
16p light mushroom (April 27, 1983)	0.85	0.85
18p mauve (April 8, 1981)	0.70	0.70
19½p grey-green (February 24, 1982)	1.50	1.60
20½P bright blue (April 27, 1983)	2.95	2.95
22p deep blue (April 8, 1981)	0.70	0.70
26p red – Type I (February 24, 1982)	0.80	0.80
28p blue – Type I (April 27, 1983)	1.00	90

The symbol on these stamps has been re-drawn and is now less close to the top of the design than hitherto. The original symbol is known as 'Type I' and the revised version as 'Type II' : recorded where both types exist for the same stamp.

D) Printed in litho by Questa. Perf: 15 x 14. One side phosphor

band (12p, 12½p, 13p); phosphor coated paper (16p, 17p, 31p); advanced coated paper (22p, 26p, 28p), or as indicated. PVAD gum.

12p emerald green (January 7, 1986)	0.80	0.80
12½p light green (February 28, 1984)	4.00	4.00
a) PVA gum	4.00	-
13p reddish-brown – Type I (October 23, 1984)	0.40	0.45
a) deep brown – Type II	2.00	2.00
b) deep brown – printed on paper supplied by Coated Papers Ltd. Type II. PVA gum (April 14, 1987)	0.80	0.80
16p light mushroom (February 28, 1984)	5.00	5.00
17p steel blue (October 23, 1984) - Type I	0.80	0.80
a) advanced coated paper - Type I	0.80	0.80
b) Type II	80.00	80.00
18p deep green (January 6, 1987)	0.65	0.60
18p bright green (one centre band) (December 3, 1991)	0.50	0.45
18p bright green (perf: 14) (December 31, 1992)	1.40	1.40
19p orange-red (phosphor paper) (November 8, 1988)	0.65	0.65
20p brownish-black (phosphor paper) (November 28, 1989)	0.60	0.50
22p yellowish-green (October 23, 1984)	0.65	0.65
22p orange-red (phosphor paper) (December 4, 1990)	0.85	0.80
23p bright green (phosphor paper) (November 8, 1988)	0.90	0.80
24p deep red (phosphor paper) (November 28, 1989)	1.15	1.15
24p chestnut (phosphor paper) (December 3, 1991)	0.75	0.65
26p red – Type II (January 27, 1987)	1.75	1.90
26p drab (phosphor paper) (December 4, 1990)	1.00	1.00
28p blue – Type II (January 27, 1987)	1.00	1.00
28p bluish grey (phosphor paper) (December 3, 1991)	1.10	1.10
31p purple – Type I (October 23, 1984)	1.00	1.00
a) Type II (April 14, 1987)	1.75	1.50
32p greenish blue (phosphor paper) (November 8, 1988)	1.25	1.25
34p bluish grey (phosphor paper) (November 28, 1989)	1.15	1.15
37p rosine (phosphor paper) (December 4, 1990)	1.40	1.40
39p mauve (phosphor paper) (December 3, 1991)	1.25	1.30

First Day Covers:

2½p, 3p, 5p, 7½p	2.00
3½p, 5½p, 8p	1.25
4½p	1.00

6½p, 8½p	1.00
10p, 11p	1.00
7p, 9p, 10½p	1.75
12, 13½p, 15p	1.25
11½p, 14p, 18p, 22p	2.00
12½p, 15½p, 19½p, 26p	2.00
16p, 20½p, 28p	1.75
13p, 17p, 22p, 31p	2.00
12p	1.50
18p	1.50
14p, 19p, 23p, 32p	2.00
15p, 20p, 24p, 34p	2.75
17p, 22p, 26p, 37p	2.75
18p, 24p, 28p, 39p	2.75

NB: the **18p** with side phosphor band and **24p** chestnut with two phosphor bands come from prestige stamp books.

E) Stamps with an elliptical perforation along each vertical side, Printed in litho by Questa. One phosphor band (**19p** and **20p**), two phosphor bands (others).

19p bistre (December 7, 1993)	0.60	0.65
19p bistre (band at left)	1.75	1.75
19p bistre (band at right)	1.30	1.30
20p bright green (July 23, 1996)	1.75	1.75
25p red (December 7, 1993)	0.75	0.75
26p red-brown (July 23, 1996)	1.75	1.75
30p olive-grey (December 7, 1993)	0.85	0.85
37p mauve (July 23, 1996)	2.50	2.60
41p grey-brown (December 7, 1993)	0.90	1.00
63p emerald (July 23, 1996)	2.75	2.75

NB: some of these stamps are also found in prestige stamp books, including the **19p** with the phosphor band to the left or to the right.

F) Stamps with an elliptical perforation along each vertical side. Printed in gravure by Walsall. One phosphor band (**19p** and **20p**), two phosphor bands (others).

19p bistre (June 8, 1999)	1.50	1.50
20p bright green (July 1, 1997)	0.60	0.65
20p bright green (band at right)	1.00	1.00
26p chestnut (July 1, 1997)	1.25	1.30
26p chestnut (perf: 14)	1.20	1.20
26p chestnut (printed by Harrison)	1.00	1.00
37p mauve (July 1, 1887)	1.40	1.40
37p mauve (printed by Harrison)	1.20	1.20
38p ultramarine (June 8, 1999)	4.75	4.75
40p azure (April 25, 2000)	1.00	1.00
63p emerald (July 1, 1997)	2.40	2.65
64p turquoise (June 8, 1999)	4.75	4.75
65p greenish blue (April 25, 2000)	1.50	1.50

NB: The **20p** with one band at right, **26p** with perf: 14 are printed by Harrison, and as with the **26p** and **37p** printed by Harrison, come from prestige stamp books.

G) Non value indicator stamp. Printed in gravure by Walsall. One phosphor band.

1st orange-red (perf: 14) (February 15, 2000)		
	1.75	1.75

1st orange-red (perf: 15 × 14) (April 25, 2000)		
	5.00	5.00

NB: this stamp perf: 14 appeared in a prestige stamp book.

First day covers

19p, 25p, 30p, 41p	5.00
20p, 26p, 37p, 63p	5.00
38p, 64p	4.00
1st, 40p, 65p	5.00

Basalt Columns (*2nd)
Patchwork fields (1st)
Linen (E, 40p, 42p)
Pattern on vase (65p, 68p)

2001, March 6
Des: Rodney Miller Associates. Printed in litho by De La Rue (E and 68p), Walsall (2nd, 1st, E, 65p) or Enschedé (2nd, 1st), One phosphor band (2nd), two phosphor bands (others).

2nd multicoloured	0.45	0.50
2nd multicoloured (Enschedé) (February 23, 2003)		
	1.05	1.15
1st multicoloured	0.55	0.40
1st multicoloured (Enschedé) (February 23, 2003)		
	1.15	1.25
E multicoloured (Walsall)	1.00	1.00
E multicoloured (De La Rue)	1.00	1.00
65p multicoloured	1.50	1.60
68p multicoloured (July 4, 2002)	1.40	1.50
First day cover (2nd to 65p)		3.00
First day cover (68p)		5.00
Stamp cards	3.00	15.00

NB: the 2nd and 1st printed by Enschedé come from the £6.99 'Microcosmos' prestige stamp book issued on February 25, 2003.

2003, October 14. Designs with white borders
Designs as for April 23, 2001 but with a white margin around the stamp design. Printed in gravure by De La Rue (except where stated). One phosphor band (2nd), two phosphor bands (others).

2nd multicoloured	0.45	0.40
1st multicoloured	0.55	0.50
E multicoloured	0.75	0.65
40p multicoloured (May 11, 2004)	0.80	0.75
42p multicoloured (April 5, 2005 – printed by Walsall)		
	0.85	0.85
42p multicoloured (July 26, 2005)	0.80	0.75
68p multicoloured	1.20	1.00
First day cover (2nd, 1st, E, 68p)		3.50
First day cover (40p)		2.50
First day cover (42p)		2.50
Stamp cards	2.00	10.00

Scotland

3d, 4d, 5d (same design)

1958-1967.
Des: G. F. Huntley (3d, 4d, 5d), J. B. Fleming (6d, 9d), A. B. Imrie (1/3, 1/6).
A) Wmk: Multiple St Edward's Crown. Non phosphor except where stated.

3d lilac (August 18, 1958)	0.15	0.15
a) two phosphor bands	8.00	2.00
b) one band at left	0.20	0.35
c) one band at right	0.20	0.35
Se-tenant pair	0.35	0.70
d) one centre band	0.20	0.30
4d blue (February 7, 1966)	0.15	0.15
a) two phosphor bands	0.15	0.15
6d purple (September 29, 1958)	0.15	0.15
a) two phosphor bands	0.20	0.25
9d green (two phosphor bands) (March 1, 1967)		
	0.35	0.40
1/3 green (September 29, 1958)	0.35	0.25
a) two phosphor bands	0.35	0.40
1/6 grey-blue (two phosphor bands) (March 1, 1967)		
	0.40	0.50

First Day Covers

3d	10.00
6d, 1/3	20.00
3d, 6d, 1/3 – phosphor	100.00
4d	7.50
9d, 1/6	2.75

B) No watermark. Two phosphor bands except where stated.
i) Gum Arabic.

3d lilac (one centre band)	0.15	-
4d blue	0.15	-

ii) PVA gum.

3d lilac (one centre band)	0.15	0.20
4d blue	0.15	0.20
4d sepia (one centre band) (September 4, 1968)		
	0.15	0.20
4d red (one centre band) (February 26, 1969)		
	0.20	0.20
5d blue (September 4, 1968)	0.20	0.25
9d green	3.50	3.50
1/6 grey-blue	1.25	1.00
First Day Covers		
4d sepia, **5d**		2.50
4d red		1.00

3½p green

1971, July 7. Decimal Currency
Des: J. Matthews.
Two phosphor bands except where stated.
i) Gum Arabic.

2½p pink (one centre band)	0.40	-
3p blue	1.00	-

ii) PVA gum. Original coated paper.

2½p pink (one centre band	0.35	0.25
3p blue	0.35	0.25
5p violet	1.50	1.00
7½p brown	1.75	1.50

iii) PVA gum. Fluorescent coated paper.

2½p pink (one centre band)	5.00	0.50
3p blue	11.00	0.25
one centre band	0.35	0.25
3½p green	8.00	-
5p violet	5.50	3.00
7½p brown	65.00	20.00

iv) PVAD gum (blue tinged).

3p blue (one centre band)	0.60	-
3½p green (January 23, 1974)	0.35	0.25
a) one centre band	0.35	0.25
4½p grey-blue (November 6, 1974)	0.35	0.25
5½p deep violet (January 23, 1974)	0.30	0.30
a) one centre band	0.35	0.25
6½p green-blue (one centre band) (January 14, 1976)		
	0.35	0.25
7p red-brown (cone centre band) (January 18, 1974)		
	0.35	0.25
8p red (January 23, 1974)	0.40	0.30
8½p green (January 14, 1976)	0.35	0.30
9p violet-blue (January 18, 1978)	0.35	0.30
10p orange (October 20, 1976)	0.35	0.35
a) one centre band	0.40	0.35
10½p grey-blue (January 18, 1978)	0.40	0.40
11p red (October 20, 1976)	0.40	0.40

B) Phosphor coated paper. PVAD gum (blue tinged).
Issued July 23, 1980.

12p yellow-green	0.40	0.40
13½p red-brown	0.55	0.60
15p blue	0.50	0.55

The lion symbol on these stamps has been re-drawn. On the original version (known as Type I) the eye appears as a circle, while the tongue and claws are thin. On the re-drawn version

(Type II) the eye is solid, while the tongue and claws are thicker. The types are recorded where the same stamp exists with either symbol.

C) Printed in litho by Waddington. Perf 131/2 x 14. Phosphor coated paper, except 11½p, 12p, 12½p, 13p, (left side band), 22p (advanced coated paper). PVAD gum (blue tinged) except 11½p and 12½p have PVA gum.

11½p mushroom (April 8, 1981)	0.60	0.45 *Cyth* ·
12p emerald-green (January7, 1986)	1.50	1.50
12½p light green (February 24, 1982)	0.50	0.60
13p light brown – Type 1 (October 23, 1984)		
	0.60	0.65
a) Type II	5.00	5.25
15½p pale-violet (February 24, 1982)	0.60	0.60
16p light mushroom (April 27, 1983)	0.70	0.75
a) printed on Harrison's advanced coated paper (November 2, 1983)	3.75	3.75
17p steel blue – Type 1 (October 23, 1984)		
	3.25	3.00
a) Type II	1.10	1.15
b) PVA gum – Type II	1.10	1.15
19½p grey-green (February 24, 1982)	1.50	1.50
20½p bright blue (April 27, 1983)	3.00	3.00
22p deep blue (April 8, 1981)	0.70	0.70
22p yellowish green – Type 1 (October 23, 1984)		
	2.00	2.25
a) Type II	30.00	20.00
26p red – Type 1 (February 24, 1982)	0.75	0.80
28p blue – Type 1 (April 27, 1983)	0.90	0.90
31p purple – type 1 (October 23, 1984)	1.75	1.75
a) Type II	80.00	80.00

D) Printed in litho by Questa. Perf 15 x 14. One phosphor band (12p, 13p), advanced coated paper (22p, 26p, 28p), or as indicated. PVAD gum. All Type II.

12p emerald-green (April 29, 1986)	1.75	1.75
13p light brown (November 4, 1986)	0.90	0.95
a) printed on paper supplied by Coated Paper Ltd. PVA gum (April 14, 1987)	0.80	0.60
17p steel –blue (April 29, 1986)	3.25	3.25
18p deep green (January 6, 1987)	0.70	0.70
18p bright green (one centre band) (December 3, 1991)	0.70	0.50
18p bright green (perf: 14) (September 26, 1992)	0.80	0.80
19p orange-red (phosphor paper) (November 8, 1988)	0.80	0.80
19p orange-red (two bands) (March 21, 1989)	1.25	1.25
20p brownish-black (phosphor paper) (November 28, 1989)	0.65	0.50
22p yellowish-green (January 27, 1987)	0.75	0.80
22p orange-red (phosphor paper) (December 4, 1990)	0.80	0.80
23p bright green (phosphor paper) (November 8, 1988)	0.80	0.85

23p bright green (two bands) (March 21, 1989)	7.50	7.50
24p deep red (phosphor paper) (November 28, 1989)	1.00	1.05
24p chestnut (phosphor paper) (December 3, 1991)	0.70	0.65
24p chestnut (phosphor paper – perf: 14) (October 19, 1992)	1.75	1.60
26p red (January 27, 1987)	2.00	2.25
26p drab (phosphor paper) (December 4, 1990)	1.00	1.05
28p blue (January 27, 1987)	1.00	1.00
28p bluish grey (phosphor paper) (December 3, 1991)	1.00	1.10
28p bluish grey (phosphor paper – perf: 14) (February 18, 1993)	3.25	3.50
31p purple (April 29, 1986)	1.60	1.70
32p greenish blue (phosphor paper) (November 8, 1988)	1.10	1.25
34p bluish grey (phosphor paper) (November 28, 1989)	1.20	1.30
37p rosine (phosphor paper) (December 4, 1990)	1.10	1.25
39p mauve (phosphor paper) (December 3, 1991)	1.10	1.25
39p mauve (phosphor paper – perf: 14) (November 1992)	2.25	2.40

First Day Covers

2½p, 3p, 5p, 7½p	2.00
3½p, 5½p, 8p	1.25
4½p	1.00
6½p, 8½p	1.00
10p, 11p	1.00
7p, 9p, 10½p	1.75
12p, 13½p, 15p	1.25
11½p, 14p, 18p, 22p	2.00
12½p, 15½p, 19½p, 26p	2.00
16p, 20½p, 28p	1.50
13p, 17p, 22p, 31p	2.00
12p	1.50
12p, 17p, 31p (Questa)	2.00
13p (Questa)	1.00
18p	1.50
22p, 26p, 28p (Questa)	3.00
14p, 19p, 23p, 32p	2.00
15p, 20p, 24p, 34p	2.75
17p, 22p, 26p, 37p	2.75
18p, 24p, 28p, 39p	2.75

NB: the 19p and 23p two bands come from a prestige stamp book.

E) Stamps with an elliptical perforation along each vertical side, Printed in litho by Questa. One phosphor band (19p and 20p), two phosphor bands (others).

19p bistre (December 7, 1993)	0.60	0.50
19p bistre (right band)	1.50	1.50
20p bright green (July 23, 1996)	0.90	0.90

25p red (December 7, 1993)	0.80	0.85
26p red-brown (July 23, 1996)	1.25	1.40
30p olive-grey (December 7, 1993)	0.85	0.90
37p mauve (July 23, 1996)	2.00	2.25
41p grey-brown (December 7, 1993)	1.00	1.20
63p emerald (July 23, 1996)	2.25	2.40

NB: the 19p with side band to right comes from a prestige stamp book.

F) Stamps with an elliptical perforation along each vertical side. Printed in gravure by Walsall (except where started). One phosphor band (19p and 20p), two phosphor bands (others).

20p bright green (July 1, 1997)	0.45	0.40
20p bright green (right band)	1.00	1.00
26p chestnut (July 1, 1997)	1.00	1.00
26p chestnut (perf: 14)	1.20	1.20
26p chestnut (Harrison)	1.00	1.00
37p mauve (July 1, 1997)	0.90	1.00
37p mauve (Harroson)	1.20	1.20
63p emerald (July 1, 1997)	2.00	2.10

NB: The 20p with one band at right and the 26p with perf: 14 come from prestige stamp books. The 26p and 37p printed by Harrison also come from a prestige stamp book.

First day covers

19p, 25p, 30p, 41p	5.00
20p, 26p, 37p, 63p	5.00

G) Non value indicator stamp. Printed in gravure by Walsall. One phosphor band. Issued on February 15, 2000, in a prestige stamp book.

1st orange-red	1.50	1.50

Scottish flag (*2nd)
Scottish Lion (1st)
Thistle (E, 40p, 42p)
Tartan (64p, 65p, 68p)

1999, June 8.
Des: A. Morris (2nd), F. Pottinger and T. Chalk (1st, E, 40p, 42p), and all adapted by Tayburn. Printed in litho by Walsall (2nd, 1st, E, 64p, 65p), De La Rue (2nd, 1st and 68p) or Questa 2nd, 1st, E and 65p). One phosphor band (2nd), two phosphor bands (others).

2nd multicoloured (Walsall)	0.45	0.40
2nd multicoloured (De La Rue)	0.50	0.55
2nd multicoloured (Questa)	0.95	1.00
1st multicoloured (Walsall)	0.55	0.50
1st multicoloured (De La Rue)	0.60	0.60
1st multicoloured (Questa)	1.00	1.05
E multicoloured (Walsall)	0.80	0.80
E multicoloured (Questa)	1.45	1.50
64p multicoloured	4.75	5.00

65p multicoloured (Walsall) (April 25, 2000)		
	1.50	1.65
65p multicoloured (Questa)	1.75	1.80
68p multicoloured (July 4, 2002)	1.95	1.80
First day cover (2nd to 64p)		3.00
First day cover (65p)		3.00
First day cover (68p)		3.00

NB: the 2nd, 1st, E and 65p by Questa come from prestige stamp books.

2003, October 14. Designs with white borders
Designs as for April 23, 2001, but with a white margin around the stamp design. Printed in gravure by De La Rue (except where stated). One phosphor band (2nd), two phosphor bands (others).

2nd multicoloured	0.45	0.40
1st multicoloured	0.55	0.50
E multicoloured	0.75	0.65
40p multicoloured (May 11, 2004)	0.80	0.85
42p multicoloured (April 5, 2005 – printed by Walsall)		
	0.85	0.85
42p multicoloured (May 10, 2005)	0.80	0.75
68p multicoloured	1.20	1.00
First day cover (2nd, 1st, E, 68p)		3.50
First day cover (40p)		2.50
First day cover (42p)		2.50
Stamp cards	2.00	10.00

Wales

3d lilac

1958-1967
Des: Reynolds Stone.
A) Wmk: Multiple St Edward's Crown. Non phosphor except where stated.

3d lilac (August 18, 1958)	0.15	0.15
a) one centre band	0.15	0.20
4d blue (February 7, 1966)	0.20	0.15
a) two phosphor bands	0.15	0.15
6d purple (September 29, 1958)	0.30	0.25
9d green (two phosphor bands) (March 1, 1967)		
	0.35	0.30
1/3 green (September 29, 1958)	0.40	0.40
1/6 grey-blue (two phosphor bands) (March 1, 1967)		
	0.40	0.30

First Day Covers	
3d	10.00
6d, 1/3	20.00
4d	7.50
9d, 1/6	2.75

B) No watermark, Two phosphor bands except where stated.

i) Gum Arabic.

3d lilac (one centre band)	0.20	0.20

ii) PVA gum

4d blue	0.20	0.30
4d sepia (one centre band) (September 4, 1968)		
	0.15	0.15
4d red (one centre band) (February 26, 1969)		
	0.40	0.15
5d blue (September 4, 1968)	0.30	0.25
1/6 grey-blue	2.50	2.50

First Day Covers

4d sepia, **5d**		2.50
4d red		1.00

3p blue

1971, July 7. Decimal Currency
Des: J. Matthews.
A) Two phosphor bands except where stated.

i) **2½p** pink (one centre band)	0.35	-
3p blue	0.70	-

ii) PVA gum. Original coated paper.

2½p pink (one centre band)	0.35	0.25
3p blue	0.30	0.20
5p violet	1.25	1.25
7½p brown	1.75	1.75

iii) PVA gum. Fluorescent coated paper.

21/2p pink (one centre band)	1.75	0.75
3p blue	7.50	1.75
3p blue (one centre band)	0.35	0.25
5p violet	18.00	3.75

iv) PVAD gum (blue tinged).

3½p green (January 23, 1974)	0.30	0.30
a) one centre band	0.30	0.30
4½p grey-blue (November 6, 1974)	0.30	0.30
5½p deep violet (January 23, 1974)	0.30	0.30
a) one centre band	0.30	0.30
6½p green-blue (one centre band)		
(January 14, 1976)	0.30	0.25
7p red-brown (one centre band)		
(January 18, 1978)	0.30	0.25
8p red (January 23, 1974)	0.35	0.30
8½p green (January 14, 1976)	0.35	0.30
9p violet-blue (January 18, 1978)	0.35	0.35
10p orange (October 20, 1976)	0.35	0.35
a) one centre band	0.35	0.35

10½p grey-blue (January 18, 1978)	0.40	0.40
11p red (October 20, 1976)	0.40	0.40

B) Phosphor coated paper. PVAD gum (blue tinged). Issued on July 23, 1980.

12p yellow-green	0.40	0.40
13½p red-brown	0.55	0.60
15p blue	0.50	0.55

C) Printed in litho by Questa. Perf 13½ x 14. Phosphor coated paper, except 11½p and 12½p (left side band). PVA gum (11½p, 14p, 18p, 22p). PVAD gum (others).

11½p mushroom (April 8, 1981)	0.60	0.45
12½p light green (February 24, 1982)	0.50	0.40
14p steel-blue (April 8, 1981)	0.50	0.50
15½p pale-violet (February 24, 1982)	0.70	0.65
16p light mushroom (April 27, 1983)	1.25	1.25
18p mauve (April 8, 1981)	0.70	0.70
19½p grey-green (February 24, 1982)	1.50	1.60
20½p bright blue (April 27, 1983)	2.75	2.75
22p deep blue (April 8, 1981)	0.90	0.90
26p red – Type I (February 24, 1982	0.80	0.80
28p blue – Type I (April 27, 1983)	0.90	0.90

The dragon symbol on these stamps has been re-drawn. On the original version (known as 'Type I') the eye is a circle, while the tongue, claws and tail are thin. On the re-drawn version (Type II), the eye is solid, while the tongue, claws and tail are thick. Types are recorded where the same stamp exists with both types of symbol.

D) Printed in litho by Questa. Perf 15 x 14. One side phosphor band (12p, 12½p, 13p), phosphor coated paper (16p, 17p, 31p), advanced coated paper (22p, 26p, 28p) or as indicated. PVAD gum.

12p emerald-green (January 7, 1986)	1.75	1.75
12½p light green (January 10, 1984)	4.00	4.00
13p reddish-brown – Type I (October 23, 1984)		
	0.50	0.50
a) deep brown – Type II	2.25	2.35
b) deep brown, on paper supplied by Coated Papers Ltd.		
PVA gum. Type II (April 14, 1987)	1.25	1.30
16p light mushroom (January 10, 1984)	1.25	1.25
17p steel-blue – Type I (October 23, 1984)		
	0.80	0.85
a) flourescent brightener omitted – Type I		
	0.80	1.00
b) advanced coated paper – Type I	0.80	0.85
c) Type II	30.00	18.00
18p deep green (January 6, 1987)	0.70	0.70
18p bright green (one centre band) (December 3, 1991)		
	0.55	0.66
18p bright green (left band)	2.00	2.00
18p bright green (right band)	2.00	2.00
18p bright green (perf: 14) (January 12, 1993)		
	2.50	2.50
19p orange-red (phosphor paper) (November 8, 1988)		
	0.75	0.75
20p brownish-black (phosphor paper) (November 28, 1989)		

	0.65	0.60
22p yellowish-green (October 23, 1984)		
	0.75	0.75
22p orange-red (phosphor paper) (December 4, 1990)		
	0.70	0.65
23p bright green (phosphor paper) (November 8, 1988)		
	0.80	0.80
24p deep red (phosphor paper) (November 28, 1989)		
	1.00	1.00
24p chestnut (phosphor paper) (December 3, 1991)		
	0.75	0.80
24p chestnut (two bands) (February 25, 1992)		
	1.00	1.10
24p chestnut (phosphor paper, perf: 14) (September 14, 1992)		
	2.50	2.50
26p red - Type II (January 27, 1987)	3.00	3.00
26p drab (phosphor paper) (December 4, 1990)		
	1.00	0.95
28p blue – Type II (January 27, 1987)	1.00	1.05
28p bluish grey (phosphor paper) (December 3, 1991)		
	1.00	0.95
31p purple (October 23, 1984)	0.95	0.95
a) advanced coated paper (January 27, 1987)		
	1.60	1.60
32p greenish blue (phosphor paper) (November 8, 1988)		
	1.10	1.20
34p bluish grey (phosphor paper) (November 28, 1989)		
	1.25	1.25
37p rosine (phosphor paper) (December 4, 1990)		
	1.25	1.25
39p mauve (phosphor paper) (December 3, 1991)		
	1.25	1.25

First Day Covers

2½p, 3p, 5p, 7 1/2p	2.00
3½p, 5½p, 8p	1.25
4½p	1.00
6½p, 8½p	1.00
10p, 11p	1.00
7p, 9p, 10 1/2p	1.75
12p 13½p, 15p	1.25
11½p, 14p, 18p, 22p	2.00
12½p, 15½p. 19½p, 26p	2.00
16p, 20½p, 28p	1.75
12p, 17p, 22p, 31p	2.00
12p	1.50
18p	1.50
14p, 19p, 23p, 32p	2.00
15p, 20p, 24p, 34p	2.75
17p, 22p, 26p, 37p	2.75
18p, 24p, 28p, 39p	2.75

NB: the 18p one band at left or right come from prestige stamp books. The 18p centre band is also found in prestige stamp books.

E) Stamps with an elliptical perforation along each vertical side, Printed in litho by Questa. One phosphor band (19p and 20p), two phosphor bands (others).

19p bistre (December 7, 1993)	0.60	0.55
19p bistre (right band)	1.50	1.60
20p bright green (July 23, 1996)	1.25	1.30
25p red (December 7, 1993)	0.75	0.75
26p red-brown (July 23, 1996)	1.25	1.25
30p olive-grey (December 7, 1993)	0.85	0.85
37p mauve (July 23, 1996)	2.50	2.60
41p grey-brown (December 7, 1993)	1.10	1.15
63p emerald (July 23, 1996)	2.75	2.75

NB: the 19p with side band to right comes from a prestige stamp book.

F) Stamps with an elliptical perforation along each vertical side. Printed in gravure by Walsall. One phosphor band (19p and 20p), two phosphor bands (others). These stamps do not have the 'p' following the denomination.

20p bright green (July 1, 1997)	0.45	0.50
20p bright green (right band)	1.00	1.00
26p chestnut (July 1, 1997)	0.75	0.70
26p chestnut (perf: 14)	1.20	1.20
26p chestnut (Harrison)	1.00	1.00
37p mauve (July 1, 1887)	1.40	1.40
37p mauve (Harrison)	1.20	1.20
63p emerald (July 1, 1997)	2.25	2.25

NB: The 20p with one band at right and the 26p with perf: 14 come from prestige stamp books. The 26p and 37p printed printed by Harrison come from a prestige stamp book.

First day covers

19p, 25p, 30p, 41p	5.00
20p, 26p, 37p, 63p	5.00

G) Non-value indicator stamp. Printed in gravure by Walsall. One phosphor band. Issued on February 15, 2000, in a prestige stamp book.

1st orange-red	1.50	1.50

Leek (2nd)
Welsh Dragon (1st)
Daffodil (E, 40p, 42p)
Prince of Wales' feathers (64p, 65p, 68p)

1999, June 8

Des: D. Petersen (2nd), T. and G. Petersen (1st), I. Rees (E, 40p, 42p), R. Evans (64p, 65p, 68p), and all adapted by Tutssels. Printed in litho by Walsall (2nd, 1st, E, 64p, 65p) or De La Rue (68p). One phosphor band (2nd), two phosphor bands (others).

2nd multicoloured	0.45	0.40
2nd multicoloured (right band)	1.10	1.20
1st multicoloured	0.55	0.50
E multicoloured	1.00	1.00
64p multicoloured	4.75	4.75

65p multicoloured (April 25, 2000)	1.95	2.10
68p multicoloured (July 4, 2002)	1.25	1.35
First day cover (2nd to 64p)		3.00
First day cover (65p)		3.00
First day cover (68p)		3.00

NB: the 2nd with band at right comes from the £7 'Treasury of Trees' prestige stamp book.

2003, October 14. Designs with white borders
Designs as for April 23, 2001 but with a white margin around the stamp design. Printed in gravure by De La Rue (except where stated). One phosphor band (2nd), two phosphor bands (others).

2nd multicoloured	0.45	0.40
1st multicoloured	0.55	0.50
E multicoloured	0.75	0.65
40p multicoloured (May 11, 2004)	0.80	0.75
42p multicoloured (April 5, 2005 – printed by Walsall)		
	0.85	0.85
42p multicoloured (May 10, 2005)	0.80	0.75
68p multicoloured	1.20	1.00
First day cover (2nd, 1st, E, 68p)		3.00
First day cover (40p)		2.50
First day cover (42p)		2.50
Stamp cards	2.00	10.00

The issues of Guernsey, the Isle of Man and Jersey are listed as GB regionals, as these issues pre-date the postal independence of the islands and are regarded by collectors as GB regionals.

Guernsey

Gathering seaweed (1d)
Islanders gathering seaweed (2½d)

1948, May 10. Third Anniversary of Liberation
Des: J.R.R. Stobie (1d), E. Blampied (2½d). Printed in photogravure by Harrison. Multiple GVIR watermark. Perf: 15 x 14.

Set 1d, 2d	0.15	0.20
First day cover		17.50

2½d, 3d, 4d

1958-68.Regional issue
Des: E.A. Piprell. Printed in photogravure by Harrison. Perf:

---

15 x 14.
i) Wmk: Multiple St Edward's Crown. Non phosphor (except where stated).

2½d red (June 8, 1964)	0.20	0.25
3d lilac (August 18, 1958)	0.20	0.25
a) one centre phosphor band (May 24, 1967)		
	0.10	0.15
4d ultramarine (February 7, 1966)	0.20	0.25
a) two phosphor bands (October 24, 1967)		
	0.10	0.15
First Day Cover (2½d)		25.00
First Day Cover (3d)		20.00
First Day Cover (4d)		10.00

ii) No watermark. Chalky paper. Two phosphor bands (except where stated).

4d ultramarine (April 16, 1968)	0.10	0.15
4d sepia: one centre phosphor band (September 4, 1968)		
	0.10	0.15
4d red: one centre phosphor band (February 26, 1969)		
	0.10	0.20
5d deep blue (September 4, 1968)	0.10	0.20
First Day Cover (4d sepia, 5d)		2.00
First Day Cover (4d red)		1.50

NB: Guernsey achieved postal independence from Great Britain in 1969 and issued its first definitives in on October 1 that year.

Isle of Man

2½d, 3d, 4d

1958-69.Regional issue
Des: J. Nicholson. Printed in photogravure by Harrison. Perf: 15 x 14.

i) Wmk: Multiple St Edward's Crown. Non phosphor (except where stated).

2½d carmine-red (June 8, 1964)	0.20	0.35
3d lilac (August 18, 1958)	0.15	0.20
a) chalky paper (May 17, 1964)	4.50	4.00
b) one centre phosphor band (June 27, 1968)		
	0.10	0.15
4d ultramarine (February 7, 1966)	0.75	0.75
a) two phosphor bands (July 5, 1967)	0.10	0.15
First Day Cover (2½d)		25.00
First Day Cover (3d)		30.00
First Day Cover (4d)		10.00

ii) No watermark. Chalky paper. Two phosphor bands
(except where stated).

4d ultramarine (June 24, 1968)   0.10   0.15
4d sepia: one centre phosphor band (September 4, 1968)
                                      0.10   0.15
4d red: one centre phosphor band (February 26, 1969)
                                      0.20   0.30
5d deep blue (September 4, 1968) 0.20   0.30
First Day Cover (4d sepia, 5d)   2.00
First Day Cover (4d red)   1.50

ii) No watermark. Chalky paper – PVA gum. One centre
phosphor band (4d), two phosphor bands (5d).

4d sepia (September 4, 1968)   0.10   0.15
4d red (February 26, 1969)   0.10   0.20
5d deep blue (September 4, 1968) 0.10   0.20
First Day Cover (4d sepia, 5d)   2.00
First Day Cover (4d red)   1.50

Machin portrait and Legs of Man (all values)

1971, July 7. Regional Decimal Issue
Des: J. Matthews. Printed in photogravure by Harrison. Perf; 15
x 14.

2½p magenta   0.15   0.20
3p ultramarine   0.15   0.20
5p violet   0.50   0.60
7½p pale brown   0.50   0.60
First Day Cover   ????
* NB: the **2½p** and **3p** exist on either ordinary coated paper or
fluorescent coated paper.

Jersey

2½d, 3d, 4d

1958-69. Regional issue
Des: E. Blampied (2½d), W.M. Gardner (others). Printed in
photogravure by Harrison. Perf: 15 x 14.
i) Wmk: Multiple St. Edward's Crown. Non phosphor (except
where stated).

2½d carmine-red (June 8, 1964)   0.20   0.25
3d lilac (August 18, 1958)   0.25   0.25
a) one centre phosphor band (June 9, 1967)
                                      0.10   0.15
4d ultramarine (February 7, 1966) 0.20   0.25
a) two phosphor bands (September 5, 1967)
                                      0.10   0.15
First Day Cover (2½d)   25.00
First Day Cover (3d)   20.00
First Day Cover (4d)   10.00

POSTAGE DUE LABELS

All the following, except where stated, were printed by Harrison in typography. Perf 14 x 15.

½d to 1/- (same design)

2/6 to £1 (same design)

Priced as unmounted mint, mounted mint and used.

1914-1923

Wmk: Crown and script GVR (Royal Cypher) (sideways). (Crown facing to the right when viewed from front of stamp). Printed by Harrison (all values except 1/-) or at Somerset House (1/2d, 1d, 5d, 1/-).

½d green	1.25	0.40	0.35
1d red	1.25	0.50	0.25
a) chalky paper	7.50	4.00	4.00
1½d brown	95.00	35.00	13.00
2d black	1.25	0.80	0.30
3d violet	14.00	4.00	0.60
4d green	67.00	20.00	4.50
5d brown	8.00	4.00	2.00
1/- blue	70.00	19.00	3.00
Set	£300	65.00	22.00

Wmk: inverted (Crown facing to the left).

½d green	1.50	1.00	1.00
1d red	2.00	1.00	1.00
1½d brown	£120	50.00	15.00
2d black	3.00	1.00	1.00
3d violet	19.00	6.50	2.50
4d green	£110	35.00	5.00
5d brown	32.00	12.00	4.00
1/- blue	60.00	20.00	15.00

In the following cases, the normal issues have the Crown of the watermark facing to the left.

1924-1931

Wmk: Multiple Crown and block GVR (sideways).

Printed by Waterlow and Harrison (from 1934).

½d green	1.25	0.50	0.30
1d red	1.25	0.50	0.10
1½d brown	50.00	27.00	9.00
2d black	6.00	1.25	0.20
3d violet	6.00	1.75	0.20
4d green	24.00	5.00	0.85
5d brown	35.00	22.00	17.00
1/- blue	10.00	4.00	0.25
2/6 purple (yellow paper)	80.00	20.00	0.80
Set	£190	60.00	24.50

Wmk: inverted.

½d green	4.50	2.00	1.50
1d red	-	-	8.50
1 1/2d brown	-	-	25.00
2d black	-	-	8.50
3d violet	10.00	5.00	5.00
4d green	50.00	20.00	20.00
1/- blue	-	-	-
2/6 purple (yellow paper)	-	-	-

Unmounted mint and used only.

1936-1937

Wmk: Multiple Crown and E8R (sideways).

½d green	7.00	6.50
1d red	1.00	1.50
2d black	6.00	6.00
3d violet	1.50	1.50
4d green	30.00	22.00
5d brown	18.00	18.00
1/- blue	8.00	6.50
2/6 purple (yellow paper)	£190	10.00
Set	£270	65.00

1937-1938

Wmk: Multiple Crown GVIR (sideways).

½d green	8.50	4.50
1d red	2.00	0.20
2d black	1.25	0.30
3d violet	7.00	0.30
4d green	60.00	7.00
5d brown	7.00	0.80
1/- blue	45.00	0.90
2/6 purple (yellow paper)	50.00	2.00
Set	£160	12.00

Wmk: inverted.

1d red	£120	-
2d black	10.00	-
3d violet	25.00	-
4d green	£110	-
5d brown	30.00	-
1/- blue	60.00	-

1951-1952

As before but changed colours.

½d orange	3.50	3.50
1d blue	1.25	0.50
a) wmk inverted	-	-
1½d green	1.25	1.50
a) wmk inverted	3.00	-
4d blue	30.00	12.00
1/- brown	22.00	4.00
a) wmk inverted	£2000	-
Set	45.00	18.00

1954-1955
Wmk: Multiple tudor Crown E2R (sideways).

½d orange	8.00	8.50
a)watermark inverted	12.00	-
2d black	20.00	16.00
3d violet	30.00	30.00
4d blue	16.00	16.00
5d brown	15.00	10.00
2/6 purple (yellow paper)	75.00	8.00
Set	£130	70.00

1955-1957
Wmk: Multiple St Edward's Crown E2R (sideways).

½d orange	4.00	4.00
1d blue	3.00	1.25
1½d green	7.00	4.50
2d black	20.00	5.25
3d violet	3.50	1.25
4d blue	16.00	2.00
5d brown	20.00	1.75
1/- brown	40.00	2.00
2/6 purple (yellow paper)	£115	10.00
5/- red (yellow paper)	60.00	18.00
Set	£240	40.00

Wmk: inverted.

½d orange	9.00	-
1½d green	12.00	-
3d violet	25.00	-
4d blue	30.00	-
1/- brown	-	-
2/6 purple (yellow paper)	-	-
5/- red (yellow paper)	-	75.00

1959-1963
Wmk: Multiple Crowns (sideways).

½d orange	0.15	0.25
1d blue	0.15	0.10
1½d green	1.50	2.00
2d black	1.00	0.30
3d violet	0.35	0.15
4d blue	0.35	0.15
5d brown	0.35	0.30
6d purple	0.50	0.15
1/- brown	1.00	0.15
2/6 purple (yellow paper)	1.50	0.20
5/- red (yellow paper)	4.00	0.50

10/- blue (yellow paper)	10.00	3.00
£1 black (yellow paper)	33.00	4.50
Set	45.00	9.50

Wmk: inverted.

½d orange	1.25	-
1d blue	12.00	-
2d black	40.00	-
3d violet	10.00	-
4d blue	30.00	-
5d brown	4.00	-
6d purple	40.00	-
1/- brown	7.00	-
2/6 purple (yellow paper)	6.00	-
5/- red (yellow paper)	10.00	-
10/- blue (yellow paper)	20.00	-

1968-1969
No watermark. Chalky paper.
i) With gum Arabic.

2d black	0.50	0.50
4d blue	0.40	0.20

ii) With PVA gum.

2d black	1.50	1.00
3d violet	0.50	0.50
5d brown	5.00	5.00
6d purple	1.00	1.25
1/- brown	3.00	2.00

1968-1969
Printed in photogravure by Harrison. No watermark.
Chalky paper. PVA gum.

4d blue	4.50	5.00
8d red	0.50	1.00

½p to 7p (same design)

10p to £5 (same design)

1970. Decimal Currency
Des: J. Matthews. Printed in photogravure by Harrison. No
watermark. Chalky paper. Perf: 14 x 15.
i) PVA gum. Original coated paper.

½p turquoise	0.10	0.25

POSTAGE DUES

1p purple	0.25	0.10
2p green	0.25	0.10
3p blue	0.40	0.10
4p sepia	0.25	0.10
5p violet	0.60	0.10
10p carmine	0.70	0.20
20p deep green	1.00	0.20
50p blue	2.00	0.25
£1 black	3.00	0.25

ii) PVA gum. Fluorescent coated paper.

1p purple	0.50	-
3p blue	1.75	-
5p violet	2.25	-
10p carmine	45.00	-
20p deep green	45.00	-
£5 orange, black	20.00	1.00

iii) PVAD (blue-tinged dextrin gum).

1p purple	0.10	-
2p green	0.10	-
3p blue	0.10	-
4p sepia	0.10	-
5p violet	0.10	-
7p red-brown	0.25	0.25
10p carmine	0.15	-
11p green	0.35	0.35
20p deep green	0.50	-
50p blue	0.90	-
£1 black	1.50	-
£5 orange, black	15.00	1.00
Set (one of each value)	9.00	4.25

iv) PVAD gum. Phosphor coated paper (giving a green phosphor reaction).

10p carmine	0.70	0.50
20p deep green	1.00	0.75

Presentation Packs

1) with PVA gum printings to £1	7.00
2) with mixed gums to £1, including 7p and 11p	3.50

1p to 5p (same design)

10p to £5 (same design)

1982, June 9
Des: Sedley Place Design Ltd. Printed in photogravure by Harrisons. No wmk. Perf: 14 x 15.

1p crimson	0.05	0.10
2p bright blue	0.06	0.10
3p purple	0.10	0.15
4p blue	0.10	0.10
5p brown	0.10	0.10
10p light brown	0.20	0.10
20p sage green	0.30	0.30
25p blue-grey	0.40	0.60
50p charcoal	1.00	1.50
£1 red	2.00	0.50
£2 turquoise	4.00	2.50
£5 dull orange	8.50	1.25
Set	14.00	5.00
Gutter Pairs	30.00	-
Presentation Pack	32.00	

1p to £5 (same design)

1994, February 15
Des: Sedley Place Design Ltd. Printed in lithography by Hopuse of Questa. No wmk. Perf: 14 x 15.
1p, 2p, 5p, 10p, 20p, 25p, £1, £1.20, £5

Set	24.00	25.00
First Day Cover	35.00	

DONT MISS OUT
ON YOUR FAVOURITE MAGAZINE

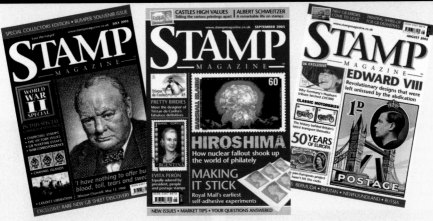

Ensure you reserve your next issue, fill out the coupon below and give it to your friendly newsagent

Dear Newsagent,

Please save a copy of Stamp Magazine, published every 4 weeks, from the next available issue, until further notice.

Name: _____ Date: _____

- ✂

Dear Newsagent,

Please deliver a copy of Stamp Magazine, published every 4 weeks, from the next available issue, until further notice.

Name: _____ Date: _____

Address: _____

_____

_____ Postcode: _____

QUEEN ELIZABETH II PRESTIGE STAMP BOOKS

Stamps for Cooks book, 1969 – Britain's first PSB

1969, December 1. £1 Stamps for Cooks
See under pre-decimal Machin definitives.
Complete book   10.00
NB: A stapled version of this stitched book exists that is much more rare. It retails at around £150.

The Story of Wedgwood book, 1972

1972, May 24. £1 The Story of Wedgwood
Panes of:

twelve 3p	5.00
six 2½p, six 3p	7.50
nine 2½p, one ½p	9.00
four ½p, two 2½p	45.00
Complete book	45.00

NB: The £45 version of the book is collectable as it is the only way that Machin collectors can get hold of the GB ½p Machin side band definitive stamp. The stamp was never issued on its own and was only ever available in this sponsored prestige stamp book.

1980, April 16. £3 The Story of Wedgwood
Panes of:

six 2p	1.00
nine 10p	2.50
nine 12p	2.75
one 2p, four 10p, four 12p	2.75
Complete book	6.00

1982, May 19. £4 Story of Stanley Gibbons
Panes of:

six 12½p	2.25
six 15½p	3.50
nine 15½p	2.50
one 2p, one 3p, seven 12½p	4.00
Complete book	7.50

1983, September 14. £4 Story of the Royal Mint
Panes of:

six 12½p (label 'The Royal Mint and America')	2.25
six 12½p (label 'Maundy Money')	2.25
nine 16p	3.00
one 3p, two 3½p, six 16p	5.00
Complete book	7.50

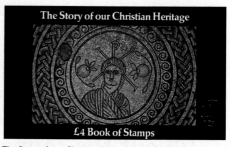

The Story of our Christian Heritage book, 1984

1984, September 4. £4 The Story of our Christian Heritage
Panes of:

six 17p	2.75
six 13p (label 'William Wilberforce')	2.50
six 13p (label 'Lillian Bayliss')	2.50
one 10p, one 13p, seven 17p	22.00
Complete book	22.00

The Story of The Times book, 1985

1985, January 8. £5 The Story of The Times
Panes of:

six 17p	2.75
nine 13p	3.75

nine 17p	3.50
two 4p, four 13p, two 17p, one 34p	8.50
Complete book	11.00

The Story of British Rail book, 1986

1986, March 18. £5 The Story of British Rail
Panes of:
six 17p	3.00
nine 12p	3.75
nine 17p	4.00
six 12p, two 17p, one 31p	10.00
Complete book	14.00

1987, March 3. £5 The Story of P&O
Panes of:
six 13p	2.75
nine 13p	3.25
nine 18p	3.50
one 1p, two 13p, five 18p, one 26p	8.50
Complete book	12.00

1998, March 3. £5 FT100 (Financial Times)
Panes of:
nine 18p	2.50
six 13p	2.00
six 13p, one 18p, one 22p, one 34p	11.00
six 18p	1.75
Complete book	16.00

1989, March 21. £5 The Scots Connection
Panes of:
nine 19p Scotland	2.75
six 14p Scotland	1.50
five 14p, two 19p, one 23p, all Scotland	10.00
six 19p Scotland	2.00
Complete book	12.00

1990, March 20. £5 London Life
Panes of:
four 20p Alexandra Palace	1.50
six 20p Penny Black Anniversary (label 'Eros')	
	1.75
six 20p Penny Black Anniversary (label 'Street Signs')	
	1.75

one 15p, one 20p, one 29p, all Penny Black Anniversary, one 2nd, one 1st, one 15p, one 20p, one 50p	
	11.00
Complete book	15.00

1991, March 19. £6 Alias Agatha Christie
Panes of:
six 17p (label 'Styles')	1.50
six 17p (label "mousetrap")	1.50
nine 22p	3.00
six 22p, two 33p	5.00
Complete book	10.00

1992, February 25. £6 Cymru Wales
Panes of:
four 39p Wintertime	2.50
six 18p Wales	1.50
two 18p and two 24p, both Wales, one 2nd, one 1st, two 33p	
	8.50
six 24p Wales	2.25
Complete book	10.00

Tolkien book, 1992

1992, October 27. £6 Tolkien
Panes of:
six 24p (label 'Runes')	2.00
six 24p (label 'Hobbit')	2.00
six 18p	1.75
one 2nd, one 1st, two 18p, two 24p, two 39p	
	6.50
Complete book	10.00

1993, August 10. £5.64 The Story of Beatrix Potter
Panes of:
four 1st Beatrix Potter	1.50
one 24p of each of Scotland, Wales and Northern Ireland, one 18p of each of Scotland, Wales and Northern Ireland	
	3.50
three 1st, three 2nd	2.50
two 2nd, two 18p, two 33p, two 39p	5.50
Complete book	11.00

1994, July 26. £6.04 Northern Ireland
Panes of:
| four 30p Prince of Wales Paintings | 1.75 |
| one 6p, one 19p, four 25p | 7.50 |

two **19p**, four **25p**, one **30p**, one **41p**, all of Northern Ireland
3.75
one **19p**, one **25p**, one **30p**, one **41p**, all of Northern Ireland
3.25
Complete book   12.00

1995, April 25. £6 The National Trust
Panes of:
six **25p** National Trust   1.75
two **19p**, two **25p**, one **10p**, one **30p**, one **35p**, one **41p**
10.00
one **19p** of Scotland, Wales and Northern Ireland, one **25p** of
Scotland, Wales and Northern Ireland 4.00
six **19p**   5.50
Complete book   12.00

1996, May 14. £6.48 European Football Championships
Panes of:
four **19p** Football Legends   1.60
four **25p** Football Legends   1.75
two **35p**, two **41p**, two **60p** Football Legends
4.25
two **25p**, two **25p** Scotland, two **25p**, Wales, two **25p**
Northern Ireland   3.00
Complete book   10.00

1997, September 23. £6.15 75 Years of the BBC
Panes of:
one **26p**, one **37p** Scotland, one **26p**, one **37p** Wales, one
26p, one **37p** Northern Ireland 3.00
four **26p** gold, four **1st** gold   3.25
three **20p**, three **26p**   2.75
four **20p** Children's Television   1.75
Complete book   10.00

1998, March 10. £7.49 The Wildings Definitive
Panes of:
nine **26p** Wilding design   4.00
six **20p** Wilding design   2.75
four **20p**, two **26p**, two **37p** Wilding design
5.00
three **26p**, three **37p** Wilding design 3.75
Complete book   12.00

Breaking Barriers book, 1998

1998, October 13. £6.16 Breaking Barriers
Panes of:
four **20p** Land Speed Records   2.75
one **20p** Scotland, one **20p** Wales, one **20p** Northern Ireland,
three **43p**   3.75
three 2nd, one **26p** Scotland, one **26p** Wales, one **26p**
Northern Ireland   3.75
three **43p**, two **10p**, three **2nd** 6.00
Complete book   13.00

1999, February 16. £7.54 Profile on Print
Panes of:
eight **1st** orange-red   3.25
four **1st** Machin large format embossed
5.00
four Machin large format intaglio   5.00
four Machin large format typography   5.00
nine **1st** orange-red   3.25
Complete book   15.00

1999, September 21. £6.99 World Changers
Panes of:
four **20p** Millennium Jenner's vaccination
1.50
four **44p** Millennium Faraday's electricity
6.00
four **26p** Darwin's theory   5.00
four **63p** Computers in brain   6.50
four **1p**, three **19p**, one **26p** 2.00
Complete book   15.00

Special by Design book, 2000

2000, February 15. £7.50 Special by Design
Panes of:
eight 1st Millennium definitive   3.50
three 1st Scotland, three 1st Wales, three 1st Northern
Ireland   4.25
four 19p, olive-green, two 38p   7.50
six 1st 150th anniversary of Penny Black definitives
                                            4.25
Complete book   15.00

2000, August 4. £7.03 HM Queen Elizabeth
The Queen Mother
Panes of:
six 2nd Scotland, two 65p Scotland   3.75
nine 1st Millennium definitive   4.00
The Queen Mother's Century miniature sheet
                                            5.50
four 27p The Queen Mother   5.00
Complete book   13.00

2000, September 18. £7 A Treasury of Trees
Panes of:
two 65p Millennium Doire Dach, Forest for Scotland
                                            2.25
four 45p Millennium Sycamore Seeds, Seed Bank, Ardingly
                                            3.00
two 65p Millennium Bluebell Wood Groundwork's
Changing Places   2.25
four 1st Millennium definitive, four 2nd Northern Ireland
                                            9.50
four 2nd Millennium Yews   1.75
Complete book   13.00

2001, October 21. £6.76 Unseen and Unheard
Panes of:
two 1st, two 65p Submarines   6.00
two 2nd, two 45p Submarines   5.00
four Flags and Ensigns   3.50
four 1st Scotland, four E Scotland   4.25
Complete book   17.50

2002, February 6. £7.29 A Gracious Accession
Panes of:
four 2nd, four E   4.00
one 2nd, one 1st, one E, one 45p Golden Jubilee
                                            3.00
one 1st, one E, one 45p, one 65p Golden Jubilee
                                            2.75
four 1st Wilding design, five 2nd Wilding design (one of the
2nd is shown tilted)   5.00
Complete book   15.00

2002, September 24. £6.83 Across the Universe
Panes of:
four 1st England, four 2nd England, one 1st Scotland
                                            3.50
four 1st Millennium National Space Centre
                                            3.25
four 1st gold, four E   3.25
Astonomy miniature sheet   3.25
Complete book   12.00

2003, February 25. £6.99 Microcosmos
Panes of:
four 1st Northern Ireland, five 2nd Northern Ireland
                                            3.25
four 1st gold, four E   4.00
two 1st and two 2nd Discovery of DNA
                                            1.50
four E Discovery of DNA   2.50
Complete book   12.00

2003, June 2. £7.46 A Perfect Coronation
Panes of:
four 1st gold, four 2nd   4.25
four 1st from the 50th anniversary of Coronation set
                                            3.25
four (different) 1st from Coronation Anniversary set
                                            3.25
two 47p Wilding design, two 68p Wilding design and one £1
1953 Coronation design   27.00
Complete book   35.00
NB: This book is becoming more rare as over half its print run
was bought by a publisher to mail out a Coronation book. Like
the 1972 Story of Wedgwood book that contained a ½p Machin
unavailable elsewhere the A Perfect Coronation prestige stamp
book contains a £1 'remake' of the 1953 1/3 Coronation stamp
that's unavailable elsewhere. In time the £1 remake is likely to
outstrip the 'Machin Wedgwood' in value because it is a
commemorative and not a definitive. Thus the pane with it on
is worth £27.

2004, March 16. £7.44 Letters by Night
Panes of:
three 2nd Scotland, three 68p Scotland 4.75
one 28p, one E, one 42p Classic Locomotives
                                            2.00
four 1st Pub Signs   1.75

four 1st gold, four 37p   4.25
Complete book   12.00

2004, May 25. £7.23 The Glory of the Garden
Panes of:
four 1st gold, two 42p, two 47p   4.75
one 2nd, one E, one 68p, one 42p RHS
                                         2.75
one 1st Iris latifolia, two 1st Tulipa, one 1st Gentiana acaulis
from the 1997 Flowers Greetings stamps
                                         5.00
two 1st, two 47p RHS   2.50
Complete book   11.00

2005, February 24. £7.43 The Brontë Sisters
Panes of:
four 2nd, two 39p, two 42p   4.00
two 2nd England, two 40p England   2.25
two 1st Brontë, two 1st Bronté   2.00
one 40p, one 57p, one 68p, one £1.12 Bronté
                                    4.25
Complete book   12.50

STOP PRESS!

2005, October 4. Battle of Trafalgar
Panes of:
four 1st, two 50p, two 68p   *
two White Ensign, one Union Flag   *
two 1st Trafalgar, one 42p Trafalgar   *
one 42p Trafalgar, two 68p Trafalgar   *
Complete book   *
* NB: At the time of going to press Royal Mail hadn't confirmed details of the exact make-up fo the panes in this book or indeed a price for the book

2006 prestige stamps books

Royal Mail has already announced that it has two main GB prestige stamp books lined up for release in 2006. They will be the February 23, 2006 issue to commemorate the 200th birth anniversary of the great engineer Isambard Kingdon Brunel and the September 21, 2006 issue to commemorate the 150th anniversary of the institution of the Victoria Cross.

Greetings books

These booklets contain the GB Greetings stamps, which are listed separately under their dates of issue. Normally the panes comprise one of each of the designs, often with additional greetings labels.

Greetings book, 1989

1989, January 31. Various designs
Cover shows elements from the stamp designs. Booklet pane comprises two of each of the five design   15.00
The stamps are all of 19p

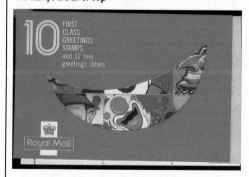

'Smiles' greetings book, 1990

1990, February 6. Smiles
Cover shows the stamps within smiling lips.
The stamps are all of 20p   12.00

'Good luck' greetings book, 1991

1991, February 5. Good luck
Cover shows good luck charms   7.00
The stamps are all 1st class NVIs

1991, March 26. Smiles
Cover shows a happy pillar box. Designs as for February 6,
1990, but inscribed **1st**   6.00

1992, January 28. Memories
Cover shows a label inscribed Memories
and pressed flowers   6.00

1993, February 12. Gift Giving
Cover shows Rupert the Bear   6.50

1994, February 1. Messages
Cover shows Rupert the Bear   7.00

'Art' greetings book, 1995

1995, March 21. Art
Cover shows a clown (the yellow strip has either the
inscription 'Pull Here' or no inscription)   6.00

'Cartoons' greetings book, 1996

1996, February 26. Cartoons
Cover shows asking for more, with bowl marked 'Love'. Stamps
are on phosphor paper   6.00

1996, November 11. Cartoons
As booklet of February 26, 1996, but stamps have two
phosphor bands   17.50

1997, January 6. Flower Paintings
Cover shows a flower   6.00

1997, February 3. Flower Paintings
Cover as for January 6, 1997, but with the additional inscription
'WIN A BEAUTIFUL BOUQUET INSTANTLY'   7.00

1998, January 5. Flower Paintings
Cover shows a box of chocolates.   7.00

1998, August 3. Flower Paintings
Cover inscribed 'Make their post memorable'   7.00

PRESENTATION PACKS

In 1964 the Post Office introduced a new product with the launch of a presentation pack to accompany the special issue to mark the Shakespeare Festival set of five stamps. However, in 1960 to mark the international stamp exhibtiton held in London (and with a sales tour undertaken by the Post Office in the USA) it was decided that it was more convenient to sell the GB definitives in pre-packaged form. Thus the low value Wildings up to 1/6, the Castle high values, the 'phosphor-Graphite' definitives and the regional stamps were each made available in packs. Each pack was priced in sterling or in US dollars, depending on where they were sold.

The stamps were 'mounted' on dark grey cards that were contained in envelopes with a large 'window' allowing the contents to be viewed. There were brief details of the stamps on the reverse of this. Thus many GB collectors regard these as the 'real' first ever GB presentation packs.

Since then presentation packs have regularly been issued for GB special stamps, as well as for issues of new definitives. Some have been issued in foreign language versions and any packs that vary from the norm are also listed as a) directly underneath the original listing. To find out more about the origins of GB presentation packs turn to pages 26-30 of this book.

SPECIAL ISSUES

as a result of a competition round through scools around Britain. Since then Great Britain has issued a Christmas issue every year in a variety of secular and non-secular designs.

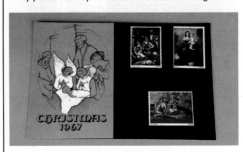

Christmas pack, 1967

1967
EFTA	3.00
British Flowers	3.25
British Paintings	3.00
Discoveries	2.00
Christmas*	1.50

* NB: For Christmas 1967 Royal Mail issued a 'presentation pack style' gift pack. Since 1967 Royal Mail has issued a year pack every year – prices for these are listed later on in this presentation pack section of the book.

1964
Shakespeare	15.00
Geographical Congress	85.00
Botanical Congress	85.00
Forth Road Bridge	£425

NB: The Forth Road Bridge pack of 1964 is now quite rare as only 13,000 were ever printed. Low printings tend to be the reason behind rare GB presentation packs.

1965
Churchill	45.00
Parliament	45.00
Battle of Britain	45.00
Post Office Tower	5.00

1966
Robert Burns	45.00
Westminster Abbey	45.00
World Cup	11.00
Birds	5.25
Technology	9.00
Battle of Hastings	4.00
Christmas	4.00

NB: Christmas issues were introduced in Britain in 1966 with the issue of 3d and 1/6 stamps that were designed by children

1968
British Bridges	2.00
Anniversaries	2.00
Paintings	2.00
a) German version	10.00
Christmas	2.00
a) German version	7.00

British Cathedrals pack, 1969

1969
British Ships	2.50
a) German version	20.00

Anniversaries (German language version), 1969

b) Cunard version	5.00
Concorde	7.50
a) German version	20.00
Anniversaries	3.00
a) German version	50.00
Cathedrals	1.75
a) German version	18.00
Prince of Wales Investiture	1.75
a) German version	18.00
b) Welsh version	40.00
Post Office Technology	2.00
Christmas	2.00

Christmas pack, 1969

1970

Cottages	3.50
Anniversaries	2.00
Literary Anniversaries	2.25
Commonwealth Games	2.00
Philympia	2.00
Christmas	2.00

1971

Ulster Paintings	3.50
Literary Anniversaries	3.50
Anniversaries	3.50
Universities	4.50

Christmas	2.75
a) Heinz version (six 2½d)	25.00

NB: For the first time, in 1971, the Post Office's Philatelic Bureau in Edinburgh ran the Heinz soup promotion. The offer consisted of exchanging the labels from eight different Heinz soups for six 2½d Christmas stamps that were sent to recipients in a presentation pack format.

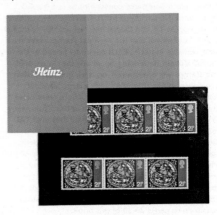

Heinz promotional Christmas pack, 1971

1972

Explorers	2.75
Anniversaries	2.50
Churches	5.00
a) Belgica pack	5.00
BBC	2.50
a) BBC staff version	15.00
Christmas	2.50
Royal Silver Wedding	2.50
a) Japanese version	5.00

BBC presentation pack (staff version), 1972

NB: To mark the 50th anniversary of the BBC the Chairman, Board of Governors, Director-General and Board of Management sent a special version of the BBC pack to its staff 'as a memento of the occasion for BBC staff'.

PRESENTATION PACKS

1973

EEC	1.75 ✓ ~~Booth~~ /350
Oak	1.50 ✓
Explorers	1.75 ✓
Cricket	2.50 ✓
Paintings	1.85 ✓
Inigo Jones	1.85 ✓
Parliament	1.85
Royal Wedding	1.50
Christmas	1.85

1974

Chestnut	1.50
Fire Service	2.00 ✓
UPU	2.00
Great Britons	2.00
Churchill	2.00 ✓
Christmas	2.00

1975

Turner	2.00 ✓
Architecture	2.00
Sailing	1.50
Railways	2.00
Parliament	1.25
Jane Austen	2.00
Christmas	2.00

1976

Telephones	2.00
Social Pioneers *Reformers*	2.00 ✓ *2 sets /6.50*
USA Bicentennial	1.00 ✓ *+ 2oths*
Roses	2.00 ✓ *+ other*
Caxton	2.00 ✓ *+ rest of corners*
Christmas	2.00

Cultural Tradition

British Wildlife (National Trust Scotland) pack, 1977

1977

Racket Sports	2.00 ✓
Chemistry	2.00 ✓
Silver Jubilee	1.25 ✓ *2 3*
Heads of Government	0.75 ✓
Wildlife	1.00 ✓ *+ Scotland w private pack*

Christmas	1.50

NB: The British Wildlife pack of 1977 was produced in a special 'private version' by the National Trust in Scotland.

1978

Energy	1.75 ✓ *+ 1 set 5 5*
Buildings	1.25 ✓
25th anniversary of Coronation	1.25 ✓
Horses	1.25 ✓
Cycling	1.25
Christmas	1.25

1979

Dogs	1.25
Spring Flowers	1.25
Elections	1.25
Derby	1.25
Year of the Child	2.75 ✓
Rowland Hill	1.25
Police	1.25
Christmas	1.25

1980

Birds	1.25
Liverpool and Manchester Railway	1.25 ✓
London 1980	1.25
Landmarks	1.25
Authors	1.75
Conductors	1.25
Sport	1.25 ✓
Christmas	1.25

Royal Wedding (souvenir book version) pack, 1981

1981

Folklore	2.25
Year of the Disabled	1.35 ✓
Butterflies	1.35
National Trust	1.50
Royal Wedding	1.75 ✓
a) special Japanese pack	4.50
Duke of Edinburgh Award	1.35 ✓
Fishing	1.35 ✓

christmas ✓

Christmas   1.50

Charles Darwin pack, 1982

1982
Darwin	1.50
Youth Organisations	1.75
Theatre	3.00
Maritime	2.50
Textiles	1.50
Information Technology	1.00
Cars	1.50

NB: A new style of presentataion pack was introduced from the pack issued to mark the death centenary of Charles Darwin in 1982. This style has remained more or less the same since.

1983
Fish	1.50
Commonwealth Day	1.50
Engineering Achievements	2.25
British Army	2.00
Gardens	1.60
Fairs	1.60
Christmas	1.75

1984
Heraldry	1.75
Cattle	2.00
Urban Renewal	1.60
Europa	2.75
Greenwich Meridian	1.75
Mail Coaches	1.60
British Council	1.60
Christmas	1.75

1985
Famous Trains	3.00
Insects	2.25
Composers	3.00
Safety at Sea	1.75
Royal Mail	1.75
Arthurian Legends	1.75
British Film Year	2.50
Christmas	2.00

Christmas folder, 1986

1986
Industry	2.00
Halley's Comet	2.00
The Queen's 60th birthday	2.75
Conservation	3.25
Medieval	2.00
Sport	2.50
Royal Wedding	1.25
RAF	2.50
Christmas	2.25
Christmas folder	8.50

NB: In 1986 the Christmas stamps were also made available in a special folder that contained 36 of the 13p The Glastonbury Thorn design.

1987
Flowers	2.25
Newton	2.25
Architects	3.25
St John Ambulance	2.25
Heraldry	2.25
Victorian Life	2.25
Pottery	2.25
Christmas	2.25

1988
Linnean Society	2.25
Welsh Bible	2.25
Sport	2.25
Transport	3.25
Australian Bicentennial	2.25
Spanish Armada	2.25
Edward Lear	2.25
Christmas	2.25

1989
Birds	2.25
Food and Farming	2.25
Anniversaries	2.50

Toys	3.25	Medical	2.75
Industry	2.25	Christmas	2.50
Microscopes	2.25		
Lord Mayor's Show	2.25	**1995**	
Christmas	2.00	Cats	3.25
		Springtime	2.50
1990		National Trust	2.50
Penny Black	4.00	Peace and Freedom	3.00
RSPCA	2.50	Science Fiction	2.60
Buildings	3.25	Shakespeare	2.60
Queen's Awards	2.50	Communications	2.60
Kew Gardens	2.25	Rugby	3.00
Thomas Hardy	1.25	Christmas	3.00
Queen Mother	3.50		
Gallantry	2.25	**1996**	
Astronomy	2.50	Robert Burns	2.50
Christmas	2.40	Wildfowl Trust	2.50
		Cinema	2.50
1991		Football	3.50
Dogs	2.50	Olympics	2.40
Science	2.40	Women	2.50
Europe in Space	3.25	Children's Television	3.00
Sport	2.40	Classic Cars	3.50
Roses	2.40	Christmas	3.00
Dinosaurs	3.00		
Ordnance Survey	2.40	**1997**	
Christmas	2.40	King Henry VIII	4.50
		Missions of Faith	2.75
1992		Legends	2.50
Wintertime	2.40	Architects of the Air	4.25
Happy and Glorious	3.50	The Queen's Horses	3.00
Tennyson	2.50	Sub Post Offices	3.00
International	3.25	Enid Blyton	3.00
Civil War	2.40	Christmas	3.00
Gilbert and Sullivan	2.50		
Greener Environment	2.40	**1998**	
Europe	1.25	Endangered Species	3.50
Christmas	2.25	Princess of Wales Memorial	4.50
		a) Welsh version	75.00
		The Queen's Beasts	2.50
1993		Lighthouses	3.25
Harrison Timekeepers	3.00	Comedians	3.25
Orchids	2.50	National Health Service	3.00
Art	3.25	Fantasy Novels	3.25
Roman Britain	2.40	Carnival	3.00
Waterways	2.40	Speed	3.50
Autumn	2.40	Christmas	3.25
Sherlock Holmes	2.50		
Christmas	2.75		

NB: The Diana, Princess of Wales memorial pack was produced in a special limited edition Welsh language version that was onyl ever available at post office counters in Wales. It's believed that its print run was only in the region of 6,500 so its value has increased greatly over the past seven years.

1994	
Steam Locomotives	3.25
Prince of Wales Paintings	2.50
Picture Postcards	2.50
Channel Tunnel	2.50
D-Day	3.50
Golf	2.60
Summertime	2.50

PRESENTATION PACKS

Inventors' Tale pack, 1999

1999

Inventors' Tale	3.75
Travellers' Tale	3.75

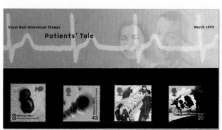

Patients' Tale pack, 1999

Patients' Tale	3.75
Settlers' Tale	3.75
Workers' Tale	3.75
Entertainers' Tale	3.75
Royal Wedding	2.00
Citizens' Tale	3.75
Scientists' Tale	3.75
Farmers' Tale	3.75
Soldiers' Tale	3.75
Christians' Tale	3.75
Artists' Tale	3.75
Millennium Timekeeper	16.00

Penny Black (1840-2000) pack, 2000

Her Majesty's Stamps pack, 2000

2000

Above and Beyond	3.75
Fire and Light	3.75
Water and Coast	3.75
Life and Earth	3.75
Art and Craft	3.75
Her Majesty's Stamps	60.00
Penny Black	10.00
People and Place	3.75
Stone and Soil	3.75
Tree and Leaf	3.75
Queen Mother's 100th birthday	12.50
Mind and Matter	3.75
Body and Bone	3.75
Spirit and Faith	3.75
Sound and Vision	3.75

NB: The Her Majesty's Stamps and Penny Black packs were produced specifically for the Stamp Show 2000 international show held at Earl's Court, London.

Queen Mother's 100th birthday pack, 2000

2001

Hopes for the Future	3.75
Occasions	5.00
Cats and Dogs	11.00
Weather	6.50
Submarines	5.50
Double deck buses	5.50
Hats	4.50
Pond Life	4.50
Punch and Judy	3.25
Nobel Prizes	5.50
Flags and Ensigns	11.00
Christmas	3.75

2002

Just So Stories	11.00
Golden Jubilee	3.50
Occasions	2.75
Coastlines	4.50
Queen Mother Memorial	3.25
Circus	3.50
Aircraft	3.50
Football World Cup	3.25
Commonwealth Games	3.50
Peter Pan	3.50
London Bridges	3.50
Astronomy	3.25
Pillar Boxes	3.50
Wildings I, 50th anniversary	47.50
Christmas	3.50

NB: The Wildings I pack was issued on December 5, 2002 to mark the 50th anniversary of the first ever Queen Elizabeth II Wildings designs. It's rumoured that only 8,500 were ever in circulation – the remainder of the print run was believed to have been destroyed by Royal Mail as the packs as said to have contained printing errors.

2003

Birds of Prey	4.75
Occasions	3.25
The Secret of Life DNA	3.50
Fruit and Veg	40.00
Extreme Endeavours	4.25
Coronation Anniversary	20.00
Prince William	20.00
British Journey: Scotland	4.25
Pub Signs	3.80
Toys	3.80
British Museum	4.25
Christmas	5.50
Rugby World Cup Win	3.50

NB: The Fruit and Veg pack from 2003 has become rare because it was a self-adhesive issue brought out with accompanying stickers to add on facial features to the stamps. This proved popular and many packs may have been used rather than being collected in mint condition. Also, the pack

was produced in shrink wrap packaging that may have decreased total sales. After one year Royal Mail destroys the excess packs so any left over will have been burnt.

2004

Classic Locomotives	17.50
Occasions	3.25
Lord of the Rings	11.00
British Journey: Northern Ireland	4.25
Entente Cordiale	2.25
Ocean Liners	4.75
Royal Horticultural Society	4.50
British Journey: Wales	4.50
Royal Society of Arts	4.80
Woodland Animals	4.80
Crimean War	5.50
Christmas	5.50

NB: The Classic Locomotives pack from January 2004 was meant to herald a redesign of GB presentation packs to make the stamp 'mounts' integral to the whole pack. A few early prints of this were produced but then the redesign of the pack was scrapped due to 'technical problems'. It's believed that a handful of the redesigned packs may exist but none have come to market as yet. Both the Classic Locomotives and Lord of the Rings packs have proved popular with thematic collectors. The Classic Locos pack with 'train collectors' (and other rail enthusiasts) and the Lord of the Rings pack with fans of the Lord of the Rings films and collectors of J.R.R. Tolkien (the Lorsd of the Rings author) memorabilia.

2005

Farm Animals	4.80
British Journey: South-West England	4.50
Jane Eyre	5.50
Magic!	5.25
World Heritage Sites	5.50
Trooping the Colour	5.50
Motorcycles	5.50
London host city to Olympic Games 2012	5.50
Changing Tastes	5.50
Classic ITV	5.50
Battle of Trafalgar	5.50
Christmas	5.50

DEFINITIVES

Forerunners

1960

Wilding definitives: priced in Sterling	£175
Phosphor-graphite: priced in Sterling	£175
Regionals: priced in Sterling	£175
Castle high values: priced in Sterling	£1100

1960

Wilding definitives: priced in Dollars	$275
Phosphor-graphite: priced in Dollars	$275
Regionals: priced in Dollars	$275

	Castle high values: priced in Dollars	$1600

Low value Machin definitives
1967
¼d to 1/9	2.50
a) German version	20.00

Britain's first decimal stamps pack, 1971

1971	½p to 9p	2.25
1971	Scandinavia Tour	12.50
1971	NABA stamp exhibition	55.00
1971	½p to 10p	6.00
1977	To 50p	2.75
1981	To 75p (pack no. 129a)	9.50
1983	To 75p (pack no. 1)	25.00
1984	½p to 75p	21.00
1987	1p to 75p	25.00
1988	14p to 35p	6.00
1989	15p to 37p	5.00
1990	Penny Black Anniversary	4.00
1990	10p to 33p	5.00
1991	1p to 75p	15.00
1991	6p to 39p	5.00

Self-adhesive definitives pack, 1993

1993	Self-adhesive booklet	8.50
1993	19p to 41p	4.50
1995	1p to £1	7.50
1996	20p to 63p	6.00
1997	2nd and 1st	4.50

1997	26p and 1st	4.50
1998	2nd, 1st, 1p to £1	8.00
1999	7p to 64p	5.25
2000	Millennium 1st	3.00
2000	Jeffery Matthews Palette	55.00
2000	8p to 65p	5.50
2002	2nd, 1st, 1p to £1	7.50
2002	37p to 68p	3.75
2002	Wildings (part 1)	47.50
2003	Worldwide and Europe	3.25
2003	Wildings (part 2)	12.00
2004	1st, Worldwide Postcard, 7p to 43p	4.25
2005	Re-issued Wilding Castle definitives	4.50
2005	9p, 35p, 46p	1.50
2005	1p, 2p, 5p, 9p, 10p, 20p, 35p, 40p, 42p, 46p, 47p, 50p, 68p, £1, plus self-adhesive 2nd, 1st, Europe, Worldwide and postcard	10.00
2005	Definitive Collection folder, containing the low value definitive pack (2005), high values pack (2003), Country stamps packs (2003), Country 42p stamps pack (2005)	32.00

High value Machin definitives
1969	2/6 to £1	6.50
	a) German version	50.00
1970	10p to 50p	4.50
1971	20p to £1	7.00
1977	£1 to £5 (pack no. 91)	13.50
1987	£1 to £5 (pack no. 13)	£145
1987	£1.60	20.00
1988	Castles £1 to £5	16.00
1992	Castles £1 to £5	17.00
1993	£10	15.00
1995	£3	14.00
1997	Castles £1.50 to £5	85.00
1999	Small size Machin £1.50 to £5 (Enschedé)	35.00
1999	Small size Machin £1.50 to £5 (De La Rue)	18.00
1999	Small size Machin £1.50 to £5 (gravure)	17.50

Postage Dues
1971	½p to 5p, 10p, 20p, 50p, £1	15.00
1977	½p to £1	7.50
1982	1p to £5	27.00
1994	1p to £5	35.00

Greetings stamps pack, 1993

Scotland pre-decimal definitives pack, 1970

Greetings stamps

1992	Memories	7.50
1993	Gift giving	9.50
1994	Messages	9.50
1995	Art	9.50
1996	Cartoons	9.50
1997	Flowers	10.50

Country stamps

ENGLAND

2001	**2nd, 1st, E, 65p**	4.00
2003	**2nd, 1st, E, 68p**	2.75

NORTHERN IRELAND

1970	**3d, 4d** sepia, **4d red,**	
	5d, 9d, 1/3, 1/6	2.00
1971	**2½p, 3p, 5p, 7½p**	1.75
1974	**3p, 3½p, 5½p, 8p**	1.40
1974	**3p, 3½p, 4½p,**	
	5½p, 8p	1.65
1976	**6½p, 8½p, 10p, 11p**	1.40
1981	**7p, 9p, 10½p, 11½p,**	
	12p, 13½p, 14p, 15p,	
	18p, 22p	4.50
1983	**10p, 12½p, 16p, 20½p,**	
	26p, 28p	9.50
1984	**10p, 13p, 16p, 17p, 22p,**	
	26p, 28p, 31p	10.00
1987	**12p, 13p, 17p, 18p, 22p,**	
	26p, 28p, 31p	10.00
1999	**19p, 25p, 30p, 41p**	7.50
2000	**1st, 40p, 65p**	5.25
2001	**2nd, 1st, E, 65p**	4.50
2003	**2nd, 1st, E, 68p**	2.75

SCOTLAND

1970	**3d, 4d** sepia, **4d red, 5d,**	
	6d, 9d, 1/3, 1/6	4.00
1971	**2½p, 3p, 5p, 7½p**	1.75
1974	**3p, 3½p, 5½p, 8p**	1.40
	3p, 31/2p, 41/2p,	
	5½p, 8p	1.65

1976	**6½p, 8½p, 10p, 11p**	1.40
1981	**7p, 9p, 10½p, 11½p,**	
	12p, 13½p, 14p, 15p,	
	18p, 22p	4.50
1983	**10p, 12½p, 16p, 20½p,**	
	26p, 28p	9.50
1984	**10p, 13p, 16p, 17p, 22p,**	
	26p, 28p, 31p	10.00
1987	**12p, 13p, 17p, 18p, 22p,**	
	26p, 28p, 31p	12.50
1999	**2nd, 1st, E, 64p**	7.50
2000	**65p**	5.25
2002	**2nd, 1st, E, 65p**	3.00
2003	**2nd, 1st, E, 68p**	2.75

WALES

1970	**3d, 4d** sepia, **4d** red,	
	5d, 9d, 1/6	3.00
1971	**2½p, 3p, 5p, 7½p**	1.75
1974	**3p, 3½p, 5½p, 8p**	1.40
	3p, 3½p, 4½p,	
	5½p, 8p	1.65
1976	**6½p, 8½p, 10p, 11p**	1.40
1981	**7p, 9p, 10½p, 11½p,**	
	12p, 13½p, 14p, 15p,	
	18p, 22p	4.50
1983	**10p, 12½p, 16p,**	
	20½p, 26p, 28p	9.50
1984	**10p, 13p, 16p, 17p, 22p,**	
	26p, 28p, 31p	10.00
1987	**12p, 13p, 17p, 18p, 22p,**	
	26p, 28p, 31p	10.00
1997	**20p, 26p, 37p, 63p**	10.50
1999	**2nd, 1st, E, 64p**	7.50
2000	**65p**	5.25
2002	**2nd, 1st, E, 65p**	3.00
2003	**2nd, 1st, E, 68p**	2.75

ALL REGIONS

These packs contain the stamps of Northern Ireland, Scotland and Wales (shown as 'x 3') or also including England (shown as 'x 4').

1988	**14p, 19p, 23p, 32p** (x 3)	9.50
1989	**15p, 20p, 24p, 34p** (x 3)	9.50

1990	**17p, 22p, 26p, 37p** (x 3)	9.50
1991	**18p, 24p, 28p, 39p** (x 3)	9.50
1993	**19p, 25p, 30p, 41p** (x 3)	9.50
1996	**20p, 26p, 37p, 63p** (x 3)	15.00
1998	**20p** (centre band), **26p,**	
	37p, 63p (x 3)	10.50
2002	**68p** (x 4)	5.00
2004	**40p** (x 4)	3.50
2005	**42p** (x 4)	2.50

Souvenir Packs

1972	Royal Silver Wedding	1.00
1973	Cricket	3.50
1973	Parliament	3.00
1974	Churchill	2.00
1975	Railways	2.25
1977	Silver Jubilee	1.25
1978	25th anniversary of	
	Coronation	1.50
1981	Royal Wedding	2.00
1984	Mail coaches 3.75	
1985	British Film Year	5.75
1986	The Queen's birthday	4.00
1988	Australian Bicentennial	8.50
1990	Penny Black Anniversary	10.50
1997	Golden Wedding	25.00

Special Packs

1971	Decimal low values from	
	½**p** to **9p** (plus an	
	additional **2p** and **2½p**)	5.00
1994	Channel Tunnel	37.00
1995	National Trust	12.50
2000	Penny Black reproduction	26.00
2000	Stamp Show 2000 pack	
	of three prestige stamp	
	books	75.00
2001	Occasions: Hallmarks	
	(five packs each containing	
	a block of ten of one of	
	the stamps)	25.00
2003	Across the Universe	
	and Microcosmos prestige	
	stamp books	40.00

Year Packs

1967	1.50
1968 (blue cover)	3.50
1968 (red cover)	2.25
1969	10.00
1970	10.00
1971	25.00
1972	17.50
1973	12.50
1974	5.00
1975	4.50
1976	5.50
1977	4.00

1978	4.00
1979	5.00
1980	5.50
1981	7.50
1982	12.50
1983	12.50
1984	15.00
1985	15.00
1986	15.00
1987	15.00
1988	15.00
1989	15.00
1990	17.00
1991	17.00
1992	17.00
1993	17.00
1994	22.00
1995	22.00
1996	27.00
1997	30.00

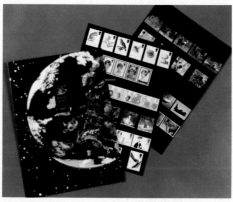

Year Pack, 1998

1998	42.00
1999	55.00
2000	55.00
2001	55.00
2002	42.00
2003	43.00
2004	43.00

Year Books

1984	45.00
1985	40.00
1986	40.00
1987	17.50
1988	17.50
1989	18.50
1990	20.00
1991	20.00
1992	22.00

Year Book, 1998

1993	27.00
1994	22.00
1995	22.00
1996	25.00
1997	30.00
1998	42.00
1999	55.00
2000	55.00
2001	55.00
2002	47.00
2003	55.00
2004	55.00

Year Book, 2000

CALCULATE WHAT YOUR GB STAMPS ARE WORTH

TOTAL

CALCULATE WHAT YOUR GB STAMPS ARE WORTH

TOTAL

CALCULATE WHAT YOUR GB STAMPS ARE WORTH

TOTAL